DOGHOUSE BLUES

CLIVE RADFORD

Black Rose writing

© 2014 by Clive Radford

All rights reserved. No part of this book may be reproduced, stored in a retrieval system or transmitted in any form or by any means without the prior written permission of the publishers, except by a reviewer who may quote brief passages in a review to be printed in a newspaper, magazine or journal.

The final approval for this literary material is granted by the author.

First printing

This is a work of fiction. Names, characters, businesses, places, events and incidents are either the products of the author's imagination or used in a fictitious or satirical manner. Any resemblance to actual persons, living or dead, or actual events is purely coincidental.

ISBN: 978-1-61296-375-4

PUBLISHED BY BLACK ROSE WRITING

www.blackrosewriting.com

Printed in the United States of America

Doghouse Blues is printed in Palatino Linotype

Dedicated to Satire Lovers

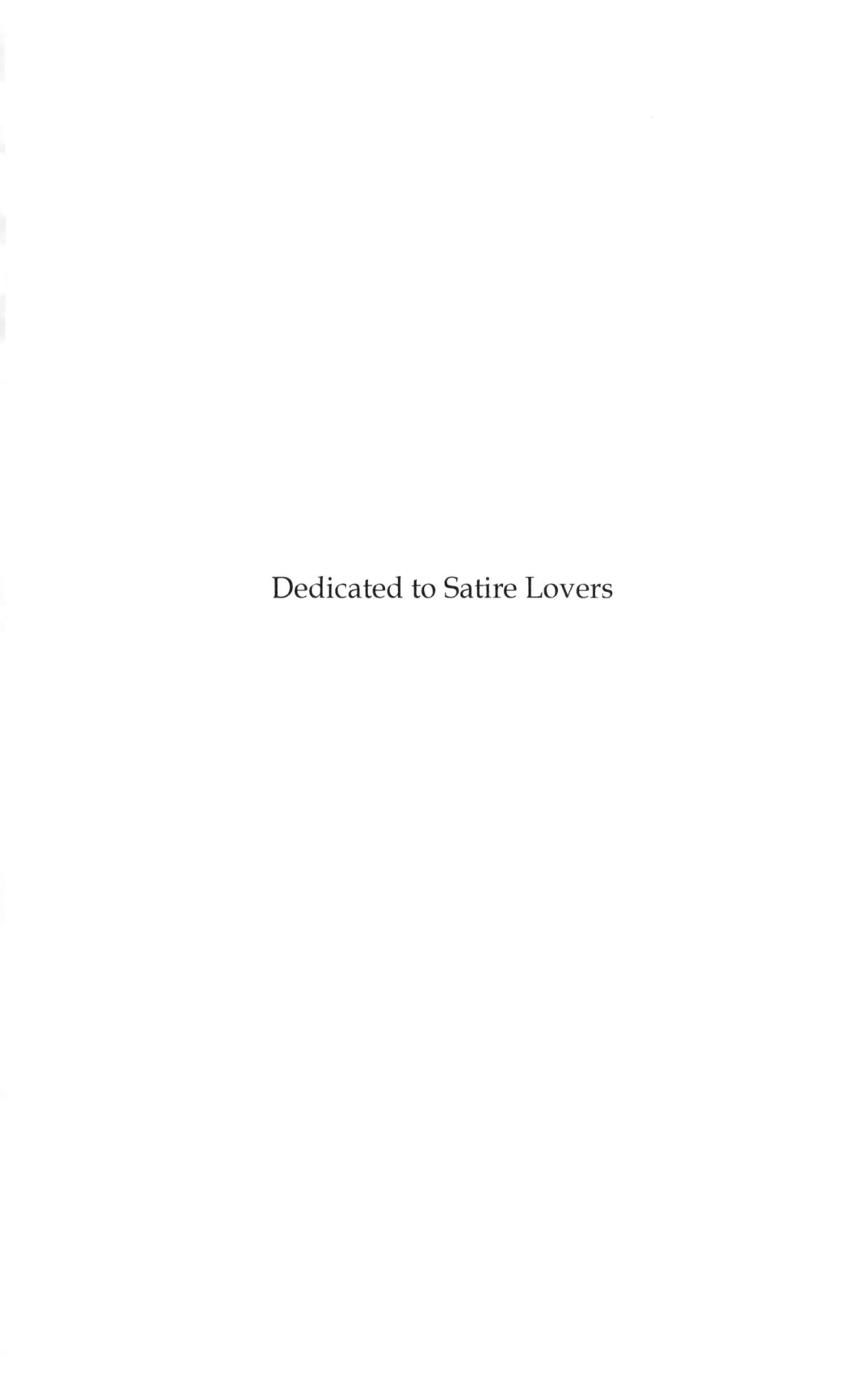

DOGHOUSE BLUES

CONTENTS

Prologue	7
Chapter 1: Art for Art's Sake	9
Chapter 2: Dongle Hell	26
Chapter 3: Hoax Call	41
Chapter 4: The Welsh Milking Maid	55
Chapter 5: Garden Party	59
Chapter 6: Lady Macbeth	88
Chapter 7: Valentine	99
Chapter 8: The Yorkshire Butchers	106
Chapter 9: The Laird of West Lothian	118
Chapter 10: Cousin Barry	132
Chapter 11: The Ayatollah's Fundraiser	156
Chapter 12: Stag Night	177
Chapter 13: Guatemala	200
Chapter 14: The Forgotten Birthday	235
Chapter 15: The Parents	259
Chapter 16: The Boyfriend	270
Chapter 17: The Big Lebowski	280
Chapter 18: The Happening	297
Chapter 19: The Babe Magnet	311
Chapter 20: Greenwich Park	324

PROLOGUE

When the clammy hand of modernity loomed into view, 40-plus Roger Fraser met it head on, his impenetrable shield of defiance protecting him from its harmful rays.

His life seemed to have become a whirl of misadventures and unforeseen potholes. *Déjà vu* memories haunted his waking and sleeping hours, and in the main had a nasty habit of reappearing and reinventing themselves in alternative guises designed to test his patience. Little surprised him, and though he prearmed himself with the necessary prerequisites to counter the threat, invariably something unexpected happened to rip apart his careful planning. Convinced that he had been hexed by a distant lover, a disgruntled client or a malevolent tax inspector, his caution to the unanticipated had become heightened to the point of alarm bells ringing as soon as his mobile sounded, or the postman delivered the mail.

Roger used to be lithe and good looking with boundless energy, but had recently gone prematurely grey, and sought the easy life away from bothersome restriction and interfering regulation. He was married to Charlotte, a striking siren who retained her youthful appearance, and found new things everyday to enrich her life, whilst making Roger's miserable. She said his shorter grey made him appear scholarly, but her husband missed his dark floppy mop.

Though lovable, Wendy, James and Heather, their three tricky and testing children, constantly challenged Roger's sensibilities on a whole variety of subjects. The Frasers' friends thought the children were angelic, but when offered for sale, they quickly retracted the accolade. Roger always questioned why.

Noticing recently that Wendy had developed into a young woman, Roger realised with pleasure that she took after her mother, being gifted with a gorgeous face and slim figure. He also wondered if the boys from the grammar school had noticed her metamorphosis into blossoming doe.

James had grown into a young version of his father, or at

least what Roger used to look like, a million years ago, or so it seemed to him. At that halfway house between manly pursuits and girl discovery, James found himself eternally attracted to the former, but snared by desires to explore the latter.

An inquisitive bundle of blonde curls and huge blue eyes, the Frasers' youngest Heather had an elephant's memory, and often became her father's greatest ally in his hour of need.

They lived in Hazelwood, a little out-of-the-way backwater in the suburbs of Kent.

When not working for the man, Roger's whole being became consumed by the family, and some of his in-laws and outlaws. Their demands called for him to surrender to the prevailing beat and back-pocket his rebellious condemnation of all things contemporary, and as he put it, designed to please the lowest common denominator.

Reality TV, false celebrity and the mendacious political classes all appalled him. In a world of crumbling values, they represented the stench of plasticity and the downward spiral of everything he held dear, including the encroachment of urban sprawl on his beloved Kent countryside, striving for excellence, and the correct use of the Queen's English. Somehow, the whole nation had been hoodwinked by this trio of fake gods. Voyeurs by proxy, viewers tuned into the inconsequential meanderings of the talentless, got sucked into fatuous debate about mediocrities, applauded badly performed old rock 'n' roll standards, and paid homage to self-appointed, self-interested social commentators, who claimed to be bastions of moral virtue.

Roger had to make a stand, push back at the overwhelming onslaught, kick against the pricks and become an avant-garde warrior, bursting their counterfeit bubbles and exposing their transparent cant.

CHAPTER 1: ART FOR ART'S SAKE

One fine sunny Saturday morning in downtown Kent county, the Fraser clan prepared to go to the Summer Exhibition at the Royal Academy of Arts. Charlotte had attended some art night classes at the local tech, and Roger's Aunt Jemina was somewhat of an art buff. Already, Roger wondered what rapacious devils waited, to add further angst and torment to challenge his powers of calm and calculation.

"Do I really have to go?"

"Yes, Roger," replied Charlotte, "you know Jemina expects it, she'll be very disappointed if you don't come."

"What does she see in this modern art thing anyway?" he asked. "I mean it's hardly in-keeping with her sophisticated tastes, is it?"

"She's exploring her dark side, besides, she's your aunt, so have a little more respect for her."

"But there's live golf on the telly, and…"

She cut him short. "Put the DVD recorder on, then."

Appearing to be running out of patience, Charlotte folded her arms together and tapped her foot on the kitchen floor in rhythmic syncopation; the usual warning signs that the red mist was about to descend.

"Very well," he agreed, "I'll record it. What time are we leaving?"

"Roger, you're hopeless, I've told you already, ten o'clock."

They packed the kids into the MPV, and headed over to Longfield Hill, to pick up Aunt Jemina; Roger's favourite aunt. Still sprightly and game for new adventures, she had a heart of gold, and invariably enjoyed her nephew's company, at least when he concurred with her views on the world. In appearance, she always reminded Roger of Joan Hickson, playing *Jane Marple*, with her bright inquisitive eyes and measured demeanour. She wore a formal hat at a jaunty angle, and a modest summer dress, ideal attire for the day's purpose, according to Charlotte.

After collecting Aunt Jemima and having barely gone a few miles along the A2, the Frasers saw a road-works sign, traffic coming to a near standstill. Roger exhaled noisily in frustration.

"You'd think they'd give us a break from it at the weekend, wouldn't you? It's more annoying than that singing git in the *GoCompare* advert, that perpetually floods our TV screens."

"Now don't start getting bad tempered, Roger," said his equally intolerant wife.

She knew that her husband knew she thought the same, but wanted to show her calm side to Aunt Jemima. Roger gave Charlotte a disdainful glare, but it just bounced off her.

"What's Roger getting annoyed about?" asked Aunt Jemima, breaking off from talking to Wendy about her homework assignments.

"Oh, it's nothing, Jemima...just a short delay," assured Charlotte.

"Short delay," Roger repeated venomously. "More like intentional sadism. The Minister for Transport knows it's a Saturday, so he's decided to be a complete twat, and cone off two lanes for ten miles, so Costain's workers can sweep the road, under supervision from 'ealth and safety jobsworths."

"What's a twat, Daddy?" enquired seven-year-old Heather.

Looking through the rear view mirror, Roger saw her blonde locks splayed against the back seat, and her blue eyes pinpointing him.

Auntie stopped talking to Wendy, and gawked up at her nephew. Charlotte nodded at Roger, her body language demanding an explanation.

"Well, sweetheart, it means that someone is..." He flustered around, trying for the appropriate softening words.

"Does it mean someone who is annoying you, Daddy?"

Heather prompted.

Roger could always rely on their youngest, to get him out of delicate situations, with a plausible explanation.

"Absolutely right, Heather," he said with enthusiasm, thinking what a lucky escape.

"Is Mister Jones from next door a twat, then?" asked Heather.

Charlotte and Roger stared at each other, bemused. Wendy and James sniggered. Shaking her head in a gesture of rebuke, Aunt Jemina stared out of the window. She wanted to remain incognito until this little episode concluded.

Her father was just about to ask Heather what she meant, but before his lips started moving, his youngest daughter came in again.

"That's what I heard Mummy call Mister Jones, when he lit that bonfire last week, and Mummy had to wash all the bed sheets again."

Lost for words, Charlotte grimaced, a mollifying glower settling on her face. She stared forward, in an attempt to disenfranchise herself from embarrassment.

"Roger, the traffic's moving," she said, "come on, we don't want to be late for the exhibition, do we?"

By Blackheath, as the Minister for Transport's cones became a distant memory, the MPV moved along at a reasonable speed. Hot and bothered, and already exhausted by the early morning challenges, Roger speculated as to what further mantraps may lay ahead in the day to ensnare him. To use an Americanism, he could virtually bet the farm on the prospect of something happening left field to cause him grief and distress, with the certain knowledge his gamble would remain safe. Segueing out of his melancholia, he became aware of the frivolities emanating from the vehicle's other occupants. The kids, bless them, he thought, were playing some tag game, whilst Charlotte talked to Aunt Jemina about the finer points of modern art, to prime her for the Royal Academy show. Back in concentration mode, as they continued to have fun, he wrestled with irate motorists, and cyclists riding in the middle of the road. He also tried to avoid getting caught on speed cameras; another prickly subject which wounded him to the core.

He was about to launch into an impassioned rendition of *I got the Chicken Shack, Fleetwood Mac, John Mayall can't fail blues*, but before he could get one note out, a dispatch rider sped past, almost taking off his wing mirror. Roger leaned out of the window, and the air went blue, with a hail of incendiary curses.

"Roger," exclaimed his wife.

"What?"

"Concentrate on your driving."

Looking suitably justified with his actions, he replied, "But I am. If I wasn't, that sod would have taken off my wing mirror."

She whispered in his ear. "What will Jemina think?"

Realising the gravity of his justified, but emotional outburst, he apologised. "Sorry, Aunt Jemina….sorry kids."

"Was that another twat, Daddy?" asked the Frasers' youngest daughter.

Still inwardly angry, Roger couldn't resist replying with, "It sure was, Heather."

"Roger," admonished his wife.

With the MPV parked at New Cross, the contingent headed for the underground. Three train changes, and 45 minutes later of enduring the most unspeakable smells, particularly on the District Line, they emerged gasping for air at Piccadilly.

Having a great time, the children gawked at the London freaks, and strained their necks gazing at skyscrapers, while Charlotte and Aunt Jemina jabbered away, oblivious to everything. A tornado could have consumed Greater London, but they would have been blind to it. Instead, the anal chat, anal as far as Roger was concerned, became about Tracey this and Damien that, Charlotte trying to impress, with her recently acquired knowledge of post-modernism. Absorbing the stream of consciousness, Aunt Jemina leisurely took it in but without showing any real enthusiasm for the subject. As well as chauffeur and financier for the whole damn trip, Roger also acted as navigator. He got the 'Oh really, Roger' look, if they took a wrong turn, or jumped on the wrong Tube train. However, with the Royal Academy only a few hundred yards west down Piccadilly, the worst seemed to be over, or was it?

***

In the courtyard, the Frasers saw a stainless steel sculpture over 20 feet tall, appearing to be emanating pastel shades in its reflected images. Gathering round the edifice, they turned to Charlotte, who had already done her homework.

"It's a Jeff Koons, called *Colouring Book*," she said.

"Can I climb to the top of it, Daddy?" enquired Heather.

Before Roger could answer, Charlotte chimed in. "Better not, darling. We don't want you falling off and hurting yourself, do we? Or Mister Koons suing Daddy for damages."

No, we certainly don't want that, Roger thought. Then suddenly he remembered the artist's name.

"Ah, I've heard of Koons, he's a septic, isn't he?"

"A septic, Roger?" asked Aunt Jemina.

Charlotte moved towards her husband, her manner threatening. "Don't take any notice, Jemina. He means, he's a Yank."

"Septic tank, Yank….oh, that's a good one, Dad," said James.

"Thank you, son, I knew I could rely on you to twig the connection."

"Oh, I see," said auntie, as she turned to Charlotte. "He always was a bit of a wag, even as a schoolboy."

Grinning, Roger basked in the adulation, before Charlotte subtly whispered in his ear, that if he wanted to continue to receive the pleasures of the flesh, he should refrain from his brand of vulgar rugby-dressing-room humour.

"Yes, dear," he told her, "message received and understood."

Thinking it would have been cheaper to see a double-header at Twickenham, Roger handed over what seemed like a small fortune for three adults and three kids, to the earnest looking receptionist. The group sashayed inside the hallowed building, the much vaunted experience moments away, their imaginations pregnant with expectation, Roger's survival training about to be stress tested.

Immediately, Heather surged forward to some curious-looking artificial decoration hanging from the ceiling, with the intention of swinging from it. The intention pleased her father. He thought maybe they would get thrown out, and he would get to see the live golf, after all. But no, just before Heather was about to take a mighty leap Tarzan style, Charlotte stepped in playing the bad guy.

"Heather." The youngest Fraser appeared to come to a halt in mid-flight. "Before you even think about swinging on that art exhibit, don't."

"That's an art exhibit?" Roger exclaimed, unable to hold back his sense of amazement.

Charlotte gave him a rueful look, nothing more to be said.

Heather found another distraction, whilst 16-year-old Wendy, and the slightly younger James, who wished he was 18, decided they wanted audio dialogue. It's a cool thing for teenagers to do, they told their father. The threesome went back to reception, allowing Roger to play involuntary financier again.

Passing over the headphones, the male attendant beamed at him joyfully, and said, "Lovely day for a family outing, isn't it, sir?"

Scowling a broken smile back at him, Roger thought he would like to go head-to-head with him on a rugby pitch in the depths of winter, and say, 'Lovely day for a scrum down, isn't it?'

Returning, they found Charlotte and Aunt Jemina involved in serious inspection of the items on display, though the latter appeared dumbstruck, by the incredulity of the exhibits.

"Oh, look at this fabulous sculpture, Jemina," Charlotte enthused. "Hasn't it got that air of power and passion about it?"

Taking a step back, Aunt Jemina made her appreciation. She began to look at it sideways, Wendy breaking into a snigger, at her unintentional lampooning antics.

"Well my dear," replied Jemina, "I think I can see what the artist is trying to achieve, but it's hardly Auguste Rodin, or even Henry Moore, is it?"

Just about to give it his two penneth, saying it reminded him of a sawn-off tree trunk, Charlotte saw her husband's lips about to move. Reading his mind perfectly, she delivered another caustic look.

"Yes Roger, we can all see what you think….no need for you to say anything."

Whistling gently to himself, hands behind his back, he stared at the ornate ceiling.

"Oh, that's magnificent."

Turning sharply to face him, Charlotte enquired, "What's magnificent?"

Pointing upwards, he smiled a smile of cultural appreciation.

Charlotte shook her head from side-to-side, appearing exasperated. "Roger, we are not here to observe ceilings." She turned to Aunt Jemina, obviously intent on soliciting moral support.

Auntie looked blank, and then broke into an admiring countenance, as her eyes fell on the ceiling. The kids followed suit.

Charlotte tut-tutted, taking no notice of her family's apparent fascination. "We are here to immerse ourselves in this fabulous array of modern art, not approve of gold-leaf ceiling decoration."

She majestically swept her arm forward, nearly knocking over one of the exhibits, and gulped in air so near-to-breathless, that she nearly destroyed the work. Contrition written on her face, Charlotte peered around nervously, convinced one of the gallery attendants had noticed her indiscretion.

"Yes darling," Roger said, amused at her unintentional recklessness.

Then he glanced forward, and saw what lay ahead on the tour, his amusement transformed to a mope. 'Oh God', he thought, 'this is a mountain to climb'. Momentarily, he transported himself to Wentworth, floating along on fairways made by angels from gold leaf, the gallery ceiling having a strong symbolic effect, Lee Westwood about to take his second shot at the 18th, for a championship winning birdie and....he felt a dig in the ribs.

"Roger, stop daydreaming," his wife intoned.

They continued with the dirge, as Roger was to later report to his work colleagues. Of course he meant 'The fabulous array of modern art', if he was quoting his wife. The party found themselves faced by an assortment of the latest products from the wacky world of post-modernism. It ranged from fairly conventional oil and acrylic paintings, and photography, some of which he liked, through to weird concoctions of the bizarre, which wouldn't look out of place on a building site, in a haberdashery shop, or a tart's boudoir.

He'd been dreading this day, since Charlotte insisted the whole family visit Tate Modern at Bankside, six months earlier. Another *Alice Through the Looking Glass* happening, where they were treated to modern art masquerading as refugees from an artificial flower shop, failed mechanical engineering leviathans, and various escapees from a kid's playground, including a huge helter-skelter. He couldn't for the life of him see any connection between this hotchpotch of buffoonery, much of it appearing to be resultant from the liberal consumption of copious amounts of LSD, and the stuff he'd seen at the National and the 'real' Tate, when he was at school, 25 years earlier. The experience had left him cold, but the kids had seemed to enjoy it. Heather had thought it like Alton Towers, Wendy making notes on the gallery for her French homework assignment, and James spending most of the day eyeing up older girls, forever wanting to be 18. Roger kept telling him that it would come soon enough, and that he'd pine for his school days, but James thought his father was weird, and didn't like girls. Roger had told him, 'I married your mother, didn't I?', but James replied, 'Mums don't count'. Roger gave up long ago, on trying for logic with their children.

The touring party then happened upon a group of BBC pseudo-art intellectuals, who according to Charlotte made a programme about the 2011 Summer Exhibition, the previous week. Immediately, Roger took an instant dislike to them. They looked like a supercilious bunch of condescending castles in the sky detached from reality types with their trendy clothing, mock Oxbridge accents, and air of superiority. They were cut from the same lofty, satirical, patronising BBC bedrock that spawned those arrogant pompous arseholes inhabiting *Have I Got News for You*, *Mock the Week* and *QI*. As the Frasers heard their falsetto tones, sermonising about the ingratitude of philistines like Roger to understand post-modernism, his dislike became intensified, he really despised them. They recognised Jannette Spliff Snorter extolling the virtues of one exhibit, to someone clearly in vehement disagreement. Roger thought it may be Brian Sewell, who looked like he loathed the pseudo-intellectual art set, as well.

"Daddy, why is that woman talking with such a strange voice?" asked Heather.

Roger began to think up an acerbic answer, but Charlotte had him in her sights, so he went for the conciliatory.

"Oh, she's got some sort of speech impediment."

Charlotte gave him a half-approving look.

"Dreadful woman," muttered Aunt Jemina. "As if a sane person would take any notice of her opinions, on anything.

She's always telling people how they must behave, but her own track record is hardly impeccable. She's another one of those 'do as I say, not as I do', holier-than-thou television pundits."

Roger's eyes lit up. "Oh, I do so agree with you, Aunt Jemina." Then he noticed Charlotte beginning to growl. "Well....she does have some good points," he added unconvincingly.

"What good points?" asked Heather. "She looks like what Daddy calls a twat!"

Grinning nervously, Roger asked, "shall we move on?"

Before they could, Charlotte took her husband's arm, gesturing forward. "Oh, look, there's Veranda Greenwoman." She pointed at the figure moving into their field of view, her gleeful admiration plain to see.

"Didn't she used to be an actress?" enquired Roger.

"She is an actress....actor."

"Oh yes, I forgot, the feminine tense has been outlawed, hasn't it?"

"She's in *New Tricks*," said Wendy.

Auntie covertly spied on Greenwoman, the narrowing of her eyes indicating she wasn't a fan. "I know her....and she's a nasty piece of work. I don't know why those other three detectives don't clock her one. I have the patience of a saint, but that, that person....gives women a bad name."

"She's just acting, Jemina," assured Charlotte.

"Hhmmm....she seems to put her heart and soul into it, like she's a man-hater," insisted Aunt Jemina.

"She is," Roger whispered to James, who cracked up.

"What was that you said, Roger?" demanded Charlotte, exuding a menacing disposition.

"Nothing dear....just talking to James about the vagaries of television character casting."

They watched Greenwoman make her way over to the BBC contingent. She showed her fully-paid-up-member of the 'I support anything which is trendy, and I'm a zealous do-gooder brigade member' pass, and was welcomed into their insular midst.

The reviewing party moved on.

One huge gallery was themed around the personal taste of a particularly well known artist, or was he a curator? Charlotte said his name, and his occupation, but Roger instantly forgot it. He tried his best to keep a straight face, but some of the patronised work on show appeared to be no better than what he'd seen in Heather's school class, where they used crayons and paint squirters, to make deformed human and animal images.

He'd restrained himself for long enough, since the wooden sculpture incident incurred his wife's wrath, so decided to ask what he thought to be quite a perceptive question.

"Charlotte."

As if intuitively knowing her husband was about to make a derogatory comment, she turned on her heels and faced him. "Yes."

"Charlotte, what is it about these works, that you find so appealing?" he enquired, venturing an encouraging smile to back up the question. "I mean, what in your view, is their particular excellence?"

Charlotte eyed him suspiciously. "Well, if you are being serious...." She twisted in Aunt Jemina's direction, seeking objective support. "It's the sheer exuberance of the creations, the lateral thought involved in their development, and the audacity of their uniqueness."

About to challenge her assertion, Roger thought better of it. Instead, he chose a non-confrontational response.

"Well that leaves nothing unexplained, but...."

"Yes, Roger?"

Examining his wife quizzically, and being careful how he

framed his next words, he ventured, "do eh....do people really buy this stuff?" He started to lose it. "I mean, you'd have to be pretty much living with the faeries, to want to part with your hard-earned readies to buy demented-looking pixies, lines of glassware, and bits of 'Frank Spencer' standard woodwork."

Charlotte didn't answer. She just shook her head from side to side again, and moved on.

Turning to Aunt Jemina, Roger asked, "Was it something I said?"

"Oh, Roger....you'll be in the divorce courts, if you carry on ribbing Charlotte. Try and be a little more empathetic."

"But....but I thought I was. I thought....Charlotte, Charlotte...."

Continuing to navigate through the melange, the day trippers watched people's reactions to the exhibits, collapsed in the odd chair to take a well-earned rest, and found relief from the heat under the air-conditioning outlets.

The sense of dedication and endurance characteristics some people employed to get through the show, appeared faultless. Roger noticed many in group parties, clearly seemed worse for wear, but still they sustained the trek. It's a matter of honour, he supposed. They knew failure to complete the marathon would incur the wrath of their co-patrons, a permanent black mark, barring them from such future events.

Strolling through the concourses, Roger began to question himself, as to why people visit galleries. He used to think it was because they inspired the onlookers, but few at the Summer Exhibition appeared stirred. In the main, like him, they had their eyes set on the last bend, taking them to the finishing line. Once crossed, they would beam relief, and charge headlong for the exits, breathing in fresh air, well relatively fresh air. They would become liberated, and think 'Never again'. But then he tempered his assertion, it may be wishful thinking anyway. Maybe he conjured up looks of despair on their faces, that weren't there. Perhaps he saw the look on his face, in theirs!

"Roger, you're daydreaming again," exclaimed his irritated wife. "Stop thinking about golf, and start appreciating these wonderful exhibits."

"Yes dear," Roger replied, going into a mock Basil Fawlty voice, stopping short from saying *Careful not to tread on any landmines, dear.*

In the central hall, the Frasers were faced with a curious stack of kitchen chairs, at its epicentre. At first, Roger thought the gallery attendants had stacked the chairs, but Charlotte assured the reviewing party that it was in fact an artist's exhibit.

James did a 360 around the stack, then carped, "Oh, come on Mum, this can't be an exhibit. It's just chairs, arranged to approximate a pyramid, with the top cut off."

Charlotte breathed out scornfully, exasperated that as well as her husband, her son was also a barbarian.

It was a similar story in Gallery 7, where a Tracey Emin impersonator had added a telephone to an unmade bed. Roger and the kids stared at the exhibit, blanching the natural desire to want to make the bed, and put the phone back on its cradle. Difficult to believe a smart business man like Chas Satchel would shell out a 150 thousand of the folding stuff, for the Emin-like puerile attempt at post-modernism, thought Roger. He made the point to Charlotte, but she waved him away with a dismissive gesture. Roger's suggestion that since Charlotte was a post-modernist aficionado, she should make Chas aware of the unmade bed, and in the process make them a fortune, only brought a further bout of wifey discontent. Her dismissive motion became a flurry of expletives, whispered in her husband's ear, so the rest of the contingent couldn't hear.

Whilst Charlotte drooled over another worthless-looking object, Roger subconsciously propped himself up against one of the floor-mounted sculptures. Pondering how this little escapade could be brought to a swift conclusion, he heard a deep authoritative voice in his left ear say, "You're leaning against an exhibit, sir."

A gallery attendant, having the appearance of a Zulu wars period British Army regimental sergeant major, replete with flashy moustache and long sideburns, stood at Roger's side, his eyes burning censure into Roger's soul. He gave Roger a disciplinary glare, as the modern art heretic balanced his weight away from the object. Roger thought about telling the sergeant major to go get himself treated by a taxidermist, but then thought better of it. Charlotte had seen the incident, and was rushing back in his direction.

"I'm so sorry," she pleaded to the RSM. "My husband is a bit clumsy."

"That's alright, ma'am," he replied, almost saluting. "May I suggest you make sure he keeps away from the floor-standing exhibits....just in case he lapses again."

"Of course," Roger's ingratiating wife confirmed.

'Cheeky bastard', Roger thought, but bit his lip, forcing an agreeing smile.

Later, the faction moved into a salon, containing paintings and the odd sculpture.

Noticing a circular object, lying beneath two hung canvasses on a wall, Roger said, "Oh, look, some workmen have left a piece of stonework. I bet the curator is furious about that."

Sidling up to him, Charlotte informed, "That's the winner of the Charles Wollaston Award." She dug her husband in the ribs. It would not be the last time that day. "Now don't embarrass me, Roger."

"But it can't be....you're joking....it's, it's just a round stone, with a hole in it, that's been filled with some resin."

Another dig in the ribs came his way, this time harder, the pain acute, but temporary.

"But I wasn't trying to be sarcastic, I...."

Charlotte forged on ahead to the next room, whilst Roger searched Aunt Jemina's face, seeking sympathetic support.

"Roger, stop goading her," implored Jemina. "I know most of this is complete rubbish, but she is on a voyage of discovery….so oblige her."

"But Aunt Jemina, I wasn't, I….oohhh."

Auntie scowled, and strode off in pursuit of Charlotte.

Sauntering up to her father, the youngest Fraser asked, "Are you in trouble again, Daddy?"

"I'm always in trouble, Heather."

After nearly two hours of wonderment or torment, depending on your particular view of post-modernism, the kids were on the verge of seeking new ventures, and Roger needed a drink, preferably a long cool beer, but his darling wife still had her modernity penchant to be satisfied. They'd actually gone around the complete show, but Charlotte wanted to revisit the most interesting work, whatever that was, her husband thought.

They trudged along after her, Aunt Jemina in particular doing a sterling support role. By now, Roger's even temper had waned. All he really wanted to do was to smash most of the airy-fairy exhibits, and make a massive bonfire of them. Wendy also seemed bored, on the edge of saying 'When can we go home', which of course her father hoped she'd say. Though also appearing bored, James was still enthralled by the hordes of late teenage girls, trying so desperately to be hip, so he sidelined boredom, quite content playing the distant watcher. Heather too, still seemed in two minds. When focused on the fun the exhibits offered, she had a ball. To her, the exhibition still equated with Alton Towers. She couldn't wait until nobody was looking, to swing from the hanging exhibits, and trample over the floor-mounted sculptures.

Needing temporary relief from the combat zone, Aunt Jemina went off to buy an exhibition catalogue. Roger could tell she'd just about had enough, but would remain ambassadorial in her outlook.

"Oh, we missed that one earlier," said Charlotte, pointing to what appeared to be a child's climbing frame in the Lecture Room, but in fact intended to represent 'The endless struggle of man, in his efforts to find freedom', according to her. Roger sympathised with the artist's intent, since that appeared to be his struggle, as well.

Now packed with enthusiasts, the curious, and doubters like Roger, all searching their exhibition maps trying to find a reference point, the Royal Academy approximated Heathrow Terminal 5, in that nobody quite knew how to find what they were looking for, but they knew it existed somewhere. The physical atmosphere became close, noise levels rising, waves of conversations hovered over the crowd, like balloons drawn by a cartoonist. Roger felt very hot, and beyond caring about cessation of bedroom pleasures.

Despite his new found empathy, cynicism returned, as he peeped sideways at some incomprehensible piece of worthless rubbish.

"Oh, dear me….this is a bit wanky, isn't it?" he whispered to his wife.

"It is not wanky at all, as you call it. It is superb," insisted Charlotte, in a determined, louder than normal voice.

"What does wanky mean, Daddy?" asked Heather, ever the inquisitor with her 'w' questions.

Roger opened his mouth, about to invent something plausible on the hop, but again Charlotte beat him to the draw.

"It means Daddy may be sleeping in the spare bedroom tonight," predicted his wife, a withering look of evil intent spreading across her anguished face.

After taking a well-earned rest, Wendy wandered up to rejoin the collective.

"What's happening?" she asked.

"Daddy just said a rude word," declared Heather.

Roger's mouth opened again in surprise, astonishment written on his face.

"Heather, how do you know it's a rude word?"

"Oh, I've heard James say a word like that, and Mummy scolded him."

Still consumed in girl watching to this point, suddenly James decided he needed to exit, stage left.

"I'll be back in a minute," he advised. "Just seen someone I know from school."

"James," his father called after him, but he'd vanished into the melee of modern-art seekers.

Turning to look at Charlotte, tapping her foot and metaphorically throwing darts at him, Roger said, "You didn't tell me James had said that word."

The foot tapping rate increased.

Trying to diffuse the situation with a lateral escape ploy, Roger said, "Oh, look at that sculpture, that's good, isn't it?"

But the ploy failed. Charlotte's foot tapping reached a crescendo.

"Roger, you're absolutely hopeless."

"What's he done now, Charlotte?" asked Aunt Jemina, returning to the fray.

"Oh….molluscs," replied Charlotte.

"Daddy, you still haven't told me what wanky means."

CHAPTER 2: DONGLE HELL

After the rigours of the Summer Exhibition, the Frasers retired to Chiquito's in Leicester Square, everyone ravenous and the menu looked mouth watering. Roger ordered enough burritos to feed a small army, a pitcher of margaritas, and orange for the kids, although James persisted in his demands to be included in the cocktails. They munched their way through the feast, everyone lightening up, after the seriousness of post-modernism appraisal. Rapidly gaining brownie points with Charlotte for the restaurant choice, Roger's scathing comments about modern art began to fade, as the tequila-based drink took effect. Having a whale of a time, it was Aunt Jemina's first experience of a Mexican restaurant. Her food slid down like liquid honey, helped by lashings of margarita. Suddenly, Roger sensed the women were getting high. Charlotte had volunteered to drive them back to the suburbs, but already she was way past fulfilling that commitment. He would have to be the responsible parent. Reluctantly, he put down his margarita, and joined the kids on orange juice, wondering at the same time if Lee Westwood had prevailed at Wentworth.

Resigning himself to abstinence, he leaned on the table, resting his chin in his left hand, whilst listening to Wendy telling him about her latest maths challenges. Then out of the blue, Ben Stapleton and his family came into his view. Stapleton used to work with Roger, but was a complete arse, a vacillating puff adder, known for his outrageous capacity to drop people in the nasty stuff, and then watch them writhe round in whatever embarrassing situation devoured his victim. Charlotte also knew Ben, and his Barbie wife, Deborah. Roger nudged Charlotte's arm.

"What?" she asked.

Indicating ahead, he said, "Look who's coming."

Glancing in the given direction, his wife muttered, "Oh no."

Charlotte despised Deborah because she attracted men, like moths to a flame. Deborah's Barbie persona was a man's paradise; easy, relaxed, non-confrontational, in many ways the antithesis of Roger's wife, whose natural constituency constantly bordered on the testing.

"Smile darling," prompted Roger, "remember Stapleton now works for one of my company's clients….and he's on the buy side."

"Roger," said Ben, grinning gregariously, "I thought it was you. How are you? Charlotte, good to see you again."

The adults made the necessary introductions with the Frasers' three children, and the Stapletons' four, swapping corrosive views about Simon Cowell, and discussing the latest iPhone apps. Chewing gum relentlessly, the lower-middle Stapleton boy, Simon, appeared to be in a world of his own making, oblivious to his surroundings. James mooned at the eldest Stapleton daughter, Stephanie, who clearly enjoyed teasing him. She took after her mother, and was a junior Barbie, though it shined better on her than Deborah. Meanwhile, Charlotte and Deborah exchanged daggers, curt with each other like circling gladiators.

"What have you been up to, Roger?" asked Ben.

"Oh, we've been to the Summer Exhibition, at the Royal Academy of Art."

"Really, modern art?" Ben clarified. "Hey….I seem to recall you saying that all modern art is rubbish."

Beginning to look concerned, Roger noticed Charlotte's ears had pricked up, the situation fast becoming prime territory for one of Stapleton's infamous mire dowsing episodes. Roger could already see himself squirming around, up to his rear end in alligators, trying to fend them off, when he'd been charged with draining the swamp.

"No….are you sure that was me?" pleaded Roger. "Wasn't it Talbot in corporate accounts who said that?"

Ben considered for a moment, Roger thinking his

predicament had been recognised."Yes," Ben answered, "Talbot didn't like modern art....but it was you who said it was all rubbish."

Now fully alert again, Charlotte prowled, wanting to play Witchfinder General to wheedle out modern-art heretics. Roger could feel her eyes piercing his body, searching for vulnerable organs to torture, like Superman's x-ray vision cutting through steel. The swamp beckoned.

"Are you in trouble again, Daddy?" asked Heather.

"Daddy's always in trouble, darling!"

Whether immediate, or stored up for a future sortie, the Frasers' youngest tried to relieve her father's impending wife attack, by launching into impersonations of Jannette Spliff Snorter. She was definitely Daddy's girl. The Stapleton kids knew the scary Jannette woman as well, breaking into fits of laughter at Heather's voice impressions. Roger gave their daughter ten out of ten for artistic expression, whilst Charlotte forced a wry smile. Charlotte's archenemy, Deborah, gawked with quiet contentment, basking in Charlotte's obvious minority-liking of Snorter.

Thankfully, the conversation moved onto what the Stapletons had been doing, the Frasers all make-believing interest, in Ben and Deborah's account of their day. Then Heather yawned, almost knocking her glass of orange juice over Deborah, much to Charlotte's delight, but protocol surfaced, and Charlotte scolded Heather, her daughter looking suitably contrite. Heather almost winked at Roger, indicating the glass contents spillage in Deborah's direction, an intentional act. Inwardly, her father bristled with pride.

After what seemed like years of unabated tedium, the Stapletons finally concluded, by telling the Frasers about their trip to the Natural History Museum, and about their next target, the IMAX. The adult's conversation then dropped into teenage relationships, leaving Wendy and the Stapleton upper-middle son, Steven, wriggling in their seats with embarrassment. Like an old hand, Stephanie took it in her stride, seemingly a mature 16, going on 32, whilst James, near to dribbling, continued to be mesmerised by her.

Suddenly, Heather squawked, "I've got a boyfriend as well."

Having gained the adults' attention, she grinned contentedly, pleased with herself.

Charlotte smiled at Deborah, a first as far as Roger could remember. "She has this special relationship, with a boy in her class."

Gazing at the youngest Fraser like a matriarchal classroom assistant, the look incongruous considering her obvious bodily charms, Deborah asked, "Do you mean you are friends, Heather?"

"No, lovers."

Charlotte and Roger exchanged discomforting laughs, then he explained, "She's very grown up for her age."

Seeing a debasing front page headline in the making, that Ben could exploit to her nephew's detriment, Aunt Jemima interjected with, "Charlotte, tell them about that fabulous hanging exhibit at the Royal Academy."

A seasoned survivor of child-based mortifying situations, Charlotte embarked on an impassioned account of the said work. Despite her synthetic looks, Deborah was quite knowledgeable about modern art, challenging some of Charlotte's views, and offering an alternate take on the piece. After a few minutes of Q&A between all three enthusiastic women, Aunt Jemima faking it of course, a slight lull in the conversation brought temporary silence.

Quickly turning to Roger before the women started up again, Ben said, "And what did you think of this masterpiece, Roger?"

Whilst Roger tried to form the appropriate, put-on, erudite words, Heather chipped in with, "Daddy thought it was a bit wanky."

Flabbergasted by the remark, the Stapletons gaped. Even Simon abruptly stopped chewing on his gum.

Breaking into an uneasy laugh, Charlotte opined, "Kids, where do they get it from?"

***

By the time the Kent-bound travellers got back to the MPV, the children were getting fidgety, Aunt Jemima as well. She had finally reached the end of her very long diplomatic tether, and made noises about needing a good cup of Darjeeling, when she got back home.

With rush hour developing on the A2, early-evening traffic backed up to Bexley, causing temperatures to rise. The Minister for Transport had decided to have more fun, by allowing a Costain Group clean-up crew onto the east-bound side of the carriageway, reducing it to a single lane. Irate motorists gestured their fury, as they passed workers appearing to have little enthusiasm for the job. In turn, the workers responded back with V signs, and shouts of 'Piss off, you hooray Henry'.

Frustrated by yet another delay, Roger said, "It takes all the pleasure out of driving."

"What does, dear?" Aunt Jemima asked.

"Oh," he agitated for a moment. "All the rules and regulations, the hidden cameras, police directed to catch errant motorists, whilst letting off real criminals scot-free, intentional road works designed to drive the private motorist off the roads….it's all too much."

Turning around in her seat to face Auntie, Charlotte advised, "He's been watching *Top Gear* again."

"*Top Gear*?" Aunt Jemima questioned.

"Yes, *Top Gear*," clarified Roger, earnestly. "You know, Hammond, May and the great Jeremy Clarkson. We never miss it do we, James?"

"Never, Dad."

"Oh yes, I do know *Top Gear*," Aunt Jemima confirmed, now fully in gear, if you'll forgive the pun.

Starting to twist around in amazement at the enthusiastic recognition, Roger nearly crashed into the car in front, before regaining vehicular control.

"Are you sure?" questioned Charlotte.

"Quite sure," verified Aunt Jemina. "I do like that Jeremy Clarkson, he's very funny, and the show is quirky, very humorous."

"Do you know Aunt Jemina, there are more women watch *Top Gear*, than men?" Roger asked.

"Doesn't surprise me, most of my lady friends tune in to *Top Gear*."

"And more women," continued Roger, "fancy Jeremy Clarkson than Jeremy Paxman."

"That's someone else, I don't like," said Aunt Jemina.

"What, Paxman?" Roger asked.

"No, that nauseating woman on *Newsnight*, oh, what's her name, er...."

"Oh, I know who you mean, Aunt Jemina," surmised Roger, "Khristy Squawk."

"Yes, that's her. She always talks down to people. I don't like that."

"I know what you mean," Roger said. "Looks like she's got a bug up her rectum, and is exceedingly pompous, sanctimonious, high-handed and toffee-nosed. Wouldn't have been out of place with those other BBC zealots, we saw at the Royal Academy. She's another charmless Celtic nerk, in the same vein as Gordon Brown and Candy Murrey."

Hearing her husband's demolition of the *Newsnight* presenter, the burgeoning look of amazement on Charlotte's face became priceless, a picture to behold. She loathed *Top Gear*, Clarkson in particular, and thought Squawk was the dog's bollocks, even the donkey's bollocks, as they say in Essex.

"Don't sugar coat it, Roger, tell us what you really think," she said sarcastically.

In a role reversal, Roger's wife had said to him, what he usually said to her, when she was off on one of her diatribes, about Wayne Rooney or David Starkey.

Ignoring the acid rebuke, Roger continued to act as *Top Gear* publicist. "Do you know Aunt Jemina, the politically correct brigade at the BBC want to pull the programme, but the senior management won't allow that?"

"No....no, I didn't."

"Well," blurted Roger, "*Top Gear* is syndicated to over a 180 countries, with I think, 350 million viewers worldwide. Can you imagine how much revenue the holier-than-thou BBC earns from that?"

"No, I can't, Roger."

"Put it this way, it's enough to keep the top echelon, and all their overpaid, so called stars, in champagne and Rollers for life, plus subsidise their unpopular politically correct soap operas, so the politically correct brigade have to grin and bear it." Turning to Aunt Jemina, this time in full vehicular control, he said jovially, "It's great, isn't it?"

"Plus every episode of *Top Gear* is downloaded by over 300 thousand people," pushed James, "and there are over eight million followers on Facebook."

"I watch the *Top Gear* repeats on Dave," said Wendy.

"So do I," added Heather.

Charlotte's mouth had become wide open in total disbelief of her family's passion for Clarkson and co, it just wasn't her day.

* * *

By the time the happy wanderers had tea at Auntie's, the mood had become tranquil, Darjeeling working its magic. Charlotte and Aunt Jemina engaged in small talk, allowing Roger to relax, fully spaced out, and looking forward to watching the golf, when they got back home.

The children pretended they were contestants on Simon Cowell's show, asking each other asinine questions, and singing Girls Aloud songs. James did a very good, flat voiced impersonation of Cowell, while the girls united in their rendition of *Sound and Vision*. Of course, Roger could remember when David Bowie first did it.

Just when he thought the worst calamities of the day were over, Charlotte began to revisit the Summer Exhibition with

Aunt Jemina, poking him yet again in the ribs to join in the conversation.

"Of course," said Charlotte, with an assured sense of informed authority, "it wasn't as challenging as Susan Phillips, Richard Wright or Mark Leckey....or even Jayson Ferry."

"Who dear?" enquired a puzzled Aunt Jemina.

Trying to help her out, Roger said, "Oh, I recognise that last name. Isn't he the guy who dresses like a woman, even makes his face up?"

"Is he a transvestite?" asked James.

Before his father could reply, Charlotte charged to the defence.

"No, James, he is simply making an artistic statement."

"By looking like a woman?" retorted James, half smiling. "Does that mean all transvestites are artists, then?"

"No, it doesn't work like that. You see, Jayson has an alter ego he calls Claire. When he wants to stop being a man for a while, he assumes the persona of Claire."

"Isn't that what all transvestites claim?" quizzed James.

Really enjoying the opposing conjecture, Roger's son was doing all his usual work for him. The pros and cons of alter-ego Claire were batted, to and fro between Charlotte and James, with Aunt Jemina refereeing, but looking even more mystified.

"What's a transvestite?" asked Heather.

Roger had been waiting for that one, with bated breath. Heather had addressed the question to her mother, so he was off this particular hook in the explanation stakes.

Clearly trying to assemble the right words, Charlottefinally said, "Well, darling, it's a man who doesn't feel quite right about his sexuality, and tries to find his real self by dressing in women's clothes." She finished with a bright smile, sure that the question had been answered.

Heather considered for a moment, then said, "Is that the same as what Daddy calls a poof?"

Wendy and James began to snigger.

Aunt Jemina tried to escape the apparent *faux pas*. She

melted into the back of her chair looking disconcerted, then asked, "What's a poof, Roger?"

Before he could make a calculated retort, Charlotte leapt in. "It means gay, Jemina."

"Gay...." Jemina clarified, "You mean they are happy people?"

Deciding not to risk shocking Aunt Jemina further, Charlotte replied, "Something like that."

After a suitable pregnant pause, Roger's wife resumed her eulogising of post-modernism artists.

"You know, they put a great deal of effort into their work," she insisted. "Much more than meets the eye." Stopping momentarily to make further consideration, she then made her final point. "It takes a great deal of talent."

Satisfied with her endorsement, Charlotte sat back, with an air of pre-eminence.

Feeling a bit more confident that he wasn't the only non-believer in the room, Roger took up the assertion. "Great deal of effort....great deal of talent," he said, with obvious vitriol. "Oh really, Charlotte, how on Earth can you say that? I remember when some Herbert constructed a rectangle of house bricks at the Tate in 1998, and had the audacity to pronounce it art. Does that mean if Fred Appleton, who does house repairs, made a wall in our back garden, it would be proclaimed as a progressive piece of post-modernism?"

Charlotte peered at Roger astonished, and then the inevitable head-nodding from side to side began. "You are just not attuned to post-modernism. You don't understand all the complexities which go into making something, which appears very simple, but in actual fact is multifaceted, requiring a great deal of talent....isn't that right, Jemina?"

On the spot, Roger wondered if auntie would be truthful, or go for the softly, softly approach.

"Well, I have to say, if what I saw at the Summer Exhibition is representative of post-modernism as a whole, then it is a poor progression from the great genres which have preceded it." She put her hand on Charlotte's knee to reassure her. "Oh, I liked some of the paintings, my dear, but those other things, bits of this and bits of that, wouldn't be out of place in the soft furnishings department at House of Fraser. I'm sorry Charlotte, but on this occasion….and I don't like to admit it." She glanced at her nephew. "Roger is right."

Charlotte became dejected, while inwardly Roger beamed. However, he didn't go in for the kill, fearing deep and repeated retribution later, *Pulp Fiction* style.

Scrutinising the gathering, and determined to give it one last try to get her family to see the light, Charlotte said, "I do appreciate what you are saying, Jemina." She faced her husband. "And Roger….but these new modern artists are trying to differentiate themselves, from what has come before. They are trying to reflect contemporary society in their work. Sometimes, it's challenging, and to make their offerings into commercial propositions, they need publicity and patronage. The Royal Academy provides the publicity and people, like Chas Satchel, the patronage."

What my darling wife said is quite true, Roger thought to himself. That's the way it's always been, for every succeeding genre of the art form.

"What you say is correct, and has some credence, Charlotte," he supported, going for the rational."All artists of any kind, whether they are writers, musicians or painters, need a sponsor, a visionary. But there is a world of difference between what came before, and what has appeared over the past 30 years. If the likes of Hirst and Emin could paint like Picasso, but choose not to, instead creating peculiar works, we could respect them. But clearly, they can't. Their idiosyncratic work is a poor substitute, an attempt to compensate for an inability to be even a mediocre painter. Pickling is no recompense for painting."

Feeling a bit guilty about her own condemnation, Roger's auntie said, "Oh Charlotte, I hope I haven't upset you."

"No….no, Jemina, you haven't."

Aunt Jemina cast a heartening look at her nephew, still

apparently basking in his son's earlier scathing commentary. "Roger, you didn't mean to upset your lovely wife, did you?"

Avalanching out of near-daydream, he said, "Of course not, I love her."

"Then give her some encouraging remarks," half-ordered Jemina.

Roger went blank.

"Go on Roger," she insisted.

Deciding the statesman-like approach was best, Roger fulfilled auntie's request.

"Don't get me wrong, I fully understand the need for a business to create demand. In the case of post-modernism, patronage from a few…let's call them far sighted billionaires, certainly helps create kudos, and provides endorsement to generate traction." He paused to make sure Charlotte appeared content with his approach. Her body language seemed to suggest happiness, so he continued. "But to expect the general public to glibly go along with it is….gilding the lily." Lingering again, he hoped to engender neutrality. "I mean, we all stand in awe at the works of the great renaissance painters through to early twentieth-century artists, such as Matisse or Pablo Picasso. We do so, because we intrinsically recognise that their creations are beyond the realms of the ordinary, something very few people can hope to emulate. But to apply that acid test to post-modernism is crass, because the work is not extraordinary….just about anyone who has an inkling of creative talent could come up with most of what we saw today." He halted attempting to lessen the blow. "I'm sorry, Charlotte….but that's how I see it."

"Well, Roger," said Aunt Jemina, "that was very well put. I can see there is more depth to you, than you've ever shown me before." She turned to Charlotte. "I think the world of you, my dear, but Roger is right on this occasion."

Feeling quite elated, never having made an argument like that before, Roger begun to wish he'd recorded it on a dictaphone for reuse, even posterity.

"One last comment, if I may?" he said.

"Go ahead," encouraged Aunt Jemina.

"We all could be entirely wrong about condemning post-modernism....and Charlotte could be proved to be right. New art movements have invariably been lambasted by both the art establishment and the general public, since the renaissance. Later in time, they were re-appraised in the context of current fashions, and adjudged to be not so bad after all. We're going to look pretty silly, if in 50 years time, what we have seen today is recognised to be masterful art."

"You make a very good point, Roger," agreed auntie.

Close to tears, Charlotte buried her head in her husband's shoulder, planting a kiss on his cheek.

"Thank you, darling," she said meekly.

Looking suitably self-conscious, Roger returned the gesture.

"Errrrr....oh brother, oooohh," derided James, as he glanced away from the happy couple.

"Shush, James," scolded Aunt Jemina. "Your parents are having a tender moment."

Charlotte and Roger finished their embrace, remaining partially entwined.

"Look," Roger began to suggest, "we've been talking about modern art all day. Why don't we discuss something else?"

With Charlotte's and Aunt Jemina's facial expressions giving him encouragement along this line, he glanced around the children, still embroiled in the Simon Cowell show.

"Hey, Wendy, you're into social networking. What's the big new thing happening on Facebook?"

She gave her father a sideways look, as if to say 'You're too old for social networking', and then grudgingly told her family about her burgeoning friend-set on Facebook. James was also a Facebook member, and Heather would be, if her parents would let her.

"What else, Wendy?" enquired Charlotte, now snuggled up close to Roger.

"Well, we're all really getting into reading online

publications, such as short stories on iPhone."

Marvellous, isn't it? Roger thought. His two eldest kids have iPhones, as does Charlotte, and all he has is a basic mobile. Something definitely wrong there, but he refrained from making the point.

"Oh, what have you been reading?" asked Charlotte.

Wendy came over a little shy, before answering. "I suppose you'd call it chick-lit, but I think some of the stories are very good."

Breaking into a wicked smile, James beseeched, "No they're not, Mum, they're complete girlie dribble."

"How would you know?" demanded Charlotte.

Yes, Roger thought that as well, hoping his rugby-playing son had not been reading girlie stuff. That would be worse than being a 'Chelski' supporter. James fudged his unconvincing response, Wendy reiterating her mother's question to him. He finally confessed, that in a moment of curiosity leading to weakness, that yes, he had logged onto a chick-lit website.

"But I was only confirming my worst suspicions, about it being crap," bleated Roger's slightly embarrassed son, as his father frowned at him.

The conversation continued, about computing in general, and the internet in particular. Wendy and James seemed to know all the latest terminology, as did Charlotte, even Heather. But Roger's greatest surprise came when Aunt Jemina joined in, telling everybody about the new classical art software, she was running on her Windows 7 platform. Feeling like a bystander, eavesdropping on scientists' conversation about the future, he suddenly grasped the limitations of his computing dictionary.

"It would be good to be able to connect my laptop to the internet," posed Wendy, "away from Wi-Fi hot spot areas."

"Oh, you'll need a dongle for that," advised James.

"A what?" asked Roger, screwing his face up, in disbelief at the word.

"A dongle, Dad," confirmed James. "It's a universal serial bus device which plugs into your laptop, and provides mobile broadband services."

Looking around his family, Roger noticed that everybody seemed to intrinsically understand the meaning of the word dongle, without question. Beginning to laugh, he said, "Well....well, where I come from, a dongle is a....".

"Yes, Dad?" said Wendy.

Trawling his memory bank, he searched for the right softening words, to infer it meant tally-whacker. Fortunately, before he blurted out something, like 'beef bayonet' or 'giant redwood', Charlotte came to his rescue.

"What your father is trying to say is that dongle means a man's private part."

James almost fell off his chair laughing, whilst Wendy merely smirked.

Suddenly, Roger detected Aunt Jemina, eyeing him intently, her look of criticism palpable.

"Roger, I know it's a double entendre, but really," she said, rebuking her nephew with a wagging finger.

"But....I didn't say anything. It was Charlotte."

Aunt Jemina just shook her head. The brownie points Roger gained only moments earlier, were now spent. Charlotte released from their mutual entwinement, no longer wanting to play the lover, her sense of indignation surfacing.

Then suddenly, Heather, who had been unusually quiet, said, "What's a man's private part?"

"Well, Roger?" said Charlotte, her hackles starting to rise.

"It's, it's a....oooohh, er...." He peered to the heavens, Captain Kirk never around, when he needed him.

He had that familiar *déjà vu* feeling again, the one where you are certain history is repeating itself, for at least the sixth time that day. Those misadventures, and oh too familiar potholes, had Roger Fraser in their grasp yet again. It was time to circle the wagons and repel boarders, or failing that, show his hand, and throw himself on the mercy of his empathy-immune relations, in the hope of compassion.

"Are you in trouble again, Daddy?" enquired Heather.

Panning round his family, he saw they were all expecting an answer. Then turning to face Heather, he said, "To quote from my schooldays Latin, *'genitor est omnimodo in molestia'*."

"What, Daddy?" Heather asked again.

Charlotte, Aunt Jemina and Wendy virtually translated in unison, saying, "Daddy's always in trouble!"

CHAPTER 3: HOAX CALL

The Frasers decided to have a garden party for friends, in-laws and outlaws, alike. Nothing too grand, just something in tune with expectations, resultant from all those times when they had attended someone else's event, and said something like 'We really must have a summer party this year'. Well, at least that's what Charlotte said, to show that the Frasers could also roll out the red carpet for the community.

With a few days to go before the great event, Roger had been tasked with the usual male demarcation duties; preparing the barbeque, buying alcohol, and hiring garden fixtures and fittings. The erection of latter to be arranged on the day, the arranging, he intended to delegate to his dextrous children, if only.

He'd learnt through bitter experience, what and what not to cremate on the 'barbie', as his antipodean colleagues called it. In his nascent twenties, still green and largely inexperienced in the ways of the world, an American visitor had asked what was on the barbeque. Roger had told him steaks and faggots, to which the septic replied, 'You mean you fry homosexuals, here in England?' Clueless at the time, Roger found out later that rear gunners are called faggots in the U.S From then on, he meticulously explored foreign phrase and word interpretations, before entertaining anyone from overseas.

"Roger, you won't forget the drinks order, on your way home from work, will you?" requested Charlotte, half-expecting him to forget, her voice hovering over the sound of frying food, and DJ's squawking their inane chat.

"Of course, my sweet, your wish is my eternal command."

"It's a bit early in the morning for your brand of condescending, rugby-changing-room sarcasm, isn't it?"

"Sarcasm?" he exclaimed, pretending surprise. "Oh, you

must mean the reference, to my unerring devotion to you."

She gave him a derisory glare, about to wade in with another soul-destroying rebuke, when they heard the sound of buffalo, trampling down the stairs.

"Can you please pick your feet up on the stairs?" shouted Roger's ever child-tolerant, but insistent wife.

A few seconds later, their little rat pack, Wendy, James and Heather, bounced into the breakfast room beaming widely, so as to diffuse Charlotte's reproachful agenda and avoid further scolding. It worked, such a sucker for their children feigning innocence, just like Roger.

All feeding times in the Fraser household bore a close resemblance to vultures gorging on prey, breakfast being the highlight. It was the time when collectively, they were all still waking up, more susceptible to clumsy table manners, and misaimed food flying over shoulders, instead of into welcoming mouths. If a television crew were filming the spectacle, it would end up in the news, or as a documentary under the heading 'families verging on the dysfunctional'.

"Can I have Coco Pops this morning, Mummy?" asked the youngest daughter.

"Of course, darling," confirmed Charlotte, now smiling, her buffalo ballet annoyance already a past memory.

Heather changed her breakfast menu, more times than the Frasers' local MP changed his mind on controversial issues. Sometimes, it happened halfway through breakfast, when she would suddenly announce that Crunchy Nut Cornflakes or Frosted Flakes no longer made her boat float. Or she would come out with some obscure logic, as to why they made the ice cap melt, thereby endangering polar bears, anti-animal she would call it.

Usually famished, first thing in the morning, James consumed pancakes with maple syrup, to be followed by the full-Monty English traditional. He also watched his iPhone intently, as if expecting news that World War III had begun, but in fact it would probably be a text from one of his dippy pals, detailing the latest sexual conquest, probably failure. Roger knew when that happened, because suddenly his son would stop knife and fork action, just below his expectant mouth, whilst an expression of drooling envy devoured his face.

Wendy was on a diet, or so she claimed. Near to a size zero already, she picked at a piece of buttered toast, washed down with pineapple juice, whilst fixing her stare at some distant imagined object, presumably considering the vagaries of teenage angst. She only consumed the meagre rations, because her mother maintained that her elder daughter would faint in class, without some sustenance.

In general, Charlotte insisted her family breakfast like kings, lunch like a prince, and dine like paupers, saying it was good for the digestion. However, often the inverse happened, evening meals becoming a major banquet. Worse still, Roger's wife remained under the impression that he had a sensible low calorie lunch, but often he gorged out in the city fleshpots, unbeknown to her. For Wendy, sensible calorie intake had become a vocation. She ate like a mouse, morning, noon and night, a conscious decision brought on by the knowledge that fat is the worst word, in the teenage girls' vocabulary.

Peripheral to the children's breakfast rituals, Charlotte entertained her muesli bowl, dipping in for the occasional nourishment, whilst reading her latest arts and crafts magazine. Long past caring about sustaining his once Dionysian shape, Roger tucked into a stack of bagels and coffee. He justified the intake on the basis that bulking up is good for rugby, didn't hurt so much when he got tackled. Yes, he still played, even though past 40, and only marginally overweight. At least it appeared that way, when he held his stomach in.

It became the usual feeding flurry for some Frasers, unable to resist the magnetic attraction of the cholesterol fuelled fry-up, whilst others observed their predator-like eating habits with critical expressions. Semi-disgusted by their mountains of food, they pulled faces at the gluttons' ravenous consumption.

Blaring out in the background, Chris Moyles added to the

circus-like fracas. Roger couldn't say he particularly liked his DJ style, or choice of music, but James and Wendy paid homage to his show, for reasons they said their father would never understand. Roger mentioning stalwarts, such as Alan Freeman and Kenny Everett from his youth, only brought blank stares in response from the teenagers. With a sneering expression, Wendy and James would ask who they were, knowing it would annoy Roger's sensibilities, though his wife swore that her husband and susceptibility never coexisted in the same space-time coordinates. Insulated from such trivial distractions by her own agendas, Charlotte had a great ability to switch herself off completely from background noise when reading. That included Roger, so Chris's melodious tones washed over her, undetected.

Heather swung along to Beyoncé, 'bouncy', as Roger called her, and Lady Gaga, while at the same time flicking Coco Pops at James with her spoon. She got one piece to half-balance on his nose, before it fell into his breakfast, like a small bird sucked into the mouth of a volcano. As it plopped into his egg yolk, she burst into hysterical laughter. Not even this brought Charlotte out of concentration. It was left to Roger to reprove their youngest daughter, but before he could say anything, James responded in kind, flicking a lump of marmalade at Heather. She ducked and it ended up on her father's chin, dripping onto his bagels.

It was just another familiar weekday start in the Fraser household. To a fly on the wall, or come to that, a spaceman making regular inspections of their breakfast time habits, the disorder and pandemonium would seem quite normal.

* * *

After the battle of breakfast, Charlotte drove Roger to Saint Mary Cray rail station, before depositing their brood at various schools. Often, Roger said to them that when he was their age, he either walked or cycled to school, but invariably the nostalgic comment was met with jeers of 'Oh, that's so un-cool', or 'Hadn't cars been invented then?' It always became a losing position, he quickly conceded, because early morning meant mental preparation for the day's work ahead, so he would sit in the passenger seat meditating, not even Charlotte's erratic driving capable of drawing concern.

One day, she had nearly run over a traffic warden, whilst waving to one of her mumsy friends en route, though no bystander, let alone the occupants of their MPV, had any sympathy for him. Traffic wardens were hardly an endangered species, their numbers were in fact on the increase. They needed to be culled, according to Aunt Jemina.

At the rail station, were the usual array of businessmen, day trippers and school children heading for London. Innes Farmer, or 'Instant Karma', as Roger called him, caught his attention by raising his furled umbrella.

"Good morning, Roger."

"Morning, Instant."

"What?"

"Sorry, I was thinking about something else, morning Innes."

"Have you seen the Telegraph this morning?"

Roger had started to read the Telegraph's business section at breakfast, but in a second misdirected retaliation against Heather's Coco Pops attack, it had got covered in marmalade by James, so he had given up.

"Er, no," he confirmed. "It somehow got away from me during breakfast."

"There's a good article on page seven of the financial section," Innes informed, with enthusiastic verve, "about gilt-edged securities."

The relevance of the fascination was that when the family released Roger into the community, he spent his working day at a well-known, if not semi-notorious investment house, colloquially known as 'the firm', by all in the financial services industry, analysing stock nine to 5:30, and advising traders what to buy and sell.

'Instant' filled him in with the salacious info, keen to emphasise his own interpretation of the material, and recommend a suitable course of action. He didn't work in investment banking, but thought he had the Midas touch, when it came to picking winners. Making the appropriate thankful noises, Roger immediately deleted the information from his mental record. It was old news anyway, something he'd dealt with the previous day, trading positions already in place. But of course being a pleasant, empathetic chap in public, and not wishing to insult Innes, he didn't tell him that, allowing him to drone away like a demented siren. They were halfway to the capital, before Innes finally ran out of advice. However, Roger had developed the art of appearing to listen, while at the same time thinking about something else, his work schedule in this instance, so no harm done.

Normally a candidate for the grand title of train journeys from hell, it turned out to be a good day on South Eastern. Innes and Roger actually had seats, so instead of being drained by train fatigue when they reached London Bridge, a feeling of unfamiliar sustained refreshment pervaded them. After saying cheerio to his amateur, stock-market guru buddy, Roger headed for the Jubilee Line, taking him to Canary Wharf.

There, he would spend the day doing battle with investment products including index-linked gilts and bonds, known as debt security to Joe Public, and feed hot leads to veracious traders from Billericay and Basildon; Essex boys with attitude according to Roger, who didn't look much older than James and had barely begun shaving. He exaggerated slightly, some were from the old school. Pinstripe suited, bowler-hat-wearing gents, with constantly rolled-up umbrellas, but their numbers had declined sharply in recent times.

One of the Essex set, a particularly vain, irksome, pimply wide boy called Lawrence Springs, which Roger thought sounded like a spa town, came into the office.

"Hey Rog," Lawrence said in a jaunty barrow-boy manner, a

pencil wedged between his left ear and Nicky Clarke hairstyle, his designer glasses perched so far down his nose, that they balanced on a recently grown, military-style moustache. He was what Aunt Jemina would call an odious little runt. Leastways Roger thought it was runt, yes, it must be.

"Yes," he said, presenting an air of disassociation, completely neglected by the trader's senses.

"What about those Japanese bonds, buddy?" jabbed Lawrence. Despite his appalling Essex accent, he had slipped into American trader vernacular. "Boy, what a white-knuckle ride, really seat of pants stuff, brought out the gambler in me, had me creaming in orbit, what an orgasm."

Translated into English, that meant the lead Roger gave him came up trumps, and he made a fortune for the firm and himself, Roger getting a share as well.

"I'm so pleased for you," Roger responded, hinting at irony, but again it flew over the trader's impenetrable head.

"Got anything else for me, Roger baby?"

How about a swift kick in the wedding tackle? Roger became tempted to say.

"Maybe something later….but first I have to analyse these latest American stock forecasts….there's movement on the U.S Federal Reserve, which could present some lucrative opportunities for corporate investors, and I also have a mergers and acquisitions conference with Frankfurt to prepare for."

"God, you're really good at what you do, Roger." He shot a toothy grin at the stock analyst. "All the guys say so," he added, still in Uncle Sam mode.

Curling the left side of his mouth in derision, Roger said, "So glad the trading floor appreciate my efforts."

Now that Lawrence was about to leave, Roger noticed that the stock-gambling Cincinnati Kid had the beginnings of a beard, incomplete though it was, and suffering dreadfully from bum fluff.

"Lawrence." The Kid turned to look back at him. "I'd stand a bit closer to the razor, if I were you."

"Huh," Lawrence retorted.

There you go, Roger thought to himself, a hat trick of non-connections, and this is the guy who's being groomed for one of the top slots in the corporation. How can the executive board bet the business on a schmuck like that? 'Oy vey', as his Jewish friends might say.

Thinking he had gone, Roger turned his attention to the American stock forecasts, but then heard, "Hey Rog, forget to tell you, I'm going scuba diving this weekend. It's gonna be awesome."

"Don't forget your concrete flippers."

Yes, it went straight over his head yet again, not even bothering to see if there was any sign of activity existing between his ears.

During the course of the morning, more Gordon Gekko wannabes entered Roger's hallowed domain, in search of gold-plated opportunities. Of course, most of them were still in nappies, when 'Gordo' first strutted his shtick in the 1987 film *Wall Street*. When they recoiled at the effort needed to convert opportunities into trades, Roger reminded them in true Wall Street fashion that money never sleeps, and not to get emotional about stock. They responded back with 'Yeah, you're right, Roger', or 'I guess an old timer like you doesn't get to your position, without knowing the markets'. That last one irritated Fraser. He was only just about into his forties, well a few years in, and these young Turks thought him ancient.

After a break from their incessant intrusions, enabling him to get on with the morning's schedule, the predators started to congregate again outside his office, during a lull on the trading floor.

One of the more superstitious traders, Trevor Evans, gaunt, nervous with spiky hair and near-albino skin tones, gingerly crossed Fraser's office threshold. Roger knew it to be Trevor, without having to look up, catching sight of his trademark, long-toed designer shoes, which curled up so much, he swore that when Trevor bent down, they would touch his nose.

"Roger, do you have a moment?"

"You're a bit previous, aren't you? Our meeting is not until three o'clock."

"Something else has come up."

Roger never had a moment, but beckoned him forward anyway. "Yes, what is it, Trevor?"

When Roger glanced up, he saw the designer shoes aficionado had a six foot, stuffed brown bear with him. "What on Earth is that?"

"It's my lucky mascot, for when there's a bears market in full flow."

Jerking his head back slightly, Roger took in the full extent of the spectacle. "Yes, it seems to have the same lofty intellectual appearance of stock traders."

Like for Lawrence Springs earlier, the acidic comment remained unprocessed by Trevor's brain. He gawked at the ever-busy stock analyst, flummoxed, as if awaiting permission to speak from a commanding officer.

"Well, come on, what is it?" pushed Fraser.

"Ahhh, you remember that commodity stock, you gave me yesterday?"

"Yes."

"Well, I spread bet it across some private investors."

"Yes, yes."

"Roger, it's gone through the floor, we've taken a bath on it." Trevor almost fell to his knees. "When Ricky Henshaw finds out, he's going to fire my arse."

Now Ricky was Roger's kind of trading floor sales manager. Brutal, vicious, psychotic, all the necessary attributes needed to keep the traders in line.

Turning his attention to Trevor's problem, Roger made a few keyboard strokes, and the computer screen displayed the commodity stock. Sure enough, falling like an Essex girl's knickers, it would soon hit rock bottom, and all hell would be let loose. Trevor would be unceremoniously excommunicated from the firm by Ricky, fed to rapacious journalists, still in search and destroy mode seeking traders to fry after the 2008 worldwide meltdown, then turfed out by his ear to fend for himself amongst the down and outs inhabiting the bottom tier of the financial services world, known as high street retail banking.

"Why didn't you go for the corporate investors," Fraser complained, "like I told you to do?"

"There's more margin with the private investors."

"Yes, but these are long-term investments, not the short-term trades that attract private investors, who are really corporate raiders in disguise anyway."

Biting his finger nails, which judging by the rate of consumption would soon be worn down to the knuckles, Trevor said weakly, "I know, I know. When the market started to dive this morning, they sold, and the stock price fell apart."

Near to tears, the dejected trader searched for salvation.

"Okay," Roger advised, "here is what you do. Buy back all the stock you sold yesterday, and resell it to corporate investors, mainly off-shore Asia Pacific, global size companies. If you pitch the right price, then by close of business today, the stock should have recovered to about its original buy price. Henshaw is out of the office all day, so God willing and the creek don't rise, when the London markets open tomorrow, you should be in the black. Check the Hong Kong stock market at midnight, and then do some further trading with Hong Kong, Tokyo and Shanghai through the night….and make yourself a huge pot of coffee."

"Yes, yes, that sounds great….oh, thank you, Roger, thank you, thank you."

He nearly bent down to kiss Fraser's hand, but the stock analyst got up before he could make contact. Instead, Trevor became in danger of smooching with his pointy footwear.

"It's not a holy relic, you know," Fraser said, with lightness of touch, trying to bring some levity to the trader's challenging situation.

The pithy comment went straight over Trevor's head without

stopping, and he was meant to be one of the more intelligent Essex-set traders. Apparently, he once read a book, and it didn't have any pictures in it, proof positive of superior intellect over his contemporaries.

He took one more look at Roger, as if gazing on a deity, then rushed away with his mascot, to begin the recovery task.

Roger thought to himself, if only my family could see me in action, they wouldn't think I was such a prat. Hey ho, there goes another daydream.

* * *

Towards lunchtime, as Roger made his way through accounts, returning from a mergers and acquisitions Frankfurt teleconference, he got a whispered call from Craig Stevens, deputy to the chief accountant.

"Hey Roger, come here."

Craig dragged Roger inside one of the meeting rooms, where five other people from accounts were gathered.

Mystified by their behaviour, Roger enquired, "What's happening, Craig?"

"Dave Stratton is going to call Sarah, and mimic Nigel."

Craig referred to a long running soap opera, involving Nigel Brooks from IT support, and Sarah Williams from accounts. Sarah had enormous tits, and Nigel was completely besotted by her, or rather her huge chest. Every so often, he plucked up courage, to ask Sarah if she would go out with him, whilst simultaneously being transfixed by her overpowering mammaries. She always answered that she had a boyfriend, and must decline his invitation.

"Oh, I see, that should be interesting," gushed Fraser.

Cowering down, they spied on Sarah, who by that time had started to eat her lunch.

Dave made the call.

"Hello, accounts, Sarah Williams speaking."

"Oh hello, Sarah, it's Nigel."

"Hello Nigel," replied Sarah, already expecting the usual request from the persistent IT specialist.

"Sarah, I know you have a boyfriend, but I would really like to take you out."

"You know I can't do that, Nigel. He would be furious, and probably beat you up."

"But Sarah, I really like you. In fact, I really love your massive tits, and I must have them."

"What?" exclaimed Sarah, almost falling off her seat, in disbelief.

"I said I must have your tits, Sarah, I must have your tits," determination growing in the caller's voice.

The one sided dialogue went on for a few more minutes, Dave building his Nigel impersonation to a crescendo, whilst the occupants of the meeting room, Roger included, tried desperately not to laugh, but it became very difficult.

Taken aback by what she heard, Sarah could scarcely breathe. From their vantage point, the audience could see her mouth lingered between tight-lipped annoyance and wide-open shock. The same sandwich she started nearly five minutes earlier remained in her right hand, going stale through neglect.

As fate would have it, just as Dave reached the peak of his plea, the real Nigel walked through accounts.

As he passed her desk, Nigel said, "Hello, Sarah, how are you?" He kept on walking.

Naturally, Sarah said, "I'm fine, Nigel," in an involuntary reaction, whilst she concurrently listened to Dave's rant.

Twigging something was rotten in the state of Denmark, she started to scan around the office, her senses drawn by the guffaws emanating from the accounts meeting room, Dave still in the throes of his pleas to must have her tits. So consumed in his delivery, by this time, the impersonator foamed at the mouth.

Sarah rose from her seat, sandwich in hand now going

moldy. Fixing her gaze on the meeting room, she started to move forward. Someone behind Fraser saw the mammary queen approaching, and alerted the rest of the co-conspirators. As she bore down on them, they made a hasty withdrawal, but it was too late to leave. Trembling at the back of the meeting room, they expected the worst. Only Dave remained blissfully unaware of her imminent arrival. As she entered the meeting room, her caustic look immediately vaporising the onlookers, he was still in full delivery mode.

"I must have your tits, I must have your tits, " he shouted down the phone, and then realised that his accomplices had moved away.

He turned to see Sarah, replete with her massive chest, towering over him.

"Aaaarrrggghhh," he gulped.

Now Sarah Williams had a reputation for being a very temperate person, who never swore, or lost her cool. The meeting room occupants' impression of her was about to radically change.

She picked up a large A4 binder, and started to lay into him with it shouting, "You fucking bastard, I'm going to kill you."

He manfully scurried around the meeting room like a demented toad, trying to evade her, but she was lethal with the binder, connecting with him several times. Eventually, he managed to escape through the meeting room door, with her starting to chase after him. She momentarily stopped to look at the rest of the culprits, before continuing the chase.

"Don't think I've forgotten about you lot, I'll deal with you later."

Then off rushed the mammary queen, and caught him before he could leave. She hounded him around the office, the binder flailing furiously, sometimes catching him on the head. He squealed with pain, as he ducked and dived between desks and chairs. Those left in the meeting room exchanged glances, then broke into the theme from *Loony Tunes,* imagining that Sarah and Dave were *Tom and Jerry.*

It was just another typical lunch hour session, behind the scenes at Canary Wharf.

What would the punters think?

CHAPTER 4: THE WELSH MILKING MAID

The working day over, Roger returned on the six ten from London Bridge. He went into the local off license at Saint Mary Cray, ordered a selection of alcohol to keep guests anaesthetised at the forthcoming garden party, and then grabbed a taxi for home.

Charlotte's art set were having a special event at the local tech that evening, so the Frasers had guests. Bruce Honeywell would stay with Roger, whilst his wife, Rosemary, along with Charlotte, and some others who had gathered at the Fraser house, intended to play art connoisseurs. Roger really liked Bruce. He was good company, and not even remotely connected with the financial services sector. So he wouldn't be bombarding Roger with questions about the best stock options to invest in, or plaguing him with requests to dish the dirt on the latest investment banking misdemeanours, such as the Sarah Williams incident.

Relatively quiet in the Fraser household, Wendy and James were in their rooms doing homework, and Heather played *Who Wants to be a Millionaire*, with her as Chris Tarrant, and a myriad of stuffed animals acting as contestants.

Bruce and Roger retired to the lounge, with a bottle of Gevrey Chambertin for company. The Honeywells were older than the Frasers, their off-spring having already left home. Lucky blighters, Roger thought, they were free for any pursuit of their choosing. Bruce used to be production manager, for the daily print run of a well-known national newspaper, but he left a few years ago, sinking his disposable capital into his own printing company.

"How's the printing business going, then?" Roger asked.

"Couldn't be better, Roger, we're 100% loaded, and just recently a publishing house has engaged us, for print-on-demand requirements."

"How many people have you got working for you, 12 isn't it?"

"22, now."

"Wow, business must be good."

"Yes, when you consider we are only in our third year of trading. It begs the question, why didn't I do this, long ago."

They continued their dialogue about the newspaper and printing industries, touching on Bruce's early career.

"Do you know," he explained, "when I first started, printing was a fine art. Now of course it's all computerised, and those old skills I learnt as an apprentice are dying out. Setting typefaces and photo sets is largely a thing of the past." With the burgundy taking effect, he stretched out in his chair before continuing. "You probably won't believe this, but one of the apprentice initiations I went through, all those years ago, was ball-blacking by the production workers with newsprint ink….it's virtually impossible to wash off with soap and water. You need to let it wear off, takes some time, let me tell you. I used to have nightmares about the production workers rounding on me, and the ball-blacking initiation being carried out again. Went on for years, huh."

Thinking of a similar watershed experience, Roger said, "That reminds me of a business trip I made to Milford Haven, not long after I started my career. The visit ended up giving me nightmares."

"Oh, what was that?"

Making himself snug and cosy, Roger launched into his tale. "I had to assess investment potential for a proposed gas pipeline to be run by energy companies. As it happens, the project became shelved for over ten years, but at the time, it appeared to be a real goer. My company had billeted me in a quiet little backwater pub, about ten miles up the coast. 'A stranger is it?' said the landlord, in a deep Welsh baritone accent, when I arrived. 'Yes,' I said, 'I have a reservation in the name of Roger Fraser'. Anyway, the landlord's wife showed me to my sea-facing room. I noticed there were metal shutters on the windows, and asked what they were for. She said, 'There's a shingle and stone beach below this window. When the tide comes in, and it's blowing a gale, stones get thrown up. The metal shutters protect the windows'."

"You didn't have to sleep with sheep, did you?" smirked Bruce.

Laughing at the inference, Roger said, "No, nothing like that."

"Because you know why Welsh shepherds carry a lipstick in their left boot, don't you?" he persisted.

"Yes....just in case they get an ugly one," Roger replied, joining in with the old joke.

"That's right, Roger," confirmed Bruce, as if he had personal experience."Sorry, I interrupted you....please, go on."

"I had arranged to meet a colleague for an evening drink. He was staying at another pub in the same village. So after dinner, I went into the bar at my pub, and asked the landlord for directions. 'Well boyo,' he says, 'it's only a half a mile walk from here, so I'll get Rhiannon to guide you on her way to chapel, you know, for the evening service'. 'Rhiannon,' I said questioningly. 'Yes, here she is'. So I look round, and can't see anybody. Then a dwarf-like creature with a grotesque face, dressed in a bright-red raincoat and yellow wellies, emerged from behind the landlord. Well....I was taken aback, Bruce....I recoiled at the sight of her, sucking in breath to prevent myself from saying, 'aaaarrrggghhh'."

"Jesus, dwarfs can be frightening," agreed Bruce.

"The landlord looks at me, like he thinks I'm a complete wimp. He says, 'It's alright man, she won't bite you, she been fed this evening. She milks the cows for us, you know.' He peeked down at the creature. 'Don't you, Rhiannon?'"

Bruce sniggered, enjoying the discomfort Roger suffered.

"A grunting sound emerged from the mini-beast as she smiled, displaying rows of fangs, looking like they were experienced at tearing flesh apart. 'Now Rhiannon, you show

Mister Fraser the way to the Seven Bells, on your way to chapel, there's a good girl,' says the landlord. Rhiannon reaches up, grabs my hand, and we are away. It's extremely dark outside, because there's no street lighting, so I'm already having visions of being chopped up and consumed by the cursed dwarf. She has my hand in a pincer-like grip, gargling and grunting, as we walk along. Then I see a figure, emerging out of the dark in front of us. I think this is it. She has an accomplice to help her chop me into little pieces. 'Evening, Rhiannon, that your new boyfriend, is it?' says the shadowy figure, as he passes. The creature just groans in response, and we continue along, what I think is my final journey. Just when thoughts of an excruciating end are going into overdrive, she releases my hand, grunts, then points down a lane, indicating the Seven Bells. I breathe a huge sigh of relief, and say, 'Goodnight Rhiannon'. 'Nnrrgghh,' came the reply. I wondered if she was speaking Welsh, but didn't wish to chance my luck any further, so quickly moved towards the Seven Bells."

"She sounds like a right little bundle of joy."

"Quite. Anyway….later that night, I'm having a really terrifying nightmare, about Rhiannon torturing my private parts, by throwing red hot coals on them. I woke up in a sweat, panting away, to hear the clatter of stones being thrown up against the metal window shutters by the stormy sea, the combination of the noise allied to my dwarf experience, responsible for my nightmare."

Bruce laughed so hard, that tears rolled down his face. "Dear me, Roger, that could only happen to you."

"Yes, you are quite right. Unfortunate things, like the Rhiannon episode, seem to constantly blight my life. As I say, it gave me nightmares for ages. From then on, I've always been wary of sleeping in hotel rooms with metal shutters, and landlords who employ sub-normal height milking maids."

CHAPTER 5: GARDEN PARTY

The great day arrived. During the morning's preparation, the Fraser house resembled a piranha's feeding frenzy. Husband and wife dashed around like meerkats on heat, up against the clock and hampered by their uncooperative children. Always a stickler for detail, Charlotte wanted to make sure everything went ahead smoothly, and without controversy. She had a list of items to be actioned, most of which were delegated to her husband. Taking the list from her, it unravelled to the floor in Roger's grasp, before he had reached the end of its instruction schedule. His jaw had dropped lower and lower in consternation, as examination revealed the required actions.

"Charlotte, you must be kidding....it's a garden party, not a banquet for David Cameron and Nick Clegg."

Giving him one of her disparaging looks, she demanded, "If we're going to do this, it's going to be done properly."

"But there are enough actions on this list, to keep a small army occupied for weeks, and I...."

"I nothing, Roger....the garden party was your idea."

"Yes, but...."

"But nothing, Roger, just get on with it, and don't come back until you have finished."

Charlotte was a disciple of the late, great Brian Clough, in that when Roger and her were in dispute, they got around the table, mulled it over for 20 minutes, and then they, or rather she, decided what was right, and Roger did what she told him to do.

Giving his wife a mock Seig Heil salute, he said, "Yes, my little commandant," breaking into *Fawlty Towers* mode, and thinking Basil had it easy with Sybil.

Meanwhile, the children caught on to the fun to be had at their father's expense, during the morning's preparation for the afternoon event.

DOGHOUSE BLUES

A wayward grin came at Roger from Wendy. "Mum's right, you're hopeless, Dad."

Directing an indifferent smirk at their eldest, Roger said, "Thanks a lot, Wendy. I'll remember that, the next time it's pocket money review time."

"You mean allowance?"

"Allowance….pocket money when I was your age, either way." He pointed to his noggin. "I will store that away, my girl."

"Bet you forget," she merrily replied, then wandered away down the hallway, attending to her ringing iPhone.

Shooting a disdainful glance in her direction, he caught a glimpse of James, stretched out in the lounge, like a satisfied cat that has had the cream. James had been delegated with putting out garden tables and chairs for their legions of guests, but instead of attending to his duties, he still watched an episode of *The Inbetweeners*, he'd recorded on the DVD player the previous night.

Observing the lecherous nonsense on the television screen, Roger warned, "I hope you're not going to grow up, to be like one of those malcontents."

Spinning around in his chair, James lazily said, "Oh….hello Dad."

"Well," Roger pressed.

"Huh."

"That's disgraceful," Roger continued, noticing more curious goings-on. "How can you possibly think that is comedy?"

"I thought you were preparing for the garden party," James replied, poking fun, and hoping his father had forgotten about his allocated task.

About to further chastise him, Roger's attention became drawn by the lewd and lascivious images his son drooled over. "What on Earth is happening there? It's, it's…."

"Great?"

"I was going to say, disgusting."

Breaking into a juvenile laugh, James extolled, "Oohhh, *The*

Inbetweeners is the best thing I've seen in ages. All my school mates watch it, it's really cool."

"Really cool?"

"Yes, everyone at school wants to be either Simon or Jay."

"Oh, I see, what about the other two oiks?"

"What, Neil and Will? They're naff."

Roger became conscious he had begun to engage his son in meaningless debate about a programme, which even by his libertarian standards approximated a crass and debased spectacle, the key reasons of course why male teenagers liked it.

"Look," Roger cautioned again, "I've not come in here, to discuss the finer sub-cultural points of a juvenile TV show. You're meant to be putting out the tables and chairs."

Suddenly Charlotte appeared out of nowhere. "Better listen to your father, James, or you could end up a brain-dead, deranged deviant." She lingered, and then muttered under her breath, "Like your father." And then, in a louder voice, "Are you still here, Roger?"

"I was just trying to get our son and heir motivated, to do his share of preparation duties."

"I can still see you, Roger," she plagued, beginning to exude danger signals.

As usual, her anger characteristic quickly rose to warning amber, and then even more quickly climaxed to alarm red.

Not in the mood for playing 'George and the Dragon', Roger chose to be deferential. "Okay, okay, I'm going."

After truculently wandering down to the garden shed, mimicking Charlotte's demanding voice tones to himself, he began dusting down the barbeque set, task number one, of what seemed to be at least a couple of hundred 'to do' actions. As he busily brushed away at last year's debris, he saw Heather on the other side of the garden. At first, he just smiled to himself, thinking what a sweet, guiltless girl she still was, playing with her dolls and stuffed animals. The next time he looked, that impression became dispelled. He watched, as she bashed one cuddly toy with a stick. Curious to know why the doll incurred

DOGHOUSE BLUES

her displeasure, he first checked to make sure Charlotte didn't hover in the background, then walked over to where their youngest still admonished the naughty soft toy.

"What's Miss Piggy done, to annoy you now?"

"She's given me too many wrong answers, and didn't bank."

"What game are you playing?"

"*The Weakest Link*, and I'm Anne Robinson, and I don't tolerate contestants, who keep on getting answers wrong."

Scanning around the rivals, he saw some familiar faces. As well as the offending Miss Piggy, Kermit the Frog and Fozzie Bear from *The Muppets*, a Fisher doll, and a Disney princess were positioned around 'Anne Robinson'. He also noticed Papa Smurf, plainly experiencing a hard life. With one ear missing, he had obviously already been the object of Heather's discontent. Finally, there were two Teletubbies, one of which reminded him of some docile Herbert from the office, and various other characters from kids' television programmes.

"Daddy, do you want to be a contestant?"

"Well I have to…."

"Good, you can sit between Kermit and Fozzie."

Roger sat down cross-legged, but before he could ask about the rules of engagement, Heather assumed the mantle of the legendary quiz queen.

"Okay contestants, this is *The Weakest Link*," she harshly announced, "and I am your quiz mistress, Anne Robinson. I'm going to ask you some questions, and don't forget to bank, if you get the answer right. Miss Piggy didn't bank. You saw what happened to her."

She grimaced at the contestants, to get them on their mettle.

"Round one, Papa Smurf, who is the main judge on *The X Factor*?"

Imitating Papa's voice, she answered, "Simon Cowell."

"No, Louis Walsh," she replied to herself, reverting back to ruthless Anne Robinson mode.

"Kermit the Frog. Who won the last series of *Strictly Come Dancing*?"

She went into a Kermit voice, "Kara Tointon, bank."

"Yeessss," she spurted, jubilantly falling out of her Anne Robinson impersonation.

"Daddy. Who is the judge on *Britain's Got Talent*, who is also a comedian?"

An appearance of blankness came over him, his mind in neutral, refusing to even come up with a plausible candidate.

"The clock is ticking, Daddy."

"Er." He began to look anguished.

"Come on, Daddy."

"Er, Jasper Carrot."

She gave him a condescending smirk, which suggested everybody on the entire planet, apart from her father, knew the answer.

"No, Michael McIntyre," she scolded him.

"Fozzie Bear," she continued, "what is the capital of England?"

"Oh, I know that one," Roger said with renewed relish.

"It's not your turn, Daddy. Be quiet, or you will be disqualified."

She turned her attention to Fozzie. "Well?"

"London," she said in a Muppet voice, which he didn't recognise to be that of Fozzie Bear.

"Yeessss….but you didn't bank!"

Out came the stick, Fozzie taking a beating.

Still smiling at her antics, he suddenly heard, "Roger, what are you doing?"

It's his trouble and strife, looking down at him from above, hands on hips, and shaking her head.

"You're supposed to be preparing things for the garden party."

"I er, I was just…."

"Daddy's just been voted off *The Weakest Link*, Mummy."

＊＊＊

DOGHOUSE BLUES

All the family invited guests, and the Frasers were expecting at least 70 people at the shindig. They invited Aunt Jemina, but she declined, citing conflict with another event, code for she didn't want all the fuss and noise, that she knew would inevitably dominate the event. The Frasers would miss her. It was the same with Roger's parents, who also lived nearby. They claimed an audience with the Queen prevented attendance.

Roger had bought a couple of cows, a flock of chickens, mountains of rice, salad and desserts to feed their hungry loins, all to be washed down with gallons of beer and vats of vino.

It was Saturday….it was 1:30….and it was….*Crackerjack*, no, but nonetheless, it felt like the start of a great show, as far as Roger was concerned. All the garden party preparation had been completed, including the erection of a marquee, which Charlotte said would bring a touch of chic to the festivities. However, the kiddie's paddling pool and mini-trampoline could have been said to deflate that attempt at sophistication.

Their myriad of guests started to arrive, and the fun and games began. Soon, the garden became packed with a throng of partygoers, intent upon soaking up the Sun and Roger's alcohol, whilst dining out al fresco style at Che Fraser, with him acting as head chef. After Charlotte and Roger made sure everybody had a drink, he went to work on the barbecue with his happy-go-lucky, bright and breezy, carrot-top friend Charlie Farley, who had volunteered to help cook the meat. Also known as Charlie Fairy, but not a rear gunner, he had known Roger for over 30 years, and only had eyes for the fair sex. Charlotte had laid out the accompanying salad and whatnots on a long row of trellis tables, which James had finally erected, after she hauled him away from *The Inbetweeners*. The guests lined up, and loaded their plates to overflowing with food.

While Charlie and Roger played 'Gordon Ramsey', Alan and Francine Mallory, long-time friends of the Fraser family, appeared at chef central, and broke into a 'what have you been doing' conversation, whilst sipping a rather good Chablis, cooled to optimise its refreshing taste. Alan always had that distinguished look of refinement about him, whether dressed in a suit or casuals. He also had a dimpled chin, which Roger invariably seemed to stare at. Like his host, Alan worked in investment banking, but neither of them would be talking about the markets today. They had enough of that during their working lives, so the subject would remain strictly verboten. An ex-Miss South London, or it could have been North Kent from the mid-1980's, Francine had retained her luscious beauty-queen looks. She was also much vaunted among Charlotte's art set, because her painting and sculpturing skills had resulted in her winning several prizes, in local art competitions.

"I hear you've seen Freda's latest bit of pottery," Francine said, scarcely hiding the hidden syntax.

Turning to face her, and already aware of the inference, Roger said, "Yes….so you probably know I got into trouble for my comments."

"Oh, you do surprise me, Roger," Alan sniggered, "fancy you getting into trouble."Fraser's reputation for putting his foot in social get-togethers went before him. "What have you said this time?" pressed Alan.

Holding his arms up in defence, Roger bleated, "It was all perfectly innocent."

"I'm sure it was, but what did you say?" asked Francine, hungry to hear confirmation of Roger's latest, in a long line of social gaffs.

Other people had started to listen, hoping to find something out to their advantage, which could be used against Fraser at a later date. As Joseph Heller taught, Roger wasn't paranoid, but that didn't mean they weren't out to get him. Roger ushered Alan and Francine into a quieter spot in the garden, leaving Charlie to head cook duties.

Looking around, to make sure they had at least some limited privacy, Roger whispered, "Well, Charlotte dragged me over to the Fortescues'. She wanted to see Freda's latest clay creation. Of course, I expected a vase or a tea cup, you know, the usual amateur potter's disasters. However, Freda has got quite friendly with the guy who takes the pottery classes, and she asked him to make a clay bust of her, to give to Gregory. When we arrived, Greg said it had just been unveiled, but Freda didn't really want to show it to us. Charlotte insisted, so Freda took us into the kitchen, where she uncovered the piece. 'Hideous, isn't it?' Freda said. Well….no one was saying anything in response, so I said in all innocence, 'It's quite a good likeness'."

Bursting into laughter, Alan exclaimed, "Oh Roger, that's a classic. What on Earth possessed you?"

"Charlotte said lack of sensitivity, but I really was trying to be nice."

The mortifying topic concluded, they moved on to the usual adult topics, who's shafting who, who got hair lacquer on their dog, did the vicar have a penchant for choirboys, the kind of highbrow banter expected at an urbane garden party. Then the topic changed to oddballs who have somehow become successful, along life's unexpected highways and byways.

"Do you know," Roger said, a look of incredulity beginning to spread across his disapproving face, "there's a Young Turk trader at the firm, who can barely speak English, let alone read. Yet I'm told he's heading for the top, despite some horrendous *faux pas*….appalling, isn't it?"

"Yes, I know what you mean, Roger," agreed Alan. "I remember a company event we had in the mid-nineties, to test school entrants for a trainee scheme. We set them tests…."

"Don't tell me," Roger interrupted, holding his hands aloft. "They couldn't read, write, or do sums, but were tremendously socially integrated."

Chortling at the cynicism, Alan replied, "Yes, that as well….but to test creative skills, we had them write a short essay about someone or something, they considered to be special. I was on the assessment team, part of the job being to check what they were writing. One boy had headed his essay 'Henri Leconte'."

"What, the French tennis player?" asked Roger.

"Yes, that's right," Alan confirmed, "and here's where a *faux pas*, unintentional or otherwise, came into it. His spelling of Leconte was in the same vein as a ladies private part."

"Oh dear," said Francine, not quite knowing where to look.

"Quite," Alan agreed. He gave his wife a sideways look. "Haven't I told you this story already, darling?"

"I don't think so….I would have remembered something like that."

Alan half-chuckled, then resumed, "And I also had to tell him that Leconte was a French 'cult' hero….not what he'd written."

"You mean another example of a lady garden?" Roger enquired.

"Yes….and I still don't know if the boy had done it on purpose, or whether he genuinely thought how he'd spelt 'Le Conte' and 'cult hero' was correct."

Starting to snigger, Roger said, "that reminds me of something….do you remember Eric Simonson, when we were at school?"

"Old Simonson, oh yes….few years older than us, quite a tearaway wasn't he?"

"He was, but your story has put me in mind of a similar incident, from our youth."

"Go on."

"Simonson got a job one summer, at the Odeon." He frowned quizzingly. "You sure you don't know about this?"

Shrugging his shoulders, Alan replied, "No."

"Well, one of his tasks was to put up the signs over the cinema's entrance, advertising the films showing, and who starred in them."

"Oh yes, I'd quite forgotten about those lettered signs," said Francine, now beginning to enjoy the conversation.

"Well, a Clint Eastwood movie was showing, so for devilment, Simonson arranged the L and I to be connected together, so it spelt..." He lowered his voice. "Cuthbert Ulysses Norman Timothy Eastwood."

"What?" enquired Alan.

Roger lowered his voice even more. "C-u-n-t Eastwood."

Francine's jaw dropped, and her mouth hung open. She wasn't enjoying the conversation, quite so much now.

"Ooohh, that's worse than Alan's sinful boy," she said, near to reproving the pair of them.

"Yes, I agree," Roger said. "It took three days of movie goers cackling and guffawing, before the theatre manager noticed, then fired Simonson."

Near to having hysterics, Alan said, "Do you know, that was typical Simonson, what a clown. I wonder what he's doing now?"

"He's the managing director of a well-known national cinema group."

* * *

After the entrées had been barbequed, and stored in warmers, some unintentionally burnt to a crisp, Roger chatted away to Gordon Anderson, and his lovely wife, Rachel. A fellow rugby player, Gordon became one of the few authorised by Charlotte to attend the event. Roger had compiled a list of prospective attendees, mainly from the rugby club. But she had red-lined most of them, leaving only a handful of surviving names. There had been one or two incidents in the past involving rugby players, that had incurred her wrath. She said, in no way would she allow the garden party to degenerate into a beer swilling, rude-song singing, rugby-player debacle.

Always great company, Gordon's pointed and pertinent witticisms were invariably accentuated in delivery, through a roguish grin, and a David Niven sounding voice. Just as gregarious, Rachel had a buoyant personality coupled with classical good looks. Consequently, she had become a favourite, amongst the men in the various Fraser social groups. They formed a very attractive, easy-going couple, the Frasers often socialising with the Andersons at local events, especially at the rugby club.

They engaged in cordial conversation, Roger reprising his garden party preparation challenges, including James partiality for *The Inbetweeners*, and his derisory performance on Heather's *The Weakest Link*, much to Gordon's and Rachel's amusement. The Andersons responded, recapping their own latest domestic misfortunes and calamities. Then turning to acknowledge Charlotte, running between the kitchen and the barbeque, like her rear end had caught fire, Gordon saw another mutual friend, Steve Hunt, in the food queue.

Also a fellow rugby player, Roger had to get special dispensation from Charlotte, to allow Steve to attend. Already on nine penalty points out of 12, as far as she was concerned, for three previous, socially unacceptable misdemeanours, Roger knew that the slightest infringement of social etiquette, would see his wife issuing the red card to his friend, and Steve would be banned from *Che* Fraser, indefinitely.

Over the years, Steve had become a natural storyteller. Not a raconteur with polished anecdotes, but someone who could communicate the salient points of an event, with complete believability. Consequently, never unable to resist seizing upon embarrassing situations to maximise their effect on unfortunate victims, Steve had cultivated a reputation for acidic humour and caustic criticism. Being self-deprecating, the mocking also applied to his startling shambles and fiascos.

Three summers ago, whilst in the Camber sand dunes with his family, he developed a sympathetic resonance for Tippi Hedren, the actress who played the lead in Hitchcock's *The Birds*. Suddenly standing up from behind a dune, an unsuspecting low-flying seagull got impaled in the back of his neck. The way Steve told it, Roger got the impression that he had to have the offending projectile surgically removed, the image beyond tangible folklore.

A solicitor by trade, Steve's occupation drew many good-natured hisses and boos from the Frasers' social group. He was a partner in a local firm of solicitors, Lunt, Hunt and Cunningham. Now there's another potential *faux pas* in the making. He loved his food, and in recent times had started to balloon, making him look like his lawyer hero Horace Rumpole, or so he claimed, to justify the increasing bulk.

His long suffering wife, Colette, a waif-like beauty with a mass of black wavy hair and saucer-shaped cornflower-blue eyes, was engaging Charlotte not far from Roger and his pals, with tales of domestic woe regarding Steve's rapacious appetite. Colette had a constant battle to keep her husband away from the larder, reputably having a combination lock on it, its opening code known only by her.

"Hey, Hunt," said Gordon. "Don't eat too much, or you'll be putting on weight."

Jerking up his head from examining the culinary delights on display, Steve sneered at the remark. "Very droll, Anderson, I must remember to thrash you at squash next week."

One of Charlotte's arty-farty friends, Machayla, stood behind Steve in the queue, filling her boots, metaphorically speaking, with salad. She was a vegan, or was it Vulcan? Anyway, she was a veggie.

"Oh, all the rice has gone," she exclaimed, wide-eyed and innocent.

This presented a golden opportunity for Steve, tailor made to suit his semi-vulgar wit.

Winking at Gordon and Roger, he turned to face her, and said, "Oh...." He peered intently at the Vulcan, er vegan. "Would you like me to give you some of my rice?" Rugby club code for man sperm.

"Oh, that's very kind of you," she replied, clearly immune from such suggestive language. "Can you give me some?"

Casting a wicked grimace in his friends' direction, and about to say something like 'yes, come behind the bushes with me', policewoman Charlotte arrived out of nowhere, with a fresh bowl of rice.

She scowled at him, then Gordon and Roger, before smiling

at her goody two-shoes friend. "Machayla, darling, no need for Steve to give you his rice, here's a fresh bowl."

Machayla tucked into the rice hill, smiled innocently at the men, and joined her arty-farty set, whilst Charlotte sidled over to her husband, about to reprimand him.

"Roger, don't take advantage of Machayla….you know she has led a sheltered life."

"But, but, but, it wasn't me, it was Steve," he protested, sounding like a frantic Kentucky chicken with Colonel Sanders in pursuit.

Too late, his wife already on her way stared back threateningly, leaving her husband open-mouthed and stumped, as she played mine host with other guests.

Steve and Gordon began to titter.

"Roger, you're always in trouble, aren't you?" Rachel said.

"Even when I'm perfectly blameless of the crime." Directing a threatening look at Steve, he said, "I'll get you for that, Hunt."

The three of them began some alpha-male bluster, with Rachel looking on, shaking her head at their primitive banter.

"Men," she said, tutting away, before joining a gaggle of wives, girlfriends and mistresses.

"Roger, who's the guy in the clowns trousers?" asked Steve.

Scanning around the foreground, he replied, "Oh, that's Pablo Pringle, Charlotte's arts and crafts teacher."

"Pablo Pringle," exclaimed Steve, in an extremely derisory voice. "Sounds like a lunchtime snack….he looks a bit effeminate, doesn't he? Poncified even."

"Is that a syrup he's wearing?" speculated Gordon.

Glancing over at the gent, Roger replied, "No….I don't think so, his mop top looks real to me."

"Hhhmmm," said Steve, "I think Gordon's right, it is a syrup. Think I'll go over, and test the theory."

Grabbing Steve by the shoulder, Roger urged caution. "I wouldn't do that, if I were you."

"Why, what's he going to do….blow me over?"

Being on the large side, a terror in the civil action law courts, and a fellow rugby player, he had scant regard for fear, but Roger felt inclined to advise him against the intended action.

"Er, no." Roger reinforced his grip on his friend's shoulder. "On first sight, he may appear like easy meat, but don't be fooled by that Joseph-Grimaldi-like appearance....I wouldn't cross him."

Joining in the disbelief, Gordon said, "Oh, why's that?"

"He also doubles as the martial arts instructor at the tech."

"Oh, a double-hard bastard, then," observed Steve.

"Yes" Roger confirmed, relaxing his grip. "Despite that limp-wristed appearance, I'm given to understand he's eased a few challengers, so I wouldn't test him."

Looking at Roger sideways, Steve started to snigger. "You're having us on, Fraser. What a load of old tosh."

"It's true, Steve, I'm not trying to fool you."

Steve took a second gander at the karate kid in waiting. Setting his face into distrustful mode, he remarked, "No, can't see it. I think he's one of your financial services brigade. Now I look more closely, he seems like one of those shady guys.... you know, Gordon, the ones that sell dodgy investments like Roger does, a widow wobblier I think they call them, trying to sign them up for a widows and idiots fund."

Throwing doubt on the ethics of 'the square mile' had become a constant source of rib-tickling for Steve. Some cheek, what with him being a solicitor, Roger thought. Often, the stock analyst would say to him, 'What do you call a bunch of solicitors at the bottom of the ocean, in a stricken submarine? A good start.' But the disdain would rebound off Steve, his turtle-wax hard exterior imperious to the flurry of insults, that close friends like Roger poured on his profession. However, privately, Roger knew in principle that his friend was quite right, the money business and morality do not necessarily coalesce, let alone co-exist in the same sphere. But with hand on heart, Roger could assure sceptics that he didn't do that. Some people he knew might, in fact did, but in his domain, the blue-chip corporate stratum, where they expect to 'do unto others, as they would do unto you, but do it first', he gave as good as he got, and so slept easy at night. He never came close to the doddering elderly, or those with brain cell deficiency, least-ways not in the client base. This Steve knew, but could never resist trying to bait his pal.

"Bollocks, Steve."

A broad grin spread across the burley solicitor's playful face. "Nearly got you, and I still say it's a syrup."

* * *

Later, Roger noticed James and his dubious friends, eyeing up some of Wendy's guests.

"Cor, she's a cracker," he heard one of them say.

Then they all broke into *The Inbetweeners* speech code, making bets on the viability of various target sexual conquests. If only one of them had the courage to approach the girls, thought Roger.

"I bet she's a goer," said another one of them.

"Which one?" Roger asked, standing behind the wolf pack, their tongues hanging out, and drying in the sun.

"The one with the big set of…." the errant boy started to say, as he turned around to see Roger. "Oh, hello Mister Fraser, great party, we were just, just…."

"Just eyeing up the girls?"

Wary of his father's unforeseen arrival, James went on the defensive. "We were just assessing Wendy's friends."

"Assessing?" Roger verified, with a hint of reproach.

"Yes, Mister Fraser," chimed in Neville Matthews, reputably James' best friend. "We have this English homework assignment, which is designed to test our observational skills."

That's a good one, Roger thought to himself. Since he was at school, teenager invention on the hop seemed to have improved.

"Observational skills," Roger repeated, "and what are you

DOGHOUSE BLUES

observing today?"

"Form, Mister Fraser," explained Jeremy Payne, another James-like dilettante, when it came to spying on the opposite sex.

"Form, hhmm....I see."

They were sat on the grass to get the best view of the 'form' they desired. Roger crouched down to their level.

"Correct me if I am wrong, but when I was at school, form was considered to be an art-class attribute."

Beginning to look alarmed, the boys thought their quasi-peeping-Tom escapade had been undone.

William 'Billy' Swan, one of the least intelligent members of the James gang, ogled the gaggle of girls, saliva starting to drip from his vulgar mouth.

"I wouldn't mind having carnival knowledge of that Roxanne Harrison," he informed his fellow voyeurs, dribbling rapaciously at the end of the sentence.

God knows how he passed the 11 plus, thought Roger, probably sent in a ringer to do the examination for him.

"You mean carnal knowledge," Roger advised, correcting him.

"Yeah, that's right, carnival knowledge," he confirmed, whilst wiping away the dribble with a slice of carrot cake, that ventured too near his mouth.

Shaking his head, Roger wondered if he ever sounded like that, at age 15. Probably, he conceded to himself. Aunt Jemina would confirm it. He dismissed the empathetic thought, determined to try and improve the boy's attraction skills with the opposite sex.

"This may sound old fashioned, but in my day, we used to talk to girls, instead of just leering at them."

"Talk?" said James, becoming mystified.

"Yes, you know....'hello', 'how are you'....pleasantries like that."

Looking at each other nonplussed, the testosterone set hunched up their shoulders, the Eureka moment yet to take effect.

"Talk?" one of them repeated, like Roger had asked them to recite the Gettysburg Address verbatim.

"Ahh," said another.

The penny began to drop.

"But what do we say, after 'hello' and 'how are you'?" asked Billy, his passion for discovery spurred on by his carnival desire.

Gazing to the heavens, Roger answered, "What you lot need is a crash course in communication and interpersonal skills."

Leaving them mulling over the revelation, like they had just discovered the Holy Grail, he headed towards the girl pack.

"Good afternoon, girls," he breezily said.

"Good afternoon, Mister Fraser," they returned, virtually in choral unison.

Catching her father's eye, Wendy seemed mortified by his unappreciated appearance.

"Hello, Dad."

"Are you all enjoying the garden party?" he asked.

The responses came cascading back with enthusiasm. 'Oh, yes', 'It's great' and 'Thank you for inviting us', the girls replied.

Smiling at them, and impressed by their courteous manners, he discovered they could actually use the Queen's English to communicate, without resorting to grunts, like the boys did.

"You see that bunch of miscreants over there?" he said, pointing back at the James gang.

"Yes," they all replied, again in perfect unison, apart from Wendy.

With her father and her friends in the same time-space continuum, she continued with her self-conscious demeanour.

"Well, don't be surprised if they come over to you a little later, to say hello."

"Huh, they're wankers," declared Abigail Mortimer, under her breath, a devout churchgoer, he'd been given to understand by Wendy.

"What was that?" he said, pretending he'd misheard dear, sweet little Abigail.

DOGHOUSE BLUES

"She said they look like anchors," offered Wendy, in an attempt to recover her father's impression that she and her friends were refined, sophisticated young ladies.

"Anchors!" he repeated, with a perplexed expression, also playing the game.

"Yes," confirmed Abigail. "They look like a bunch of ship's anchors, thrown overboard, and lying around aimlessly on the seabed."

"Oh....I see," he confirmed, still playing the pretence game. "Well, thank you all for coming. I do hope you enjoy the rest of the party. Good afternoon, girls."

"Good afternoon, Mister Fraser," they pealed back.

As he sauntered away, feeling pleased with his youth development work, he heard Roxanne say, 'Your dad's great, I really fancy him,' then 'Shut up Roxanne' from Wendy, obviously further discomforted. A nice warm glow came over him, making him feel very satisfied with his sensitive efforts. Administering the word of experience must be a hidden talent.

* * *

With plentiful hop and grape consumption, the garden party accelerated into full swing, everybody chilled out, with some stimulated into dance motion by the background sounds of modal jazz and classic rock; one of Roger's earlier 101 delegated tasks, to erect an audio speaker system in the marquee. Of course Wendy and James wanted modern stuff. But they took a vote and Roger won, ignoring the concept of majority vote ruling, and telling them he did have his toleration limits. The thought of the Arctic Monkeys, who according to James are the new Beatles, which they're not, or the Backstreet Boys or was it the Back-passage Boys, who Wendy said were bigger than Led Zeppelin, which they weren't, drowning out adult conversation, was beyond compromise, even democracy.

Moving amongst his guests, he exchanged a few words, here

and there. Then he saw Charlotte eyeing him, with that familiar scornful look. I couldn't have done anything wrong in the past few minutes, could I, he thought to himself.

She signalled for her husband, to come into the kitchen with her. He moved at a rapid pace. Best to show willing, he thought, just in case he had unwittingly committed yet another social gaff, brought to her attention by some dobbing-in member of the thought police.

"Hello darling, enjoying the party?" he said, half-expecting a dressing-down.

"Your cousin Peter has arrived."

"Cousin Peter....but he lives in King's Lynn. What...."

"They're on the way back from France, and thought they would call in to see us, on their way home."

"They....you mean Sandra and that brood of unruly kids are with him?"

"Shush Roger, they'll hear you."

Lowering his voice, he asked, "Where have you put them?"

"In the lounge."

Eight years older than Roger and high in his affections, Peter had worldly, grey-blue eyes, and a shock of dark wavy hair, which he secretly coloured. Though Sandra suspected the ploy, she never raised the issue with him. Built like a muscle mountain, bullets bounced off him, but she knew his thatch to be his Achilles' heel. Consequently, the colouration habit remained off the marital agenda. Along with Roger's elder brother, Colin, Peter had acted as his veteran guide and mentor, during his junior school years. Roger used to raid Peter's record collection, discovering such gems as the Rolling Stones and the Who, when Gordon and Steve were still playing with Dinky toys and Meccano. Peter had been married three times. His latest wife Sandra, though nearly half his age, had the necessary gravitas to keep him on the straight and narrow, when he became tempted to indulge in risky pursuits spurred on by his drinking pals. These included abseiling off Kings Lynn Customs House and bungee jumping off the Clifton Suspension Bridge.

They had a gaggle of four to seven-year-olds, who would scare Lee Marvin and 'The Wild Bunch'. Additionally, there were four, or maybe five offspring, from his two earlier marriages. Fortunately, they would be with their mothers and adopted fathers, so the child management task ahead wouldn't be all that daunting.

Charlotte had always been stand-offish with Sandra, detested her in fact, mainly because she was younger, and God had been very kind to her bust measurement. Sandra would even mount a challenge on Sarah Williams, for the grand title of supreme chest of the year. Charlotte's condemnation seemingly had no bounds. In her more vociferous moments, she insisted that like Deborah Stapleton, Sandra, who she had christened 'Gloria big tits', were the Devil's disciples. Not quite true, Roger thought, but he had noted long ago, that irrationality ruled over common sense, when it came to women measuring up and comparing physical attributes with members of their own gender.

Gliding into the lounge, arms outstretched, Roger welcomed his cousin. "Peter."

"Roger," he replied in his deep masculine voice, which always made him a great after-dinner speaker.

The cousins shook hands and embraced.

"Sandra, darling," Roger complimented, "you look well."

Suntanned and supple, it really set off her contrasting long strawberry-blonde hair, and deep-blue eyes, making her appear like every man's vision of the classic voluptuous glamour model. Roger began to appreciate why his cousins' wife drew hisses and scowls from other woman, not so well endowed.

"Hello Roger," she said, in her silky seductive voice.

They hugged, Roger immediately reminded of why Peter found her so attractive when they first met, her extremely ample bosom engulfing most of Roger's chest, and she wasn't wearing a bra that day.

Roger then turned his attention to their children; Rowan, Peter was a big *Blackadder* fan, Basil, poor sod, Peter was also a

Fawlty Towers fan and the twins, Cecile and Pamela. "Hello kids, how are you?"

They responded back with a chorus of, 'I'm fine, Uncle Roger', then immediately made enquiries about sustenance.

"You've caught us entertaining, Peter," he said, "we're having a garden party."

"Yes, we saw the procession of cars on your driveway, and out on the road. Got room for some more?"

Shooting a glance at Charlotte, Roger knew she would be trying to telepathically contact him, to say something like 'Sorry we're full', but refusing Peter wasn't an option.

"Of course, we have plenty of food and drink."

Already, Roger could feel the stilettos, and he wasn't thinking high heels, in his back from Charlotte, but what else could he do?

"On your way back from France, then?" he said, trying to appear interested, in yet another full-blown account of someone's summer holiday expedition.

"Yes," confirmed Peter. "We've been touring in the Dordogne and Brittany. Sent you a postcard from Rouen, you should get it next week."

* * *

Charlotte and Sandra took the new children contingent out into the garden, where they joined Heather and a bunch of other sub-ten-year-olds, who were playing in the pool, and bouncing on the trampoline.

Heather immediately seconded them all into a game of Assassin, which they intrinsically seemed to know how to play, though its rules and purpose completely escaped Roger. Charlotte gave them all enough food to gorge on for a month, and a pitcher of orange juice large enough to drown in, Roger wondering if that's what she secretly hoped would happen. The last time Rowan, Basil and the twins descended on Hazelwood, the house looked like Hurricane Katrina had visited.

Charlotte then walked away with Sandra, leaving Roger pondering what little Machiavellian drama may be about to unfold. What made it worse, was that all red-blooded males, including the James gang, cottoned on to realising 'Gloria big tits' was braless. Her top set bounced along in front of her, like a couple of merry footballs. Roger could see heads, moving up and down in sync with the playful pair, Billy Swan so transfixed by the twin peaks, that he was virtually purring, or was it baying.

Symbolically speaking, Roger became absolutely sure Charlotte had her hands wrapped tightly around Sandra's neck.

Meanwhile, Peter joined him for refreshments in the marquee, and they began reminiscing about old times, as they usually did on social occasions. The pair must have gone through this process dozens of times, but still some things remained timeless, and were always worthwhile revisiting. Charlie Farley and Steve Hunt joined them.

"Hey, you'll never guess who I saw last month," said Peter.

"Go on," prompted Roger.

"Chopper Read."

"What, old Paul Read?" Roger asked.

"The very same."

"Well, I haven't seen Paul in years," reminisced Roger.

"He's even bigger than he used to be," Peter continued, "and 15 years ago, when we played badminton, he was bigger than most."

"Yes, Chopper always was a big lad," agreed Roger.

"Do you remember that incident at the Black Lion?" asked Peter.

"What....with the two butch lesbians?" Roger clarified.

"Ahh, they may have looked like butch lesbians," elaborated Peter, "but they were really man eaters, predators. Great white sharks would have steered away from them."

"That sounds interesting," observed Steve, always keen to hear a tasty tale. "What happened?"

"You tell it, Peter," Roger requested to his cousin, "I think the vino is beginning to catch up with me."

"Well, we were at the Black Lion. Brian Enderway, Paul Read, Roger and me. We usually used Castlemaine Avenue for badminton, but it was being redecorated, hence the Black Lion. Later, we retired to the lounge for refreshment. It was Roger's turn for a round, so he went to the bar, and made an order. At the opposite end of the bar, were a couple of heavy duty, pug ugly women, Grindle and Adeline types. Looked like they'd just defeated Burt Reynolds at roller ball, or gone ten rounds with Henry Cooper and beaten him." Becoming obsequious, he gawked at Roger. "You'd better carry on from here, cus. After all, it did happen to you."

"Okay," Roger confirmed with keenness. He didn't know why, because it hadn't been his finest moment. "After a few seconds, Grindle fixed me in her sights. 'Hey, dark and skinny,' she said."

"Skinny," gulped Steve, almost spilling his vino, "skinny, you?"

"Yes, I wasn't always the mature, going-grey foreboding figure, you see standing in front of you now....as you well know."

Steve seemed lost for words. He certainly did remember a time, maybe a prehistoric time in anybody's life cycle, figuratively speaking, when Roger resembled Apollo at his finest, but Steve chose to conveniently forget, after the ribbing he took about his own burgeoning size earlier.

"Anyway," continued Roger, "I mouthed 'fuck off' at them. They didn't like it. They moved towards me. I felt like a little tugboat, being approached by two massive battle cruisers. As they got closer, they dwarfed me. I'd thickened out by my mid-twenties, but compared to their massive bulk, I was still on the slender side. I gave them a dismissive look. They didn't like that, either. The next thing I know, the gruesome twosome were standing either side of me, looking threatening. Adeline scans me up and down, like she's about to snarl. I could feel her Devil's breath on my face. I thought 'fuck, I'm going to get gang banged!' Adeline backs away, hands on hips, as if about to give me an uppercut."

Steve and Charlie started to smile, Peter already laughing, because he knew the ending. Roger too began sniggering slightly, the bountiful grape having loosened decorum irrevocably.

"Now don't make me laugh," Roger pleaded, "or I will never get to the end of this tale." Recomposing himself he continued. "Having intimidated me, Adeline allows Grindle to take over. She said, 'Hey skinny, who's the big boy?' expecting a quick response. 'Big boy,' I lamely enquired. Grindle broods. She got within inches of me, radiating a look of complete indifference, at what she considers to be my puny body. 'The big boy with those other skinnies,' she said, pointing at the table, where my comrades are still discussing the finer points of badminton etiquette. I gawked over in the direction she indicated. 'Oh, you mean Chopper Read?' I enquired. Well, Grindle and Adeline look at each other, and lick their lips, like they are about to bite down on prime American rib."

"Having dined out on pork chops," added Peter.

"Quite," Roger agreed, before resuming. "Adeline said to me, 'Why's he called Chopper Read?' Now Paul had developed a bit of a reputation as a hard-tackling defender, in our five-a-side sessions, so I had rechristened him Chopper Read, in salute to Ron 'Chopper' Harris, who played in the great Chelsea team of the early 1970's."

"Great tackler," said Charlie, "harsh but fair."

"Quite," Roger said again, trying to concentrate. "So, I said, 'Oh, he's called Chopper Read because...,' Then I suddenly realise this is a golden opportunity, to drop Paul in it. Instead of telling how he got his nickname for hard tackling, I decided on an alternative course of action."

"Go on, go on," encouraged Charlie, eager to hear the final humiliation.

"Okay...Grindle and Adeline were becoming impatient, beginning to growl, a knee in my bollocks not far away. 'Well skinny....why's he called Chopper Read?' demanded Grindle. 'Because, because....' 'Yes, yes,' the monsters said in unison. 'Because he's got a massive schlong.' 'A what?' asked Adeline.'A huge dick,' I confirmed."

Tears started to form in Peter's eyes, in anticipation of the final scene. Steve and Charlie were chomping at the bit.

"Come on, come on," implored Steve, nearly wetting himself with anticipation.

"The roller ball players look at each other," Roger continued, "push me aside, and proceed to the table."

"That's right," said Peter. "In no uncertain terms, they made it clear that Brian and myself were redundant to their plans, and descended on Paul, surrounding him with their bulk, so he couldn't escape." He paused. "Took him nearly an hour to get away from the gruesome two-some, while Brian, Roger and I smiled at him from the bar. He virtually had to drop his pants, to prove to them his phallus was not as big as his nickname suggested, before they let him go."

Steve and Charlie weren't far from falling over in hysterical laughter, Peter and Roger not far behind.

The four of them continued these lurid tales from yesteryear for about a further twenty minutes; then Roger felt a tap on his shoulder. Turning around, still guffawing at Charlie's latest tale, he saw Charlotte. She appeared to be quite wet.

"Hello, darling," he said, with an air of lightness. "We were just reminiscing about old times….it is raining?"

"Raining," she replied, on the verge of meltdown, "I'll say it's raining. Come with me."

She grabbed her husband's hand, and whisked him away, his glass contents flying up in the air, narrowly missing his companions in reminiscence.

***

"Charlotte, what on Earth is the matter?" Roger asked.

She gawped at him, as if stupefied.

Realising it's not raining after all, he asked, "Charlotte, how did you get wet?"

"Get wet," she said, her warning signals starting to rise. "I'll tell you how I got wet. Those brats of your cousins started a water fight with the other kids. When I tried to stop them, that evil little Basil emptied a bucket of water over me....and all Sandra could do was laugh."

Roger began to sober up.

"Ah, I see."

"So what are you going to do about it, Roger?"

"I guess I'd better go sort it out," he said, smiling, and trying to diffuse the situation.

"Yes, I think you better had....I'm going to get changed."

Going back inside the marquee, he saw Peter, Steve and Charlie were still having a whale of a time, chewing the cud about pastimes.

"Er, Peter...." requested Roger, "we are needed for diplomatic and UN peacekeeping duties."

"Oh, something controversial happened?"

"You could say that....come on."

As the cousins approached the paddling pool area, an explosive furore ensued before them. A crowd had gathered to spur on whoever's son or daughter it was, giving it some wellie. The cousins entered the war zone, with little Julia Mallory taking aim with a bucket of water at one of Peter's twins, Cecile, Roger thought. Julia aimed perfectly, but Cecile ducked, and the load fell on Basil. According to Charlotte, Basil was a born vivisectionist, and the least tolerant of Peter's kids. Basil retaliated with a counter attack, but little Julia saw it coming, and the water hit Georgina Fortescue, who burst into tears, and ran off to find Freda, her doting mother. Roger dived in, as did Peter, trying to separate the marauding youngsters, but only having four hands between them, as fast as they took them out of the fray, the children ran back, resuming hostilities.

Then a water load intended for Bethany Anderson from Rowan, who Charlotte reckoned had 666 embossed on his head from birth, ended up hitting Virginia Loos-Smyth, one of Charlotte's arty-farty friends. Virginia gasped, as the cold water flushed through her light summer dress, then she grabbed a bucket out of Cecile's hand, dipped it in the paddling pool, took aim at Rowan, and let fly. But he was too quick, and the load drenched Bethany's mother, Rachel. Always game for anything, Rachel returned the free of charge washing in kind, but most of her load hit Hannah Tomlinson, mistress to Ethan Scott. His wife was away on a weekend residential course, bet she's glad she couldn't make it, thought Roger. Then other wives and girlfriends joined in the water battle, Steve Hunt encouraging the action with 'get in there, girl', until he too received a soaking.

Soon, the husbands and boyfriends joined in as well, whilst the James gang and Wendy's set sniggered, laughed and pointed from the wings. Finally, Charlotte emerged from the house, saw the fracas, and rushed forward with the intention of stopping it, only to receive another soaking. She screeched a deafening sound, bringing the water war to a stop, all combatants staring at the steam rising from her body. Her eyes searched around trying to find her husband.

"Roger, Roger," she shouted, the flashpoint moment very near.

He stepped forward. "Yes my sweet."

Before Charlotte could say anything more, she noticed Sandra smirking at her dishevelled state, but before Charlotte could launch into 'Gloria big tits', Heather, who had been conspicuous by her absence until this point, stepped forward with a bucket of water, and launched it at Sandra. It connected dead centre, providing an instant wet tee-shirt competition for the men to judge, the cold water enticing Sandra's braless nipples forward, causing male knees to buckle. Billy Swan virtually went into convulsions, the rest of the James gang becoming equally pole-axed, in teenage sexual heaven.

"Don't laugh at my mummy, Auntie Sandra," Heather scolded, with the authority of a seasoned matron.

Losing her customary cool for dealing with outlaw incidents, Charlotte burst into uproarious laughter. Several other lady guests, who had congregated around the soap opera, couldn't help themselves and followed suit.

Looking furious, Sandra began filling a bucket, probably with the intention of soaking Charlotte again, until Peter said, "Now Sandra, don't...."

Too late, the bucket's contents were in mid-flight, but were misdirected, the soaking heading for Steve. With his back turned to the throng, he remained oblivious, until the water collided with his head, bespoke shirt and trousers. Always a keen advocate of slapstick-type theatre, he smiled almost sweetly, dipped a bucket in the paddling pool, but instead of going for Sandra, he poured its contents over Pablo Pringle, who had remained adjacent to the combat zone, consuming ice cream. In the process, Steve's earlier theory became proven. Off came the syrup, to reveal a silicone waxed head, reflecting sunlight like a lighthouse beacon.

Though only half Steve's size, Pablo launched into him, with a flurry of karate chops and kicks. It's true, he was a martial arts instructor, and Jesus, he was good, Steve getting pulverised, squawking and squealing like a stuck pig. It took the combined efforts of Gordon, Charlie, Peter and Roger, to haul the vicious Bruce Lee impersonator off their wounded comrade, the instructor still flailing kick-boxer thrusts and screaming like a frenzied banshee.

Behind the martial arts display, other adults had joined in the water battle, using the opportunity to exercise long-held grudges against each other. All the younger children laughed hysterically, thinking it hilarious their parents indulged in the kind of behaviour resulting in punishment, if they did it. Preferring to enjoy the neo-Carry On display as spectators, the Wendy set and the James gang resisted the temptation to join in. Instead they poked fun at their elders, and stored up the debacle for a later occasion, when it could be used as a bargaining chip. They goaded on participants, applauded particularly well-directed water loads, and chortled at the attempts to disengage Pablo from Steve's throat.

Things got even worse, when Greg Fortescue received a particularly vicious load from sources unknown, sending him toppling against the main strut, holding up the marquee. The marquee came down over the water battle, consuming all participants, ironically to the sound of *Just Walkin' in the Rain* by the Prisonaires, still coming out of the surviving sound system.

* * *

Later, James showed his parents the whole event, captured on his iPhone video recording app. It had also been recorded by several of the guests, one of whom posted it on YouTube, under the title 'Garden party descends into bedlam-like chaos', with the tag line 'Teenagers and young children watch in horror, as adults lose their cool, and indulge in mindless violence and vandalism. Calls for police intervention narrowly avoided'.

CHAPTER 6: LADY MACBETH

The Frasers went on tour, allegorically speaking on safari, as Roger called it, visiting in-laws, outlaws and friends alike. Wendy and James wanted to stay at home, but after the garden party fiasco and subsequent cleanup, their parents were taking no chances.

Bright and early, the entire Fraser family piled into the MPV, and set off along the M25, en route for Buckingham to see Charlotte's mother, Davina, or Lady Macbeth as Roger called her.

Davina and Charlotte's father, Valentine, were having a trial separation, although sabbatical might have been a more appropriate expression. After 47 years, the marriage had slipped in to neutral, all the excitement and pining for each other long gone, both partners needing space, as it's euphemistically called, to reassess and re-evaluate, with the ultimate intention of living together again, renewed and refreshed.

She had retained the ancestral home, whilst he moved out, to live at his club. That had been three months ago, but there were still no signs of convergence between them. Roger knew Charlotte was secretly concerned, but she flew the supportive flag, endeavouring to justify her parents' separation. He didn't believe it would take much to reignite the flame, just a matter of sufficient time apart, from the constancy of being with each other 24 by seven. Confident that Charlotte would receive news of reunification by Christmas, Roger tried to put the affair into context, and bolster his wife's misgivings about the temporary break-up.

However, Charlotte felt awkward about the situation. She subconsciously bit at her fingernails, as the MPV headed northwest, along the world's biggest mobile car park.

"Enjoying your snack?" Roger enquired.

"Huh," she replied, still fixated by inner thoughts.

"You're devouring your fingers," he observed.

She suddenly became aware of her involuntary action. "Oh, yuck."

Still early in the day, 8:15 to be precise, their little untouchables, as Roger sometimes called them, making him feel like Elliott Ness, were fast asleep. Looking in the rear view mirror, he saw James, his mouth wide open, tempting passing flies, and making a curious gurgling noise. Wendy appeared much more serene, her north and south firmly shut, as she caught zees. As his eyes traversed further to the left, Heather came into view, curled up with Kermit the Frog and Miss Piggy, both forgiven after disastrous performances on *The Weakest Link*, hours before the even more disastrous garden party.

"Are you still concerned about Valentine and Davina?" he asked.

Charlotte exhaled noisily, releasing tension. "Yes, I am."

She began to look behind her.

"Don't worry," he assured her, "they're asleep."

"This will be the first time I will have seen my mother, without my father being present….it feels abnormal."

Slipping his left hand into her right hand, and squeezing, he said, "Don't worry, darling….it will be just a transitory blip. You'll see, they'll be back together again very soon."

She leaned across, and rested her head on his shoulder, concern quelled, at least for the time being.

15 minutes later, the wild bunch began to stir. Scanning the rear view mirror again, Roger saw James yawning so much it seemed like he'd get lock jaw.

His mouth finally returning to the closed position, he licked his lips, then enquired, "Are we stopping for breakfast?"

"You've had breakfast already," Roger reminded him.

"Oh yes, I thought that was a dream….doesn't seem natural, eating in the middle of the night."

"It wasn't the middle of the night," intoned Charlotte. "It was 6:45."

DOGHOUSE BLUES

"That's right," insisted their son, "the middle of the night."

The conversation brought Wendy back to the land of the living. "I was having a lovely dream about Justin Timberlake...." Roger always thought of him as Justin Trouser-Snake. "He was...." she continued, then recognised she about to stray into teenage girl dream confessional territory. She sat up with start, hoping her indiscretion had not been registered by her parents.

"Yes, Wendy?" asked her fretful mother.

Whoops, Wendy thought to herself, then immediately changed the subject. "Where are we?"

"Just gone past the Potters Bar junction," her father advised.

"Oh, is that all...." she yawned, "I thought we'd be there by now."

"Ahh, quite right, Wendy," Roger began, "but you forgot to allow for the Minister for Transport, having more fun and games on Britain's motorways....most of the M25 northern section is coned off, and there's a 50 mile an hour speed limit, not that we've even reached 40, since the Dartford Crossing."

Also back from the land of nod, Heather said, "Daddy." Yawning and stretching, she almost inadvertently punched Miss Piggy in the face, only for the doll to fall over, before her fist touched it.

"Yes, sweetheart."

"Can I have a pet gerbil, when we get back home?"

Charlotte and Roger exchanged glances. Where did that come from? Roger thought.

"A pet gerbil," he said.

"Yes."

"Is there any particular reason you want a gerbil?" he asked.

"Well, after Mummy murdered that rat, I think we owe a debt to the rodent family."

"I didn't murder that rat."

"Yes, you did, Mummy, I saw you," said their youngest, with some venom.

"Heather," entreated her mother, "it was already dead, when I put it on Mister Jones' bonfire."

"Yes, but you set the trap to catch it….." Heather protested, "I should report you to the RSPCA."

Trying for reason, in order to extricate his wife from the dock, Roger said, "Heather, rats are vermin….they spread disease. Mummy was only trying to keep all of us from catching something nasty….that's why she murdered, I mean set a trap for the rat."

"Well, I'm not satisfied with your answer," moaned Heather, going into Anne Robinson mode, thinking that persona would be more effective. "Grownups shouldn't kill little innocent animals."

"It's the same as when Dad killed that pigeon," added Wendy.

"I didn't kill that pigeon….." Roger objected. "How was I to know it was going to fly in front of the MPV?"

"You're a grownup," said Heather. "You should be able to tell, when a little innocent bird is about to fly in front of you, and stop the car."

"I never even saw the blessed bird coming anyway," Roger complained, "besides, if I had braked, the car behind would have run into us."

"Better that, than killing an innocent little bird," declared Heather. "Anyway, can I have a gerbil, when we get back?"

Her parents exchanged glances again.

"We'll see," said Charlotte.

"That means no," offered James.

"I hope you're not going to start as well," Roger said.

"I remember when I wanted a python, and was told, 'We'll see'," continued the Fraser son.

"James, you were six years old," Roger remonstrated again, "it would have eaten you."

DOGHOUSE BLUES

***

By 10:30, the holidaymakers were rolling into Buckingham, pulling up on the gravel drive at Vespers, so named because of its proximity to a nearby church. Set in a beautiful location, on a minor tributary of the Great Ouse, the sight of her childhood home invariably brought out the effervescent side of Charlotte's character. She broke into a satisfied smile, taking in the house and the immediate river panorama. When James was younger, he would fish the river from the back garden with his father, Valentine advising the best swims for chub and dace. Vespers also had a magnetic fascination for Wendy and Heather. Additional to the river attractions, the girls would find entertainment among Valentines collection of first edition books in his study, and Davina's plethora of tropical plants in the heated greenhouse.

Davina came out onto the drive to greet them, and soon they were all ensconced in the morning room, having a refreshing cup of tea. Always bright and alert, Charlotte's mother was a Girton College graduate, with a very sharp mind and highly intellectual-looking facial features, especially her intense greeny-blue eyes. Roger always found them quite mesmerising, impossible to look away from during conversation. She had a reputation for being a maverick philosopher, though claimed to be a realist. All in all, a very powerful woman, who Roger respected, even loved, despite her Lady Macbeth mantle. The children quickly became bored with the tea ritual, and went out into the back garden, leaving the adults to discuss the world at large.

"So this is the seat of the House of Commons Speaker," quipped Roger, knowing he had laid bait that Davina would be unable to resist.

"Furcow," she replied, glowering.

Roger nodded.

"Yes it is," confirmed Davina, "and that jumped up little

socialist bitch wife of his."

"Halley?" he enquired, with a hint of sarcasm.

"Yes, she's almost as bad as the Blair woman. Her behaviour is disgusting, sheltering under the protection of her husband's Office of State whilst, at the same time, pontificating her armchair Labour Party agenda. God….that woman needs birching." She leaned forward, malice written into her expression. "There is nothing more annoying, than middle-class hypocrites playing left-wing politics, and insisting we all wear hair shirts to purge their own consciences, whilst their noses are firmly stuffed in the gravy-train trough."

"You don't like her, then?" he suggested, nodding openly and inviting another forthright reply.

"Certainly not….odious little runt."

He wondered where he had heard that before.

"Well, don't sugar coat it, Davina, tell us what you really think."

Her son-in-law's attempt at levity only brought more vitriol, against Furcow and his wayward wife.

"Did you hear about Furcow's motoring incident at the House of Commons?" asked Roger's rapacious monster-in-law, er, mother-in-law.

"You mean," he clarified, "when he stared out of his House of Commons apartment window, and saw someone had backed into his car?"

"Yes." Davina started to smile. "I would love to have been there, when he ran up to that man who had backed into his car, and said, 'I'm not happy', to which the considerably taller gent replied, 'Well, which of the Seven Dwarfs are you, then?' That was brilliant… couldn't have happened to a more deserving, self-centred, egotistical, disloyal worm."

"You didn't vote for him at the last general election, then?" he ribbed her.

"Certainly not….I voted for Nigel Farage."

"A protest vote, then?" he prodded.

"Certainly not, the Conservatives are wishy-washy. They

DOGHOUSE BLUES

have abandoned their beliefs in a free and independent England, and joined the treacherous rabble, which are endlessly driven by politically correct politics and Euro babble. That blithering idiot Boris Johnson is a typical example."

"Oh, we're with you on that one, Davina," Roger supported. "He wants to build a huge airport in our back garden, well, off the North Kent coast, or on the Isle of Grain. Everybody is up in arms against his ludicrous proposals. There are Boris Johnson 'wanted dead or alive' posters, all over Kent. He's about as popular as an ice-pick salesman at a Leon Trotsky family reunion."

"That doesn't surprise me," agreed Davina, "I always did think he was extremely short, in the grey matter area. It's amazing that he is Mayor of London. I can't see any difference between his trendy, lefty policies, and those of his predecessor. Oh, what's his name? He sounds like a stoat with a speech impediment, loathsome little creep."

"Red Ken?" he surmised.

"Yes," confirmed Lady Macbeth.

On great form today, she sat back in her chair, and continued the diatribe. "Don't you realise, from Magna Carta in 1215, to the Representation of the People Act in 1949, our history has been a long campaign to achieve national freedom and democracy, under a sovereign parliament. Since that abject fool, Heath, conned the nation into joining the EEC in 1973, those sacred ideals have been watered down, and power handed over to a set of unelected bureaucrats in Brussels and Strasbourg." She took a sip of Lapsang souchong. "Cameron was supposed to be a euro-sceptic, but reneged on his promise for a membership referendum, as soon as he was elected. As far as I am concerned, he is a hound and rotter. Nigel wants out of the EU, so do I, like most English people. Gorging themselves silly on caviar and champagne at the taxpayer's expense....they're all rogues and vagabonds."

"Oh, Mother, the EU's not that bad," justified Charlotte.

"Yes, it is, Charlotte," Davina shot back, with a disapproving frown aimed at her daughter. "It's only since you've been running around with that progressive art crowd in Kent, that you've lost your common sense, and any notion of what's best for this country."

Shaking her head, Charlotte retorted, "Mother, it's not like that....it's just I've been exposed to some alternative points of view, since I began the arts and crafts course at the local tech....you know, people who come from different backgrounds."

"Are you talking about chavs?" her mother asked.

Roger couldn't wait to hear the answer to that one.

"They're not chavs, as you so indelicately put it....most come from very respectable homes and backgrounds, but some do have a left-of-centre leaning."

That was good, he thought. Non-confrontational, and designed to ease the conversation in an alternative direction.

"What do you mean, Charlotte?" pushed her mother.

Dear me, Roger thought, Lady Macbeth wasn't going for it.

"Oh, Mother, we're in a new millennium, in fact we've been in it for over ten years....middle-class people do not necessarily support traditional status quo ideas any longer."

"You mean they support dubious and treacherous politicians," her mother pressed, "like that Brown person?"

Charlotte pulled a halfway-house face, not intending to support or deny the possibility. "Yes, some do, some don't....but New Labour are hardly extreme left, are they?"

"I'm not talking about extreme left. Or come to that, extreme right....I'm talking about a rogue, who has done more damage to England than Hitler ever did."

"Oh, Mother."

Having none of it, Davina said, "We should all be active in the fight to restore democracy and self-government to England. We should reject EU diktats which force laws on England to our detriment, often without parliamentary scrutiny which further erodes the nation's independence. How can you possibly support a neo-dictatorship like that, Charlotte?" She paused,

DOGHOUSE BLUES

frowning at her daughter again. "Remember, England fought and prevailed in two world wars, to preserve our way of life. Tens of millions died in the process. Do you really want to belittle their sacrifice, and insult their memory, by glibly surrendering to the European Parliament?"

"Of course not, Mother....but these are different times and...."

"Different times, be blowed," stormed her mother. "What's the difference between Hitler's or Stalin's totalitarian states, and the virile empire building of the EU? I'll tell you...absolutely nothing."

"Oh, there's no reasoning with you, on this subject," Charlotte protested.

"That's what someone would say," her mother chastised, "who has buried their head in the sand."

Charlotte tutted in exasperation. Arguing with her mother did not come naturally, they usually agreed on most things.

"What makes it even worse," continued Davina, "is that the EU is a byword for waste, extravagance and corruption, on a breathtaking scale. Do you know, my girl, the EU auditors have never given its accounts a clean bill of health....and do you know why this has been allowed?" She stopped to allow a response, but it was a feint. She answered her own question. "Because all the major political parties support the EU.... now don't you find that a little strange? What other issue or organisation has this universal support, from both the right and left? None, and do you know why?" She offered the opportunity for answers, but before Charlotte could justify EU excesses, off she went again. "Because they, like the EU, are corrupt, and cannot resist the temptation to take a taxpayer-funded ride on the gravy train, and stick their noses in the trough, as well."

"You're such a cynic, Mother," Charlotte replied, her arms crossed, in an instinctive body-language act of defiance.

"Cynic," repeated Davina. "A cynic is what an idealist calls a realist. The trouble with most people in this country, is that they have stupidly bestowed all decision making with the political classes, on the basis they are acting in their best interests, when in fact, they are only acting in their own short-term interests, and don't give a damn about the country's future….it's the moral dimension, or more specifically, their complete indifference to it."

Roger could see that Davina had thoroughly researched and analysed the issue, and his wife, like most of the nation, had unwittingly gone along with the con. Sensing the exchange beginning to spiral into bruising territory, he took the initiative.

"Davina," he said, in his most polished voice, whilst flashing the gnashers, a ting of sparkle almost bouncing off them.

Lady Macbeth turned her attention to him. "Yes, Roger."

"Will we be seeing Valentine, during the next few days?"

Davina half-grinned, leaving Roger wondering what that meant. "Valentine will be joining us for lunch tomorrow," she confirmed.

"Oh, good," he enthused, sustaining his selling smile, "I'll look forward to that. I always enjoy his highbrow style of banter."

Suddenly, Charlotte saw Heather through the window, about to launch Miss Piggy into the Great Ouse tributary. Miss Piggy must have forgotten to say 'bank' again. Charlotte quickly got up, and opened the window.

"Heather, what are you doing?"

Her youngest glimpsed up.

"I'm going to baptise Miss Piggy," came the reply.

"Oh, dear," Charlotte uttered under her breath, then much louder, "wait for me, Heather, before you do anything."

She moved rapidly towards the kitchen door, Lady Macbeth and Roger not far behind. Charlotte then raced into the garden, to make sure the John the Baptist imitator didn't venture too near the river, rescuing Miss Piggy a secondary consideration. Davina and Roger waited on the terrace with Wendy and James, who were both engrossed in reading material, and oblivious to Miss Piggy's plight.

Emitting a knowing look at her son-in-law, Davina said, "Roger, you can be very diplomatic at times."

"What?" he said.

"I know you asked about Valentine, because Charlotte and I were arguing."

"Don't know what you are talking about, mother-in-law," he said meekly.

"I think you do," complimented Davina.

CHAPTER 7: VALENTINE

"Hello Charlotte. Hello children."

Valentine had arrived for lunch at Vespers, the next day. He spoke from his Morgan Aero 8 convertible, swiftly parking and jumping out of it, like a 1950's racing driver. Still very fit for someone approaching 70, he had a full head of silver-grey hair, clear blue eyes, a square jaw, and exercised everyday to sustain his body weight, not altered in over 40 years.

Davina and the Frasers, which Roger thought sounded like an indie rock band, were on the driveway, having just returned from a walk around the town. Charlotte rushed forward to embrace her father.

"Oh Dad, I'm so pleased to see you."

Returning the cuddle, her father replied, "Hello, Charlotte, how are you my darling?"

"I'm fine, Dad," she confirmed.

Next up, Heather jumped into Valentines arms. "Grandad, grandad," she bleated, pleased to see him.

"Ooohh, that's quite a welcome," exclaimed Valentine, as she almost winded him.

Wendy gave him a peck on the cheek, and James shook his hand in the expected manly fashion.

It was Roger's turn next. "It's been too long, Valentine, how the Devil are you?" he cheerfully enquired.

"Roger, my boy." He examined the stock analyst. "You look fit….I can see all that city-slicker work is good for you." Chortling a perceptive laugh, he added, "Or is it my lovely daughter?"

"Charlotte, of course….she builds me up to do battle in the city."

Valentine turned his attention to Davina. He walked forward, squeezed her, kissed both cheeks, and said, "Hello, my pretty," whilst beaming one of his marvellous smiles.

Judging by Davina's returned smile, both Roger and Charlotte determined that she was tempted to immediately suggest a return to the roost for Valentine. But then she composed herself, becoming more defensive. As the embrace broke, her body language suggested further penance expectation, though the Frasers remained uncertain, as to why and for what reason. Valentine's rakish good looks were a possibility, but Roger, in particular, doubted that temptation to stray had been the cause of the separation. Much more likely, familiarity breeding contempt had been behind the division, but hell would freeze over, before Roger would ask the true reason for the split. In this context, the Fraser family's job became to create conditions, whereby the pair became reunited, as soon as possible.

* * *

Sitting down to a splendid lunch, the conversation flowed, as the family began their starters.

"Heather, what have you been up to recently?" asked her grandfather.

Considering for a moment, the youngest daughter then went into lurid details about the Royal Academy of Art visit, the garden party, and her continuing challenge to get competitors to 'bank' on *The Weakest Link*. Several times during her undiluted account of events, Roger squirmed in his seat, recalling some of the more unfortunate episodes. Being the eternal envoy of the discreet, Valentine listened resolutely to every detail, not casting any judgmental looks at Charlotte or Roger. On the other hand, Lady Macbeth emanated a continuous set of facial contortions and half-uttered rebukes, signalling her displeasure at the goings-on.

Finally, Heather finished with, "Oh, and I wanted to baptise Miss Piggy in the river, for her poor performance on *The Weakest Link*, but Mummy wouldn't let me."

"Well, thank you for that most illuminating review, Heather," opined Valentine, ever the font of encouragement to his grandchildren.

"You're welcome," returned a glowing Heather, head tilted to one side, and appearing moved by her grandfather's tribute.

Wendy and James were also questioned by Valentine, similarly responding with examples of school experiences, and their burgeoning social lives. Expecting her GCSE results soon, Wendy told her grandfather that she was confident of some very good grades.

The lunch developed into a pleasant and cordial affair, Davina and Valentine the perfect hosts, constantly making sure that everyone was kept fed, and engaged in light-hearted conversation. Roger found it difficult to believe they were now separated, the couple looking like peas from the same pod, irrevocably put on this Earth to eternally be with each other. Highly delighted with their unified performance, Charlotte interpreted it as a sign that her parents would soon reside under the same roof, once more. Davina was an excellent cook, and her cinnamon foie gras and rainbow trout courses just slid down with a little Chablis lubrication, though Heather passed on the cinnamon starter, instead electing to go for prawn salad.

After tarte aux fruits dessert, the Fraser children excused themselves, returning to the garden to pursue their chosen ventures, on their best behaviour in front of their grandparents. That left the adults free, to exercise in more stimulating conversation. Departing the dining room, they retired to the lounge, sunk into deep-pile chairs, and hugged their brandy glasses.

Valentine had always been a bit of a card. Like Roger's cousin, Peter, he was an accomplished public speaker, so he had a canon of after-lunch anecdotes and tall stories, to keep everyone amused.

He flew Canberras and Buccaneers in the RAF, retiring as a wing commander, before joining an aerospace consultancy firm, and rising to board level. His career had imbued him with a

DOGHOUSE BLUES

plethora of experiences and yarns, which were always lively, never soporific. Further, as was the case for Roger's parents, the stock analyst had put some cast-iron investments Valentine's way over the years, producing explosive dividends. So all in all, Valentine wasn't short of a bob or two, allowing him and Davina to broaden their experience even further, adding to the life sketchbook.

"Have I ever told you about Blinky Alcansop?" asked Valentine.

Charlotte and Roger exchanged questioning glances.

"Blinky Alcansop," Roger said, "don't think so."

Valentine smiled, and rubbed his hands together. He couldn't wait to tell them the story.

"Well, Blinky and I were entrant cadets together at Cranwell. Blinky was a great bloke, but he had the most appalling taste in women. Often they verged on the canine."

"You mean they were hounds," Roger offered.

"Hounds....put it this way, Roger, they all looked like they fed on Winalot and Bob Martins. I think some auditioned for the title role in *The Hound of the Baskervilles*, but were rejected on the grounds that they were just too ghastly."

"So they panted and had shiny coats?" egged Roger.

"You've got the picture," Valentine confirmed. "In fact, Blinky once told me his favourite Hollywood actor was Rin Tin Tin. Anyway, we're having an end-of-term ball in the officer's mess, and all the Cranwell bigwigs are present, including the CO. Part of the protocol is for the cadets to introduce their female companions to them. So Blinky has invited this rather large lady, with one of those poodle hairstyles, to be his belle."

"He means a bouffant," clarified Davina.

"That's right, me dear," Valentine confirmed energetically. "When it's Blinky's turn to present his companion, the bigwigs shrank back at the sight of her. She's bigger and taller than Blinky, has a strange growth on the end of her nose, and looks like she could form the entire front row of a rugby scrum. The senior officers were courteous, but slightly brusque, still alarmed at the sight of Blinky's date. They quickly make the necessary acknowledgment noises, and moved on to the next couple....you get the picture?"

"Oh yes, Valentine," Roger said, endorsing his acknowledgement with a knowing smirk, "very graphic."

"Good, isn't it?" returned his father-in-law, with gusto. "Anyway, our flight instructor, Squadron Leader Harding, had been watching the charade from the wings. He takes Blinky aside, and says to him discreetly, 'I knew there was a touch of eccentricity about you, Alcansop, but all your companion needs is a flashy moustache, to pass for one of the burly groundcrew, who service the Gnat trainer jets."

Roger began to laugh, as did Charlotte, in fact she was way ahead of her husband, already seeing the probable end to the tale.

"Wait for it, wait for it," insisted Valentine.

"Not sure I can, Dad," spluttered Charlotte.

"You must, you must," demanded her father, also starting to show signs of gleeful breakdown. "So in reply, Blinky says, 'I like my women full and round', to which the squadron leader looks his companion up and down again, then says, 'and preferably on four legs with shiny noses?'"

Charlotte and Roger were floored, both erupting into raucous amusement. Davina stared at them, like they were demented hyenas.

"Really, Valentine, no wonder women burnt their bras in the 1960's."

Taken aback, Valentine retorted, "Oh, come on, me dear....it's just a story, no harm done, and I'm sure I told you that yarn, when we first met."

"Well, if you did, I've forgotten about it."

"Come on, Mother," said Charlotte, "I'm the one who's meant to be all uptight about women's rights, and you're meant to be the cavalier free-thinker."

Davina considered, and then broke into a smile, the iconoclastic moment seconds away.

"Do you know, Charlotte, you're right….I don't really know why I took exception."

Leaning forward, Valentine put his hand on her knee. "You took exception because you are still trying to make me suffer."

"No….no, I wasn't."

"Well, can you give me another reason…why you usually laugh like a drain, at all my RAF yarns?"

Lady Macbeth thought again. "No, no, I can't, I…."

Becoming more serious, Valentine implored, "Davina, let's stop all this silly nonsense. I can't even remember properly, how it all got started anyway."

A developing look of contrition started to come over Davina. "Yes, I can't really remember, either. I just feel that with Charlotte, Roger and the grandchildren here, something is different, something's…."

"Something's getting back to normal," suggested Valentine, "is that what you were going to say?"

"Yes, well maybe. Oh, I don't know, but I do feel differently, like a spell has been broken."

"That's very truth-seeking," observed Charlotte, "even elegiac."

Becoming the peacemaker, Valentine added more thoughts. "I think we took each other for granted, for a while….that's when the snapping at each other started. I don't think either of us did it on purpose, more the case we just fell into that mode…. maybe it takes an outside stimulus, like a visit from loved ones, to break the spell. What do you think, Davina?"

"Yes, I think you may be right."

"Me dear, good things take time, great things happen all at once," Valentine insisted, sincerity etched in his tender smile. "When we first met, that was a 'great things' moment. When Charlotte and Roger met, I believe that was also a 'great things' moment. You see, Davina, we were meant to be together….it's as simple as that."

Praise from my father-in-law, can't be bad, thought Roger. I must remember to play that card in the future, when things may not be quite so rosy.

The conversation persisted along the lines of repatriation and renewal, Valentine and Davina sitting together on the sofa, whilst Charlotte and Roger acted to encourage reparations. Roger got the distinct feeling that Valentine would be moving back into the family home, sooner than the forecast Christmas-time. It all started to get a bit emotional, wet cheeks and wavering voices. Charlotte and Roger excused themselves, joining the young ones in the garden. A while later, Valentine and Davina also emerged into the sunlight, hand-in-hand and smiling, all sources of conflict forgotten, all concerns quelled.

Deciding to change the mood, from sombre to humour again, Valentine said whimsically, "Take some advice from me, Roger...treat 'em mean, and keep 'em lean." Sustaining the playful satirical mode, he added, "All we husbands have to do that."

"Why's that, Valentine?"

"Because if we don't," he warned, tongue in cheek, "they'll be wearing trousers next and even wanting the vote!"

CHAPTER 8: THE YORKSHIRE BUTCHERS

The following day, the Frasers left Buckingham secure in the knowledge that Valentine and Davina would soon be reunited again. Appearing relaxed, like a weight had been lifted off her, Charlotte joked with the kids, and didn't get upset once, not even when Heather inadvertently managed to get ice cream into her lap. Charlotte even laughed at Roger's jokes and mordant comments about other road users, and the Minister for Transport.

Next up on the tour was Roger's brother, Colin. He lived in Harrogate, and worked for a well-known chemical company, that got taken over by the French. His wife Louise also majored in chemistry, and worked for the same company, but when they married, she soon left to have babies. Still devilishly good looking, and often mistaken for the actress Saffron Burrows, Louise had a constant radiance about her, reminding Roger of a porridge TV advert, showing glowing school children in winter, with the strap line, 'central heating for kids'. Their children, Angela and Donald, got on very well with Roger's offspring. On the night the tour party arrived, and after being shown to their rooms by Louise, 18-year-old Angela was asked if she would look after the junior brigade, whilst the adults went out to play.

Angela had filled out, and had developed into a very attractive young woman. As a child, she would have her cornsilk hair trimmed to the neck. By her early teens, allowing her hair to grow, it became wavy and slightly darker. Now she had a full-mane strawberry-blonde hairstyle, which coupled with her midnight-blue eyes and high cheekbones, produced a classic English country-girl appearance.

A year younger than his sister and still to make the transition from callow youth to young man, Donald remained slightly gawky, the unfortunate trait giving the impression he was short on brain power. But he excelled at school, and his teachers thought he might be destined for great things. However, whereas Angela had it in mind to make a career in broadcasting, Donald remained fully vacant in terms of direction, something which worried his father.

Angela and Donald would keep the southern Fraser child contingent happy and amused, whilst the adults absconded into the Yorkshire night, in search of good food. Angela and Wendy had been penpals for many years, whilst Donald had affinity with James, being virtually the same age. Both of Colin's children adored Heather, Angela in particular thinking that she would develop, into someone with character and passion, certainly Miss Piggy and Kermit the Frog bore testament to the ardour accolade.

As the adults made up their minds regarding cuisine choice, Roger noticed that Colin's once neatly-trimmed dark moustache and beard were beginning to lighten, and his face was thinner, than when they were in their twenties. Roger would have liked to say that the weight loss had been brought on by daily exercise, but knew work concerns were the cause. Colin had always been very fastidious, thorough and professional in his outlook, but his profession had taken its toll.

On the other hand, Louise remained blooming, her silky flaxen hair and chartreuse eyes little different from when they married. Domesticity suited her. She felt fulfilled, having brought up their children and supported Colin's career, rarely pining for her former life in the laboratory.

The one constant about Roger's brother lay in the ability to switch off work issues, like an avalanche. Once committed to a social venture, his natural sense of fun and games surfaced. He became as good a companion, as anyone Roger ever knew, with a wide range of conversational topics, and amusing stories regarding astonishing calamities in the chemical industry.

Colin had suggested the Chez la Vie restaurant for dinner, because of its renowned reputation for quality beef and excellent wine cellar. The diners arrived in fine form, appetites sharpened by the fresh Yorkshire moorland air, keen to sample the renowned À la carte menu. Packed with obviously contented locals and tourists alike, it seemed Colin's choice had been an excellent selection. They looked forward to a sumptuous dinner, and some riveting conversation.

"Do you remember Fiona Ferris?" asked Colin.

"Vaguely," Roger replied. "That was when you were an undergraduate at Westbrook Chemicals, wasn't it?"

"Indeed."

"And?" prompted Roger.

"I bumped into her at a conference recently, brought back a flood of late teenage memories."

"Oh, do tell," requested Louise.

Reaching across the table, Colin held his wife's hand. "Nothing to be concerned about, darling, it was a passing moment from long ago."

"So what's the significance?" asked Charlotte.

"Well, Westbrook Chemicals sponsored me for my degree. Every summer, I would go to work for them, to get some industrial experience. That's where I met Fiona, and her pugnacious father."

"Oh, yes, I'm starting to remember now," Roger said, whilst smiling at the girls. "You're going to like this."

"Now don't spoil it, junior," griped Colin, with an air of senior brother authority.

"Yes sir," Roger replied, pulling an invisible zip across his mouth.

"To continue....I was put to work in the materials lab, working for Fred Ferris, Fiona's father. Now Fred had a reputation for being abrupt, often brusque with a short fuse, and had little tolerance for ineptitude. Consequently, he had gained legions of people, who let's say didn't care for his manner. He also had the appearance of a crazed ferret....fortunately for Fiona, she had inherited her mother's genes. Further, his high-pitched voice, and the stabbing-like manner he used to emphasise things with his hands, added to the rodent impression. Consequently, Fred Ferris was known as 'Ferret Face', or 'Ferret Features', behind his back."

"This is beginning to sound like one of Roger's far-fetched stories from Canary Wharf," suggested Charlotte.

"Unlike the improbable products of my brother's vivid imagination, this actually happened," defended Colin.

"Steady on," Roger said, "all my stories are perfectly true," then jokingly added, "how dare you impugn my adventures."

Beginning to chuckle slightly, Colin assured, "only kidding, brother Roger."

"I know."

"One day, I'd been dispatched to the liquid analysis labs, on some sundry business," Colin continued. "I had to telephone back to the materials lab for some reason, which I can't remember now. Anyway, Fred's secretary, Anna, would normally answer the phone. So when I called, I naturally expected her to answer. I said, 'Hello. Is Ferret Features about?' No response. 'Hello, hello, is Ferret Face there?' Then I get the reply. 'This is Ferret Features, who the hell's that?' I quickly slammed the phone down, and sheepishly returned to the materials lab, but Fred was not about."

"So you got away with it?" Louise insinuated.

"Yes and no….as you will see," advised her husband. "Quite by chance, Fiona had invited me over to the Ferris household, for dinner that evening. So when I arrived, she led me into the lounge, where her father was reading the evening paper. Immediately, I think Fred has figured out the voice was mine, and I'm going to get a roasting, if not dismissal from the company. Instead, Fred dips his paper, and welcomes me warmly. We exchange a few courteous words, and then sit down to dinner. Everything is going splendidly. Fiona and her mother clear the table, leaving Fred and I to chat. Then Fred says, 'Do you know what, Colin?' 'What's that, Mister Ferris?' I enquire. 'You won't believe this, but some cheeky bugger called the lab today, asking if 'Ferret Features' was about.'"

Charlotte and Louise started to smirk.

"Well, of course I feigned surprise and revulsion," assured Colin. "'Really, Mister Ferris, how disgraceful,' I said. Later, after leaving the Ferris household, I believed I'd got away with it."

"And did you?" enquired Charlotte.

"Well, this is why I say yes and no. I brought up the notorious incident with Fiona at the conference. She told me her father always knew it was me. He just wanted to make me sweat a bit….the only reason he didn't tear a strip off me, was because of my friendship with his daughter….so I suppose I did get away with it."

"To quote Blackadder," Roger said quietly, "you lucky, lucky, lucky bastard."

They had not long been into their entrées, when four very large gentlemen sat down, at the table next to the Fraser contingent.With the newcomers' bombastic voices drowning out conversation, the Frasers lapsed into eavesdrop mode. From what they could gather; their dining neighbours were Yorkshire butchers from Leeds, who all bore an uncanny resemblance to the great character actor, John Savident. They seemed totally oblivious to other diners and restaurant staff alike, not bothering to lower their voices, about some of their more sensitive dining topics.

"I'll tell thee wot," said butcher number one.

"Yorkshire code for, 'I'd like to tell you something'," Colin whispered to Roger.

His compatriots carried on munching their sirloins, one managing to guffaw, "Wot's that, then," between mouthfuls.

"My wife was in Manchester, tuther day. She goes inta butchers in Deansgate, and orders a sheep's head. She says, 'it must be a Yorkshire sheep,' and do you know what the cheeky bugga of a butcher said?"

"What?" asked butcher number three.

"He shouts back inta preparation area, 'Charlie, takes the brains outta that sheep'."

"Cheeky bugga," said butcher number four. "They're all the

same in Lancashire, think we Yorkshire folk are simple."

"Aye," agreed butcher number one.

The mirthful tale had the Frasers beginning to snigger. Though the Yorkshire butchers were only a few feet away, they remained unmindful to their escalating frivolity.

A bit later, butcher number three just had to share something with his dining comrades.

"I'll tell thee wot, I'll tell thee wot."

"Wot?" asked butcher number four.

"I wer' just gettin' down t' vinegar stroke, tuther night, when front doorbell goes. I thought, 'Who the fuck's that?' So I climbs off t' wife." He turned to butcher number one. "Difficult woman, you know. Puts on t' dressing gown and t' slippers, goes down t' stairs, opens t' front door, and who should it be, but fuckin' Geoffrey Boycott? I said, 'How do, Geoff, what the fuck do you want?'"

"No need to translate, Colin," assured Roger, "I think we all got the gist of that."

Losing it, the Fraser brothers roared with laughter, the girls not far behind their husbands in losing control completely, with the rest of the patrons in a similar state of unmanageable merriment arousal. Jaws opened to their maximum extent, stomachs on the verge of cramp with riotous guffawing. Colin became so overwhelmed with uncontrollable amusement, he dashed outside to truly let loose. From inside the restaurant, his dining companions heard his belly-aching laughter, high above the general hilarity consuming other customers.

It became like one of those situations in school assembly, when someone lets rip, and those around the ripper find it impossible to not at least smirk, if not lose control completely, and blurt out irrepressible jollity, resulting in a visit to the headmaster's study, to pay penance. In Roger and Colin's day, that meant six of the best, received with pride, as a badge of honour.

Remarkably, the four burly butchers still seemed insensible

to the laughter parade they had created, carrying on with more lurid tales from the Yorkshire butchering profession, and their extra-curricular cricketing activities, whilst hardly noticing the impact their yarns had on fellow diners.

Eventually, the Frasers emerged from the restaurant, aching with mirth, and in danger of vomiting up the very expensive hors d'oeuvres, Chateaubriand and Crepe Suzette they had just consumed. An experience that personally Roger would not have missed, even for a cast-iron investment with the American Federal Reserve, the experience would rate highly in the annals of Fraser folklore, and become recounted on many future occasions.

"Is that typical for Harrogate, these days?" enquired Charlotte, as they made their way back.

"Only on week nights," advised Colin. "At the weekends, it gets even more hilarious."

"What a great night," Roger enthused. "We don't get free of charge floorshow entertainment like that, in London and Kent."

"Yes, free entertainment in Yorkshire is also rare," added Louise. "Being a tight-wad bunch, they usually charge for everything."

"I would have thought you'd got used to the cultural differences between the deep south, and the land of Geoffrey Boycott by now," remarked Roger.

"Funny you should say 'the deep south', young brother," exclaimed Colin. "We have friends in Alnwick, north of Newcastle. Last year, one of their neighbours moved to the south. They thought it would be Middlesbrough, which for north easterners is the limit, of what's considered to be the civilised world. In fact, the neighbours were heading to Sussex, the real 'deep south'."

* * *

When the Yorkshire butchers appreciation society got back to Colin's house, they found Heather in pet lovers' heaven. Morpheus, the family cat, so named for his dreamlike appearance as a kitten, had returned from a hunting expedition, the youngest Fraser joyfully playing with the feline killing machine, known as The Terminator by neighbours. If ever a rodent problem plagued the neighbourhood, the Schwarzenegger copycat was called upon to do his duty. Roger began to wonder what Morpheus would have made of Fred 'Ferret Features' Ferris.

Morpheus suffered from big cat syndrome, his favourite TV programme being *Big Cat Diary*. As far as he was concerned, he considered himself to be as big as the leopards and cheetahs, he saw on the Serengeti. Very large by domestic moggy standards anyway, he imagined himself to be even bigger than his actual size, challenging all-comers; cats, dogs, three times his size, badgers, foxes, even stoats, on what he considered to be his sacred turf.

He saw Colin coming through the lounge door, and immediately leapt up, almost knocking him down, in the style of Dino welcoming Fred Flintstone home.

"Get down, Morpheus," demanded Colin, as he became virtually pinned to the deck by the loyal, but over-enthusiastic cat.

Sat on Colin's chest, purring away, The Terminator licked his master's face tenderly.

"Morpheus, stop it, stop it," begged the senior Fraser brother, but the neighbourhood terror remained unrelenting, continuing to dispense affection, until Louise waved a kipper under his nose, and he leapt away to consume his supper.

Since the last time Roger saw him, Morpheus seemed to have grown even bigger, so the junior brother appreciated Colin's sterling efforts in trying to shift him, before the kipper intervened.

As Roger helped his brother to his feet, he said, "You should have named him Titan, or one of those other powerful deities."

"I know," Colin replied, "but as a kitten, he had such a sweet and dreamlike appearance, hence the Morpheus tag. If I could have seen a few years into the future, I would have named him Godzilla."

"Yes," agreed Roger, "I begin to grasp the resemblance."

"It's strange," Colin continued "I've seen him stalking prey, whilst keeping other predators at a distance with his threatening howls. Often, just before he strikes, I swear there's a halo-like mist above his head. Louise has seen it as well."

"Really?" Roger said mockingly, thinking his brother was joshing him.

"Yes, yes....I'll tell you something else, Roger. Because of that curious halo, and his ability to deter other aggressors, Louise has taken to calling him The Bulletproof Monk."

Immediately, Roger began conjuring visions of a four-legged feline refugee from *Crouching Tiger, Hidden Dragon*, who has the drop on all challengers. What a cat. Whilst still developing explicit illusions of 'Crouching Morpheus', he felt a tug on his arm. It was Heather.

"Daddy."

Instinctively, he knew what was coming next, but had to go through the confirming ritual anyway.

"Yes, sweetheart."

"Can we have a cat, Daddy, when we get back home?"

"Gone off the idea of a gerbil, have you?"

"Well, if we got a cat as big as Morpheus, he could look after me, and protect me from attackers."

"Attackers?" Roger exclaimed, furrowing his brow.

"Yes."

"Who are these attackers?" her father enquired, already feeling an incongruous answer would be given.

"Attackers are anyone who stops me doing, what I want to

do."

"You mean like Mummy and I?"

"Yes. If I had a cat like Morpheus, I would train it to scare off attackers, even scratch them, if they didn't stop." She clawed her hand forward, and hissed in an emulation of feline behaviour, or was it misbehaviour?

Too terrible a vision to become reality, the thought of a huge hulking brute like Morpheus greeting him every night, Fred-Flintstone-style, made Roger shiver. But what could he say to deter Heather's desire?

Roger went for the tried and trusted chestnut. "We'll see."

***

The next day, the grownups were reading newspapers in the lounge, when Colin glimpsed up and exclaimed, "Oh, no….here comes Lurch."

Angela's latest boyfriend Lurch, so named by Roger's brother, because he bore an uncanny resemblance to the character of the same name in *The Munsters*, and those odd-looking cannibals in *Popeye* cartoons, had become a thorn in Colin's side. Justin Edwards, Lurch's real name, had been banned from parking his tiny Skoda on Colin's driveway. Hence his long walk from the road, which enabled Colin to pick out his approach. The oversized Dinky toy lowers the tone of the neighbourhood according to Colin, the road as near as the Skoda now got to the house. He maintained that ex-commie country imitation cars were an effrontery to his receptivity.

Angela had fallen out with her previous boyfriend, six months earlier. Colin had liked him. He drove a BMW 1 Series, much more in-keeping with neighbourhood standards. So desperate to see the demise of Lurch in his daughter's affections, recently, Roger's brother had visited the ex-boyfriend, telling him that his daughter might be amenable to advances from him again. He was mulling it over, apparently.

"Why did she dump him?" Roger enquired.

Colin whispered, "Angela has got into tomb-stoning, much to our concern, and Joel, that's the previous boyfriend, doesn't tombstone."

"Does Lurch?" wondered Roger.

"He does now," Colin confirmed, "to keep in my daughter's good books."

"Hhmm, tomb-stoning," mulled Roger, "Maybe there'll be an unfortunate accident to the Skoda lover."

"I'm not that lucky," replied Colin, ruefully.

Justin was calling for Angela, to take her to the local ice rink. According to Colin, Justin could hardly walk, let alone skate. However, Angela asserted that Justin became transformed on ice, his usual terra firma awkwardness replaced by Torvill-and-Dean-like grace, though her father remained sceptical. His skating prowess had become the key reason, why she had fallen for the Skoda aficionado.

Angela answered the door, ushered young Justin into the lounge, and then continued to get ready for the hot date.

Turning to face his least favourite person, Colin said unenthusiastically, "Oh, hello Lurch."

"What?" said the biped-deficient youth.

"I said…been to church….before you came to collect Angela."

"Oh….no," Lurch stuttered, "I've come straight from the car showrooms in Leeds. I'm thinking of upgrading my car."

"A BMW, perhaps?" said Roger's brother, up-shifting gear in his tone and beaming with tangible encouragement.

Over two generations, BMW had become the Fraser family's de facto car of choice. Roger and Colin's father swore by German engineering, owning vehicles made by the Munich-based company, for over 40 years. Colin was on his third beamer, and Roger had an M3 convertible, tucked away in the garage. The M3 represented his one extravagance, only ever seeing the light of day, if the Met Office could guarantee rain free conditions, an extremely rare event in the Home Counties.

Charlotte's vehicle, the Mercedes Viano MPV, had been the daily Fraser workhorse for seeing the family around Kent county and beyond, since she traded in her much snazzier Audi A7 for a people carrier. Of course, Valentine believed all foreign cars were vulgar. He always went for English classics. Additional to his Morgan, he had owned Aston Martins and Jags in the past. But these days, he wouldn't entertain a Jaguar. He reckoned that the grill badge appeared like a scrunched-up silver milk bottle top, and defeated the whole objective of a premier-class marque.

"No....a bigger Skoda," informed the source of Colin's discontent.

Grimacing and growling, Colin abruptly snapped up his Telegraph to continue reading, much to his brother's amusement.

Taking over the mini social interlude, Louise exclaimed, "Sorry, Justin, we're being rude. You've not met Colin's brother, Roger, and his wife, Charlotte."

They exchanged introductions, Colin still brooding behind his newspaper. Moments later, Angela returned, and whisked her skating partner away. As they walked down the drive, Roger couldn't help but take a gander at Justin's walking action. Sure enough, his gait was something to behold. With each forward step, he raised his heel acutely, thus increasing his already tall height, by a further four to five inches. The repeated action did indeed remind the onlooker of *The Munsters* character, and definitely qualified as a candidate for John Cleese's *Ministry of Silly Walks*.

Colin watched as well. "Can you imagine that cretin, skating to *Bolero*?"

CHAPTER 9: THE LAIRD OF WEST LOTHIAN

Early the next morning, the holidaymakers made their farewells to Colin and his family, and pointed the MPV due north. It was time to do some missionary work in Jockland. They took the A61 to Ripon, and then joined the A1, which would take them all the way to Scotland's first city. Compared to the grid-locked south east, driving in the lowlands became a doddle, a sublime pleasure. Superb countryside flashed by, with about one vehicle for every mile of road, and better still, nobody ripped off Roger's wing mirrors, or cut him up, necessitating him to resort to verbal abuse. A terrible thing to admit, he thought, but the further north of cosmopolitan London you got, the friendlier and more courteous the folk became.

Traditional and seemingly everlasting, it felt more like the England that Colin and Roger knew as kids, typified by village greens, lively characters, free speech and carefree days. Where had those glorious times gone? As they bombed along, through the teal and forestgreen valleys, and over dark-orchid topped hills, he couldn't help but reflect how much the South East, and London in particular, had changed over the past 40 years. Whereas Cheshire where the brothers had been born, and Yorkshire and Scotland remained the same, as in memories from childhood visits, made with their parents, Roger could find little constancy in Kent. Once associated with the idyllic world of the *Larkins*, Kent now represented a byword for burgeoning demographic dystopia, overpopulation, airports which consumed entire communities, and motorway networks crammed to bursting with foreign juggernauts.

The Frasers arrived late afternoon in Mid Calder, just outside Edinburgh, to see Roger's old friend, Hector McIntyre, his easy-gong wife, Avril and their three children, Hayley, Robert and Steven. There were too many Frasers to fit into Hector's house, so they had arranged for reservations at the Lothian Lodge, just a few miles away.

Roger had known Hector, nearly all his life. A Scot by birth, and before moving north of the border again, Hector had spent most of his life in England, where he had met Avril. He was Chief Engineer at Parsons Peebles, an electrical rotating machinery manufacturer, once owned by Rolls Royce, where he had become a much respected authority within the industry. Roger's old mate was also known as The Laird of West Lothian, leastways that was the grand title the Frasers used on Christmas cards. 'Why is that?' a younger Wendy had asked years ago. Her father answered, 'Well, he has always pronounced the word 'lad' as 'laird'; hence the latter affords a dual use in conversations with me. It both infers a regal title for him, plus a continuing source of mispronunciation applied to the young'.

For once, foul weather had kept at bay in Jockland. The McIntyre and Fraser clans sat out in Hector's back garden, everybody taking maximum advantage of the opportunity, to soak up some sunrays. The young set's fascination with adult talk soon tired, and they all piled back into the lounge, to watch *Iron Man*.

Charlotte and Roger had always been very fond of the McIntyres, and Hector had been known to say that he loved Roger in an extremely manly fashion, not that the fashion made it sound quite right.

Invariably upbeat and bubbly, Avril had always been easy to socialise with, her genial temperament winning her many admirers. She had that precious gift to be able to talk to anybody, and make them feel welcome and relaxed. Vivid eyes and a fluffy mass of dark hair added to Avril's appeal, confirming nature had been very kind to her.

It was a similar story for the Laird in terms of personality traits. Hector and Roger hadn't exchanged a crossed word in over 25 years, but unlike Avril, Hector had become follicle-challenged in recent times. Where once he had sported a Robert Plant-style golden mane, there were now only a few spouts, here and there on top. Sometimes, Roger would hold his hand up in front of his face, shielding his eyes, and tell the Laird that the reflection of light coming off his head blinded him. Knowing it only said in jest, Hector would retort back, calling him a cheeky Sassenach bastard. What remained constant, and had gravitational pull, was Hector's vibrant personality. Roger just loved being in his company.

After they had gone through the usual 'long time, no see' chitchat, Charlotte asked, "What's been happening with you guys, lately?"

Smiling wickedly, Avril answered, "As it happens, Hector had an embarrassing incident, just yesterday."

"Really?" said Roger with eagerness, sensing a potential source of discomfort for the Laird.

Frowning at Roger, the Laird of West Lothian, started to nod his head from side to side; an indication that the incident must have been bad.

"It was nothing really," he bleated, "just one of those unfortunate situations which happen, once in a lifetime."

"Come on, Hector, tell all," requested Charlotte.

After a few more excursions around the buoy, with Avril prodding her husband to be frank with the account, he finally relented.

"Okay, okay," whined the disinclined jock. "Last night, Avril and I attended a Parsons Peebles dinner at the Witchery, near to Edinburgh Castle. Just a few of the middle managers, and heads of department, we do it about twice a year."

"It's always a hoot," added Avril. "They're really nice people."

"Well, we got talking about travel," the Laird began to explain. "Places we've been to on business, you know the kind of thing, Roger."

"Yes, indeed."

With Hector's face already beginning to take on a ruddy hue, clearly, he remained mortified by whatever indiscretion he had made. Good, thought Roger.

"Go on, Hector," enthused the sparkling Avril.

"Well, I was telling them about a visit I made to Asheville, North Carolina, many years ago, when I was still with GEC Alsthom. I'd done the business with the local electricity utility, and was on an aircraft, waiting to take off for Colorado. An elderly lady was being escorted to her seat, by what looked like her middle-aged son. Whilst he helped his mother get settled, and put her hand luggage in the overhead compartment, I suddenly tuned into his voice….he sounded just like Huckleberry Hound, and as he continued to talk, I transformed him into the shape of the cartoon character, in my mind. Ever since then, I've been of the opinion that all people who hail from North Carolina, talk like Huckleberry Hound. You, er, see where I am coming from?"

"Yes, yes," Charlotte and Roger confirmed.

"Well," continued Hector, "I'm telling this story at the dinner, much to the amusement of my colleagues and their wives, when we hear the scraping sound of a chair, being moved out from the next table. A tall distinguished-looking gent stands up, and says, 'Excuse me, sir. I'm from North Carolina, as are all the folks at this table, and I can assure you that in general, no one talks like Huckleberry Hound, where we come from."

"Wow, what are the chances of that?" Roger exclaimed.

"Precisely," confirmed the Laird. "How was I to know, that three thousand miles from their homes in the Blue Ridge mountains, a gaggle of offended North Carolinians would pitch up, on the next table to ours in Edinburgh."

"But that wasn't the end of it," added Avril. "Go on, Hector."

"Well, it's a matter of implanting the seed….until that point, the Parsons Peebles crowd had not taken in the southern United States accents, coming from the next table. But after that gent stood up, reprehending me, all our ears became attuned to their speech. You know, that southern drawl, with a sweet, relaxed, well-intentioned personality. Soon, there are whispered comments going around our table, like 'they do sound like Huckleberry Hound,' and 'when do you think Powerful Pierre and Dinky Dalton,' you know, those other 'Huckleberry Hound' cartoon characters 'will join them?'"

"Wish we'd been there," said Charlotte. "It really does sound like a hoot, as you said, Avril."

Hector's inhibitions had all but disappeared. He really put gusto into the account, now. "The folks from North Carolina sense they have become the source of further amusement for the locals. The same guy, who first took me to task, stands up again, and pronounces, 'It's not Huckleberry Hound anyway, it's Foghorn Leghorn we sound like.'"

Roger almost fell out of his deckchair, as did Charlotte. It was the funniest thing the Laird had ever told them, and resulted in a bout of Huckleberry Hound and Foghorn Leghorn voice impersonations, causing further uncontrollable hilarity.

James and Robert came out onto the patio, not even *Iron Man* keeping their attention over the adults' laughter.

"What are you lot so happy about?" asked Robert, sounding potentially judgemental, and scratching the back of his head, in disbelief.

"You're too young to understand, son," replied Hector. "We grew up on Bugs Bunny and Yogi Bear, not *The Simpsons* and *Iron Man*."

Joining James and Robert on the patio, the other children also stared in disbelief, as four grownups dissolved into further fits of uncontainable guffawing.

* * *

Later, the Frasers left Mid Calder, heading to the Lothian Lodge to check-in.

"Good evening," Roger said to the male receptionist, in a breezy voice, still high on Hector's Huckleberry Hound tale.

"Hello, sir," came the low-key reply.

Already, Roger formed the view that 'Jock' would not be the

most communicative of Scotsmen.

"Now," ventured Roger, "we have a reservation in the name of Fraser, three rooms."

Jock didn't answer. He just buried his head in a computer screen, and banged a keyboard. For a moment, Roger thought that Jock was going to tell him *computer says no* in a David Walliams drawl, but that kind of mock role play looked beyond the representative from the welcome to Jockland tourism society. Roger wondered if Jock wore a kilt, and if so, did he 'go commando', to use the modern vernacular.

Finally, un-jovial Jock said, "There are three rooms, booked in the name of Fraser."

"Yes, yes, precisely….that's what I said."

"Do you require breakfast?"

"It would be nice."

"Do you require dinner?" Jock asked, continuing his checklist with a mournful face.

"Not this evening, we're dining out with friends."

"Do you require an early morning call?"

"Er, no, we're on holiday."

"Do you require a morning newspaper?"

"Same answer."

"Do you require…."

The list went on and on, Charlotte and the kids keen to cut the crap, cut to the chase, and be shown to their rooms, or at least given directions. Eventually, the questions ground to an end. Jock issued keys and directions, the Frasers gratefully exiting reception.

"That was painful," observed Charlotte.

"Yes," Roger agreed. "There are three types of Jock. The affable, intellectual good ol' boy, like Hector. There's the likeable cheeky chappie, like Ally McCoist. And there's the dour, charmless Celtic nerk, like Gordon Brown and Candy Murrey. That receptionist guy fell into the last category."

* * *

One of Roger's favourite destinations, unlike many countries, which were merely picturesque, the land of Rabbie Burns and Rab C Nesbitt added to Scotland's obvious beauty, with mystical vistas and spiritual legends. Much more than just eye-catching glens and desolate mountain ranges, Roger thought a tangible atmosphere existed in Scotland, history's ghosts almost visible.

Hector once told him that he'd stopped at Flodden Field, technically in Northumberland, but which in 1523 was a border area, that saw the English inflict heavy losses on the Scots. Hector had walked through the famous field. He had sworn he heard battle sounds and the cries of dying men. Roger didn't doubt his friend's recollection. He'd had his own experience of uncanny events north of the border.

Attending a financial services conference on behalf of the firm in Perth, Roger had stayed at Sunbank House, a Victorian hotel set in Capability Brown-like designed grounds. Though boasting a luxurious interior, the outer grey granite stonework and austere facade equated with stories that the hotel was haunted. Roger had dismissed the yarns as folklore and tourist trap. But one night, when he gazed out from his bedroom window across the vast lawns leading down to the River Tay, a spooky figure came into view through the gathering mist. During the evening, he'd indulged in over consumption of Scottish malts with fellow conference attendees. Worse for wear, he rubbed his eyes, thinking hallucination had overtaken control of his senses, but still the eerie figure advanced. On the verge of becoming a believer in the afterlife, suddenly the apparition took on recognisable features. It turned out to be the local gamekeeper returning from the Tay, after a search and destroy mission for salmon poachers. Later, Roger concluded that the seed had been implanted on his arrival, when the receptionist took great delight outlining the hotel's ghostly past. Add the blear-inducing effects of alcohol, and his overactive mind had done the rest, but he considered the creepy experience to be typical of the supernatural and paranormal history associated with Scotland.

* * *

Early the following day, the McFraser clan travelled to Stirling, to see its celebrated castle, made even more famous in the making of the great Alec Guinness film, *Tunes of Glory*. Then they returned to Mid Calder, Roger depositing Charlotte and the kids with Avril, before driving into Edinburgh to collect Hector from work.

He parked the MPV and went into Parsons Peebles reception, asking for Mister McIntyre. A few minutes later, the Scot trotted down the staircase, from his first floor office.

"Hello laird," he said brightly, obviously looking forward to continuing some rewarding dialogue with his Sassenach visitors.

No matter how old Roger got, he would always be a laird, meaning lad, in Hector's vocabulary.

"Hello, Laird," Roger returned with equal vitality, meaning 'regal one' rather than 'lad', keen to explore more issues and adventures with his old mate.

As they walked out to the MPV, a young graduate engineer rushed up to Hector.

"Mister McIntyre, Mister McIntyre."

Swivelling around to face him, the Chief Engineer said, "Yes, laird, what is it?" Hector meant 'lad' again, of course.

"Mister McIntyre, can you sign off my calculations and expenses, please?"

"Expenses, laird," Hector replied, his upper register starting to rise. "You expect us to pay your expenses, as well as paying your salary?"

Becoming speechless, the poor laird appeared forlorn.

"Huh," exclaimed Hector, disappointed no reply had been offered. "Here, let me see those calculations first."

The calcs were handed over. Hector went through a generator's mechanical engineering design factors, mentally doing some rough order of magnitude calculations. He then took a cursory look at the expenses, nestling in the junior engineer's hand.

"Nnrrgghh," Hector said to himself, then in apparent exasperation, "Oh, dear, dear, dear, me laird, this is completely wrong. There appears to be major discrepancies in your calculations….and worse still, your expenses. Oh dear, dear, dear, me laird, what are we going to do with you? Don't they teach you anything at university, these days?" Stopping, he tutted in Roger's direction, obviously expecting his support in de-constructing the wayward engineer. "Where did you go?" Chief Engineer McIntyre asked the laird, in his mock 'Victor Meldrew' voice.

"Bolton, Mister McIntyre."

"Bolton," repeated Hector, near to astonishment. "I had no idea Bolton even has a university. Unbelievable." The Victor façade really took over now. "That's not a real university, is it?" he questioned with flagrant derision.

Near to tears, the graduate engineer remained baffled, unable to answer.

Shaking his head, Hector turned his attention to Roger again. "Just can't get the staff these days, you know."

Roger nodded his head up and down, in notional agreement, but didn't speak, simply pressing his lips together, not wishing to add to the chastised engineer's woes. When he first alighted on Roger and Hector, he walked tall. Now the lad appeared close to complete collapse, shrinking fast and disappearing into his shoes.

Re-engaging with his prey, the Laid of West Lothian said, "If you had gone to a proper university like Manchester, where I got my M.Sc., they would have taught you that accurate stress analysis can only be accomplished by using top-end equations, not the simple calculus you have used, which yields erroneous results." He paused. "Remember Wall's Law, laird, remember Wall's Law….A solid will remain in an inert steady state, until acted upon by an external force."

Roger couldn't remember Wall's Law, but he could quote Ball's Law verbatim; When the heat on the beat, equals the throb on the knob, then the angle of dangle….no, he'd forgotten the rest.

"No, Mister McIntyre," the laird stammered, "I mean yes, Mister McIntyre….sorry."

"And what's this second page of rubbish?" asked Hector.

"Oh, they're my expenses, for that visit to Hinckley Point."

Cocking his head back, Hector exclaimed, "I don't believe it." Roger could have sworn he now listened to the real Victor Meldrew, Hector's receding hairline adding to the effect. "No, no, no, laird." Hector finger-wagged the lad. "You can't claim for this, or this, or this."

The miffed Chief Engineer started crossing off items on the expense claim sheet. He scanned the mechanical calculations again, and then glared back at the expenses. "Oh dear, dear me, what are we going to do with you, laird?"

Near to suicide, the graduate appeared to be drained. Gingerly taking back both documents, he scuttled off, tail between legs, hair shirt torturing his back.

Funnily enough, Roger could remember a time, when Hector never assumed an aggressive stance with anybody, not saying boo to a goose, and was extremely shy, especially with girls. What a complete change in personality, Roger thought. But that was explained by the fact that Hector acted in role-play mode. With his Chief Engineer hat on, he had to present an unchallengeable exterior to his staff, particularly junior engineers. Away from the world of Faraday and Tesla, he reverted to the usual easy-going, fun-loving pussycat, Roger always knew.

"Bit harsh," Roger said.

"Bit harsh," repeated Victor, er Hector, whilst screwing his face up in dismissive reproach. "They have to learn, and learn quickly….no second chances in this business. If we get the design of a large generator wrong, for say a hydro-electric scheme in China, or a nuclear power station in France, the company could be sued for tens of millions….harsh but fair."

Roger took his point. Fundamentally risk averse as well, the

DOGHOUSE BLUES

firm adopted the same uncompromising measures to ensure compliance with U.S Securities and Exchange Commission regulations, at least until those irresponsible scallywag traders went to work on the gold nuggets Roger gave them.

"Yes, you are quite right," Roger said. "Come on, let's go for a quick one in the Tap Room, before we go back to your place."

* * *

Celebrated pub the Tap Room in Mid Calder, had been HQ for local Rangers supporters for over 75 years. A life-long Gers fan, Hector had joined their membership soon after arriving in the village. Settling into two pints of heavy, the old friends began chatting.

"You see that guy over there?" said Hector, pointing to an oversize, kilt- wearing jock at the bar.

Peering over in the given direction, Roger enquired, "What about him?"

"That's Bruce McKay, he tosses the caber."

Raising his eyebrows, Roger asked, "Is he a good tosser?" He couldn't resist the temptation to use the term.

Quite put out by his impertinence, the Laird retorted, "I'd say he's a good tosser, he's the current Fife district caber tossing champion."

He waved over at the caber tosser.

"Hello, Hector," said the walking Celtic man-mountain.

"Hello, Bruce, alright are you?"

"A bit of a strain in the lower-right forearm."

"Too much tossing?" Roger whispered to the Laird.

"Ssshh," the Laird warned, "he'll hear you."

Roger continued, "I thought too much tossing made you deaf."

"No, that's blind," corrected Hector.

"Hhmm, have you tried it yourself?" Roger asked, before taking a long pull on his heavy.

"What….tossing?"

"I know you've done that. What about the caber?"

"Not got the build for that, laird….but it is an impressive sight."

"Tossing?" Roger enquired, risking further looks of implied impertinence.

"Tossing the caber."

"Yes," agreed Roger. "I must say, there is a bit of a discrepancy in build, between yourself and the Fife district champion tosser. That guy is bigger than most rugby players I know."

"I've seen some even bigger."

"Bigger tossers?"

"Bigger caber tossers."

Taking another gulp of the heavy, Roger then said, "Yes, well….if we have finished with the subject of big tossers, there's another topic, I'd like to hear your thoughts on."

"Oh, what's that?"

"If you could be anyone else, Hector, who would you be, and why?"

"That's a good question, laird….takes some consideration," he replied, in a jocular academic manner.

"Anyone you like," proposed Roger, "real or imaginary."

"Hhmm, I've always had a penchant for Percy Thrower."

"Percy Thrower," Roger replied dismissively, about to pour scorn on the choice.

"Yes," explained Hector, "you'll recall whilst at university, I was always one for getting my fingers, deep into the soil….you know, connecting with nature."

Beginning to comprehend the seriousness of his choice, perhaps using Percy as a metaphor, Roger said, "Ah, you mean communing with mother Earth."

"Yes, yes….if I hadn't chosen engineering, I would probably have gone for one of the naturalist disciplines, or even botany, in the guise of say Darwin or Huxley."

"Anything else?"

"Well, being a design engineer by trade, I've always fancied myself as an inventor, in the mould of say James Dyson."

"I can't see you trading in industrial-size generator design, for domestic house appliances."

Hector reminded Roger that they laughed at Jock, when he invented the strap, then concluded with, "Maybe when I retire, I'll take up the pipedream….how about you?"

"It's something I've thought about a lot, recently. My life has seemingly always been focused on the conventional….you know, career, wife, children. So in my more reflective moments, I choose the escapism route."

"You mean existentialism?" suggested the ever-intellectual Laird of West Lothian.

"Kind of….but it's a daydream. I'm too far into conformity, as are you, and I suppose there is nothing wrong with that…."

Sensing the thought to be incomplete, Hector added, "So long as you remain alert to the possible?"

"Yes, that's my point, Laird….somehow to stop getting sucked into the conventional maelstrom completely and disappearing."

"You mean consumed by the societal machine?"

"Precisely."

"So answer your own question. Who would you like to be?"

"Hhmm….well, in my lighter reflective moments, you know, those odd occasions when I have the house to myself, and I can drift away, listening to Miles Davis or John Coltrane."

"Or come to that, even King Crimson or Joy Division."

"Quite….in such near-to-existential moments of escapism, I imagine myself to be Thomas Crown."

"The Steve McQueen character?"

Roger nodded confirmation.

"Why?" the Laird asked.

"Because like James Bond, he never gets hurt, and leads an exciting and disaster-free life. It's also that Bob Dylan thing as well…you know; 'don't follow leaders', steer away from conformity, don't let the machine consume you, be your own person. I suppose in practice, it's more Bob Dylan than 'Thomas

Crown', but for me, the Steve McQueen character is the ultimate, absolute freedom icon. *Lovejoy* is another one, of course."

"Yes, I see what you mean....though it's a bit late to jump ship, for either of us."

"Yes. I'm not sure I should have started this blessed conversation with that exploratory question. It now seems like eons since I tabled it. Sorry."

"That's alright," Hector acknowledged, as he glimpsed at his watch. "Come on, drink up, we have to go, or else Avril will be roasting my nuts for our supper this evening."

"Sounds delightful," observed Roger. "Would they be accompanied by truffles and horse chestnuts, all puréed in Haggis source with rosemary and thyme topping?"

CHAPTER 10: COUSIN BARRY

Several days later, Hector and his family wished the McFraser clan bon voyage, and the visitors headed back south to 'civilisation'. They had one final tour stopover, and that was with Roger's cousin, Barry, who lived at Headingley.

He was a reader at the University of Leeds, but also did work for the biotechs and pharmaceuticals, often working alongside Roger's brother, Colin, when things touched on chemical engineering issues. When not working or engaged with his family, Barry's next love had always been cricket. A sound all-rounder, he had played for Yorkshire seconds back in his late-teens and early-twenties, but because of his academic career, he could never wholly commit to the county-cricket level expectations of a professional cricketer. Consequently, he now played part-time for York, in the Yorkshire Premier League. He often told Roger stories of Yorkshire cricket yore, passed down through the generations.

One story that had eternally stuck in Roger's memory, centred on the late, great, 'Fiery' Fred Trueman.

Yorkshire were playing the West Indies, when Charlie Griffith and Wes Hall formed the tourists' attack. Trueman batted at number ten, and a new, young fast bowler, Chris Old, batted eleven. Hall and Griffith were finishing off the Yorkshire tail, when Old came in to face Griffith, who then proceeded to intimidate the young cricketer with some fierce bouncers and 'bodyline bowling'. Being a straight up-and-down gent, Fred turned to Griffith and said, 'Give the lad a chance'. Griffith eyed the Yorkshire man and dismissed his request with, 'Fuck off, honky.' Trueman fumed. Hall came up to Griffith and said, 'You shouldn't have said that'. 'Why?' asked the unrepentant Griffith. 'You'll see, you'll see', advised Hall, with a note of caution.

A few balls later, Old played on, and Yorkshire were all out for 387 runs. After the break, Yorkshire took the field, with Fred as opening bowler. Still incandescent with rage at Griffith's insult, and harsh treatment of the young Chris Old, Fiery Fred then proceeded to almost skittle out the West Indies, single handed. Batting number eleven, Griffith witnessed Trueman's carnage of his teammates.

Griffith took his crease position at the batting end, whilst looking at Yorkshire's premier bowler, throwing the ball up and down in his right hand, with menace. Trueman glared at Griffith, snorted like a bull, then walked back to his normal start point, for his bowling run-up. Trueman stopped, turned, and ogled Griffith with the stare of Medusa, then walked back a further 20 paces, before starting his run-in.

Fiery Fred put the first ball around Griffith's left ear, and the second just past his nose, leaving the West Indian shaking in his boots. Trueman yorked Griffith with his third ball, sending his off-stump cart wheeling backwards. The fast bowler finished with figures of eight wickets for 75 runs, Yorkshire winning the match.

He went up to a still-shaking Griffith and said, 'Don't ever call me honky, ever again, and learn some manners and fair play, before you come to Yorkshire again'. Hall had been at the non-striker's end. He wandered down the wicket, and said to Griffith, 'Told you'.

The story had probably been embellished over the years, but remained a popular anecdote of Yorkshire cricket folklore, and a thoroughly engaging yarn, which Roger had told to many people.

Barry's wife, Beverley, met Roger's family at the front door, ushering them inside for refreshments. Easy on the eye, with her pale goldenrod hair, coupled with striking navy-blue eyes, and charm personified, Beverley had always been a natural communicator, capable of persuading detractors to her viewpoint through the sheer force of her personality, without

DOGHOUSE BLUES

raising her voice. Her attractive appearance and calm approach allied to passion, ensured people listened with intent when she spoke. These characteristics, together with her gregarious nature, had Charlotte's endless approval. They were great friends, often calling each other, at least once a week.

"Barry sends his apologies," advised Beverley. "He called me earlier to say he is delayed at the university, but will be with us soon."

"Oh, that's okay," Roger said, "I often have unexpected work demands which affect my social schedule, as well."

"How was your trip to Eilat?" asked Charlotte.

Barry and Beverley's return from holiday was the reason that Roger and his family hadn't stopped to see them, following the visit to Colin's place in Harrogate.

"Very hot and humid, daytime temperatures up in the nineties, but really relaxing, and we liked the local Israelis."

"Did you get the chance to do any snorkelling?" Roger asked.

"I didn't, but Barry and Giles did."

Due to go back to Exeter in a few weeks, for his final-year Geology course, Giles, their oldest son, had caused Barry some consternation regarding his university choice. Naturally, his father had wanted him to go to Leeds, but Giles, like so many students, needed to explore the wider world, his Yorkshire passport with visa enabling him to leave the sacred county for Devon. As a nascent teenager, Giles used to be like a colt with gangling legs, but now he had broadened out, developing into a Jude Law lookalike. Roger hoped Giles was better at Geology, than Jude was at selecting good film roles. A little unkind to Jude, but some of his films were worse than Johnny Depp's, although Roger did like the latter's work in *Chocolat* and *The Libertine*.

Barry's younger son, Simon, had recently completed his AS-levels in Maths, Physics and English, but wanted to be a musician, giving Barry much heartache and sleepless nights. Simon didn't look like Jude Law, more like Paul Whitehouse, in his 'Suits you Sir' *Fast Show* tailor character. Simon played guitar in a local rock band, and by all accounts measured up in the axe-wielding stakes, capable of performing Red Hot Chilli Peppers and Rage Against the Machine numbers, note perfect. Roger had reminded Barry on several occasions, that rich could be accomplished from any number of disciplines, including rock music, so Barry shouldn't be concerned for Simon's future. Besides, the guitarist elect could always fall back on a science career, if he went on to complete his A-level studies.

"How did you get on, with the separation of meat and dairy products?" enquired Charlotte of Beverley.

"Oh, you mean having to choose one or the other, in traditional Israeli restaurants?"

"Yes."

"That wasn't a problem. None of us are really into dairy products as a main course, so we always went for the meat option."

The holiday theme continued for a while, with Giles, Simon, Wendy and James participating, whilst Heather read one her Brownie books. Heather had informed her parents that when she turned 11, she would move up to the Girl Guides, and become a leader. That, Roger didn't doubt. The way she marshalled her stuffed animals, into performing the most outrageous tasks, did take a special brand of leadership. He has this daydream, that when she turned 21, and had a degree in Business Administration, she would join the firm, and use her special brand of discipline, to mercilessly lick badly-behaving, Essex-boy traders into shape.

Whilst continuing their family oriented topics conversation, the discussion group heard the front door go, and Barry strolled into the lounge.

"Hello, everybody," he said. "Roger, Charlotte. Good to see you again."

They all embraced each other, then he settled down to tell Roger about his day, and what had been happening in glorious Headingley. Charlotte and Beverley rapped on about some current affairs issue in the kitchen, whilst the more junior members of the families moved in the direction of Barry's games room, in the cellar. Barry and Roger had the lounge to themselves.

Taking in his elder cousin more fully, Roger noticed he looked as fit as a box of frogs, as they say in some parts of Yorkshire. He had always possessed a rugged face with bright steely eyes and a weather beaten complexion, giving the impression of perpetual health. It seemed that long hours spent in the lab and handling testing undergraduates had not dulled his radiance.

"Some young marketeer," Barry began, "with little experience, and even less common sense, tried to tell me today that the future of chemicals will be forged in the white hot arena, as he called it, of Third World pesticides."

"Really?" exclaimed Roger, hinting at incredulity, not that he knew the first thing about pesticides.

"Yes," Barry explained, "that direction is strictly passé, it's been done and dusted to death for decades."

"What is the future challenge, then, Barry?"

Cousin Barry stretched out in his chair, with an air of experience and knowledge, pouring from him. "Petro-carbons emulation."

"You mean imitation petrol?"

"If you like. Behind the scenes, we've had it under wraps for a long time, waiting on hold until the oil runs out."

"What about these electric cars that Charlotte seems so keen on?"

"Oh, glorified toys, totally impracticable. I mean, to get from here to London, an electric car would need several tonnes of batteries, trailing behind it....and even then, would just about make it, before needing to sit on a charger for two days. No, they're just there to appease the Green politically correct lobby, but no one in government believes electric cars are the future. Once the oil has gone, the chemical industry will become the supplier of combustible fuels. May not always be carbon-majority based. Hydrogen could form the major constituent."

"That sounds like the same argument, as for wind farms."

"How do you mean?"

"Well, we've examined wind farm investment at the firm, but the strategic future will be with next-generation nuclear power stations, not wind farms. In economic terms, wind farms are not viable, and most of the blessed things are out of action, for most of the time, anyway. The country needs sustained and reliable power generation, and that will only come from nuclear power."

"So what you are saying is that like electric cars, wind farms are there, just to appease the Green lobby."

"Yes. We conducted a survey, got inputs from government, industry, domestic users, the full gambit. What became plain is that these wind farms will never deliver a sustained output to the national grid, not even if the whole of the UK was coated in the damn things. The politicians know that will never be acceptable to the electorate, so it's nuclear."

"Huh, I see. It is the same argument, then."

"Just returning to your plastic petrol, if you'll forgive the term."

"Yes."

"We hear a lot in investment banking, about alternative-liquid fuels having enormous investment potential, but certainly, to the best of my knowledge, there are no major stakeholders at present, just a few exploratory ventures."

"It will happen, mark my words, young cousin. The rate of black gold production is actually reducing, new fields harder to find, and even harder to exploit, in out-of-the-way places like Alaska, or miles beneath the seabed. Fuel supply companies know the resource is finite, and an alternative fuel source will definitely be needed to power the internal combustion engine. The work we're doing on petro-carbons emulation will be the solution, down line."

"Yes, makes perfect sense. It does to investors, as well. The big petroleum producers, such as Shell and BP, still dominate

DOGHOUSE BLUES

the stock markets worldwide, and they will certainly not be throwing in the towel, when the natural resource runs out. So yes, where you're headed, is the place to be."

"For sure," concurred Barry, breaking into a mischievous smirk. "By the way, you must get upstarts in investment banking as well, fast-buck artists who are here today, gone tomorrow, but don't really understand the true direction, in which the business should be headed. Come on, Roger, spill the beans, I bet you've got some real clangers."

Guffawing in agreement, Roger said, "Oh, Barry, I could bore you for hours with a plethora of sad and pathetic stories you would find unbelievable, but nonetheless, were tabled as going concerns, or risk-proof ventures."

"For example?"

"Very well, if you insist….now let me see if I can remember a real turkey."

"Investing in rust repairers, or pilotless passenger aircraft, perhaps?"

"Very good, I'll have to check those out….now, what is a really tragic example?" Roger trawled through his memory banks for a few moments. "Oh, yes, here's a good one, which will probably make some of the ill-thought-out ideas from your industry seem quite sane."

"Go on."

"One of the more speculative ideas in 2003, from a particularly over-optimistic trader at the firm's New York HQ, centred on investing in Bethlehem Steel, a once-famous U.S corporate heavy-hitter, which by the millennium, because of lack of inward investment for modernising the plant, was in its last throws of life. His great idea was to buy the failing business and convert the steel mills into Disney-style theme parks."

"Mmmm, actually that appears quite sound, on the face of it."

"There was only one problem."

"What was that?"

"It was complete bollocks, total tosh."

"What? Worse than an Al Gore sponsored scare mongering, increased taxes justified, global warming disaster film?"

"Yes....well, I'm not sure about that.... Al Gore?" questioned Roger incredulously, knowing he must have disbelief written on his boat race.

With her recently adopted 'all things left of centre must be good' buy-in, if Charlotte had heard the comment about Gore, the debate would truly have gone on until doomsday. Thank God she remained in the kitchen, thought Roger.

"Where was I?" he enquired.

"Complete bollocks."

"Oh, yes....you see, many investment ideas seem feasible, but the acid tests are always return on investment profile and risk. When the firm crunched the numbers, even on the basis of 'if we build it, they will come', which of course in itself is complete fairy-tale bollocks, it simply did not stack up as a going concern. The restructuring costs alone would have taken too many years, to return to investors with profit, and that was on the basis that a bunch of refurnished steel mills in industrial Pittsburgh would attract the same market crowd who go to Disney, in Orlando and LA."

"A non-starter, then, like my head-in-the-clouds chappie."

"Yes. Ironically, the trader who championed the idea left the firm for Lehman Brothers, and you know what happened to them."

* * *

After the wives finished feeding the 5000, the adults settled down in the lounge, with Old Pulteney and Stag's Breath for company, whilst their little darlings continued to be entranced by pastime distractions in the games room. Wendy talked to Giles about Exeter, over a game of table tennis. James became influenced by Simon's guitar playing, as the latter demonstrated his axe skills, and Heather played skittles. Later, Roger hoped to get a few frames of snooker in, with Barry.

"Our friends north of border certainly know how to prepare a quality liquor, don't they?" Roger observed.

"Best in the world," confirmed Barry.

"Don't you think you are both being seduced by kudos and branding, more than the bottle's contents?" questioned Beverley.

Appearing surprised by the assertion, Barry asked, "What do you mean?"

"What Beverley means, gentlemen," answered Charlotte, "is that you've been sucked in by the brand, rather than the liquor itself."

Obviously, the girls had been planning to test their men's drinking habits, after preparing dinner.

"Oh, that's tommyrot," insisted Barry. Looking quite put out, probably because he'd been drinking choice-quality malts, virtually since he could walk, he added, "What do you think, Roger?"

Needing to find a middle-ground, inoffensive to both points of view, because unlike his elder cousin, Roger rarely drunk malt whisky, apart from when in Jockland, he offered, "It's an interesting viewpoint, one that can be applied to many high-profile branded products, sensitive to buyer perception."

"Well, bugger me with a fish fork," exclaimed Barry, "you're not in agreement with their view, are you?"

"Branding is all about creating kudos, as Beverley quite rightly said, Barry. It's human frailty, that we gravitate towards the unobtainable, and when we finally get it, we treasure it, like its priceless antiquity. Excellence in brand management is all about creating the myth, the desire, and the recognition to be part of an exclusive club….Whiskies, particularly those of Scottish origin, rely on sustaining their exclusivity, to justify exorbitant prices."

Shrugging his shoulders, Barry declared, "Well, bless my soul, you are agreeing with them."

"Yes….and no, Barry," maintained Roger. "Yes, because fundamentally, they are right….and that can be applied to any high-quality commodity, from a Rolls-Royce Phantom to

Thornton's Belgium chocolates. No, because some products claim exclusivity, through careful market positioning and demographic targeting to gain kudos, but really, they are nothing special."

"Mmmm, I like Belgium chocolates," said Beverley, smiling at Charlotte, who also lost control, within sniffing distance of cocoa-based delights.

"Quite," Roger said. "Beverley's reaction confirms my point. Chocolate is chocolate, but surround it with fancy gold leaf and old English-style writing, then add a few special ingredients,and it takes on an elevated dimension, to justify a superficially-inflated selling price."

"But the Old Pulteney and Stag's Breath does taste remarkable," upheld Barry.

"Oh yes," agreed Roger, "but measure for measure, they are between five to ten times the price of a standard blended whisky."

"Hhmmm, I begin to take your point," Barry reluctantly conceded.

"Don't get me wrong," Roger continued, "there's nothing wrong with exclusivity….if you can afford it. But I would suggest that at least 50 per cent of the satisfaction comes from the kudos of the brand, and the remainder from its taste."

"You really think so, Roger?" asked his wife.

"Yes, I do."

"You're not just trying to ingratiate yourself with us?" pressed Charlotte, as she half-smiled at Beverley.

"Ah….that's it," said Barry. "You're on a promise, aren't you? That's why you're siding with the girls."

Grimacing back at his cousin, Roger jokingly replied, "Certainly not. I do not suck up to my wife's point of view, in return for overt sexual favours."

Barry persisted, spurred on by assumed tales of sexual depravity in Kent; known as God's Own County by Roger and his rugby-playing mates. Seeking some retribution on Roger, for not supporting his earlier assertion, he said, "Oh….what do you do, in return for overt sexual favours, then?"

Bending forward in his chair, Roger shed a wicked grin and replied, "I'll tell you that later, when we play snooker. You may learn something to your advantage, with Beverley."

That set off a sexual innuendo exchange, building layer after layer of sub-text conjecture, regarding Roger's supposed carnal desires, everyone reduced to gibbering muppets, as uncontainable giggling let loose at his expense. Charlotte confirmed the despot rules of engagement, granting him unconventional sexual favours, as she called them. Beverley suggested that such Women's Lib, wrath-incurring acts of sexual immorality, demanded a wide array of yoke-bearing domestic penalties, as quid pro quo.

After several false starts, caused by more lewd inferences, the 'brains trust' returned to the branding theme.

"It's the same, for example, with luxury cars," Roger suggested. "Take the bonnet badge off a hundred thousand pound Porsche 911 and it becomes near to the much lesser-priced Volkswagen Beetle, with a spoiler. And of course, VW own Porsche. People are buying the badge. Years ago, I used to go into Porsche dealers, and ask 'How much is this 911 Turbo?' They'd say….£80,000 pounds. So then I'd ask, 'How much without the badge?' They would just smile, knowing that the ex-works cost was probably less than £20,000, but never admitting to it, because the brand would lose its high-value kudos."

"Well, Roger," observed Beverley smiling at his wife, "Charlotte and I didn't expect to get so much support from you."

"And I didn't expect your apparent lack of support for me," Barry added, partially smarting, "or your non-neutrality."

"It's nothing personal, Barry," assured Roger. "You know that, favourite cousin. It's not even my view. That's just the way it is. Being passionate about a belief does not necessarily persuade."

"Yes, I know," returned Barry, with a warm reassuring smile, "and I agree. I have said something like that to others, not on this subject, but on something completely different. So yes, I am being staunchly partisan, without considering the true value of what I hold dear."

"We all have our little indulgences," pacified Roger, "and to balance things, I would equally point out that some feminine extravagances, let's say….in the perfumery and boutique clothes categories, fall within the same rationale."

"Huh, you've spoilt it now, Roger," exclaimed Beverley.

"Yes, I thought you were on our side, for once," added Charlotte.

"Look, darling," Roger assured her, "as I just said, it's not a matter of sides, it's more a case of recognising that human frailty for exclusivity is one of the cornerstones of retailing in particular, and capitalism in general. There's nothing wrong with it. I'm as bad as anyone else, with my kudos brand preferences. The quintessential point I'm making is that we all fool ourselves, into believing that high price tags are justified by attributes such as exquisite taste, in the case of Old Pulteney or Shag's Breath, when in reality, the premium price we pay is disproportionate to the real value of the goods. Sorry, I meant Stag's Breath."

"I like that ending, Roger," enthused Barry, sniggering, "Shag's Breath, hey? I must remember to deliberately say that, next time I order a bottle from that pompous, jumped-up do-gooder in our local off-license."

"Sounds like you don't like this person," Roger suggested.

"Oh….no one does, around here," Barry advised. "I'm talking about….what's her name, Beverley?"

"Germaine Yancey."

"That's her," confirmed Barry. "Let me tell you, Roger, I'm known for my tolerance, but I've been close to strangling that woman, at times. Even Beverley can't defend her."

"Yes, it's true," agreed Beverley.

"If ever there was a title," Barry continued, "for killjoy, humourless, tongue up Harriet Harman's rear end, politically correct bleating, greedy human rights lawyers are wonderful, do as I say and not as I do, ban everything that moves, trendy liberal lefty of the year, then Germaine Yancey is your man, er woman."

"What's he, sorry she, doing working in an off-license?" enquired Roger. "If she's such a paragon of virtue?"

"Ah, well," Barry went on, "this is where the complete hypocrisy of the woman comes into play. We have heard from third parties that she justifies her employment in the liquor distribution trade, by making customers feel they are morally reprehensible, for consuming alcohol."

"Ah," said Roger, "I begin to understand your reference to Harriet Harperson. It's alright for me to send my children to private schools, but you mustn't."

"Can we please return to the subject in hand," requested Charlotte, "as I am liable to go on the defensive for this woman, and Roger won't like that. Besides, I'm on holiday. I spend enough of my time frightening Roger, as he calls it, by supporting left-of-centre issues. Only a few days ago, I got a dressing-down from my mother, so please don't let me go down that route."

"Point taken," said Barry, "understand your position, my dear. Now where were we?"

"Branding and kudos," confirmed Beverley. "It's got my attention. I find it fascinating."

"Is it?" questioned Barry. "I was looking forward to putting my feet up, chilling out over a few noggins of....what did you call it, Roger, Shags Breath? I wasn't planning on debating the finer points of brand awareness."

Taking no notice of her husband's desires, Beverley blithely carried on, oblivious to his request. "I suppose it's like all advertising is aspirational, and designed to seduce by association. Kate Moss uses Coty. Therefore, if I want to be like Kate Moss, I should use Coty as well."

"I would certainly agree with that," said Charlotte. "The number of times I have come out of a shop, and thought 'I've just been had', seduced into buying something because of its association value."

"Actually," Roger suggested, "they do sometimes produce some great mimics."

"Mimics, what do you mean?" enquired Barry.

"You remember the Whiskas advert, where a housewife talks about her cat's favourite food, Whiskas?"

"Yes," Barry confirmed.

"I've heard that mimicked," explained Roger, "as 'Missus Jennie Jones talks about her cat's favourite food….mice'! That's real black humour, hey?"

"Ha, ha, ha," chortled Barry. "I see what you mean."

"Yes, it is a corker," Roger enthused, "but be careful about repeating it, in earshot of Heather. If she hears, we can expect a visit, not only from the RSPCA, but the SAS and MI6, as well."

"Fancy some more Shags Breath, Roger?" invited his cousin.

***

The next morning brought another beautiful day in the North Riding, so both families went off to Castle Howard, and then on to Rievaulx Abbey for a picnic. Unlike the final chapter of the Fraser's garden party, everybody conducted themselves in a highly civilised and well-mannered way during lunch. Heather had been boisterous at Castle Howard, wanting her father to find her a swing to play on, a task even beyond his inventiveness in a stately home. However, it became the first time she'd been to an ancient abbey, its reverent atmosphere clearly affected her behaviour, and instead of charging around, she assumed a somewhat passive manner. Despite Henry VIII's efforts to completely destroy it, much of the superstructure still survived. A feeling of tranquillity pervaded the grounds and Roger could only put her sanguine behaviour down to its aura. She always asked a thousand questions about any place they visited, most very challenging and unanswerable, for example 'Why does Chartwell not allow dogs in Churchill's art studio?' But for some reason, Charlotte and Roger were yet to figure out,

Heather appeared to be quite fascinated by Rievaulx Abbey, like she had entered a new phase in her development. The questions she asked were answerable, like 'Why was Henry VIII so fat?' It might have been a temporary state, brought on by the holiday, but her parents enjoyed it.

Whilst everyone else explored the abbey, for a second time after lunch, Barry and Roger stretched out on the grass, watching fair weather cumulus pass overhead, under a pale turquoise sky.

"Barry."

"Hhmm."

Catching him, before he drifted away into sweet dreams, Roger asked, "If you had Dr Who's Tardis, which way would you travel? Into the future, or back to the past?"

"Huh, that's a good one. What's brought that on?"

"Oh, I suppose change, and not necessarily change which I like, or even have any control over, or opportunity to debate and approve."

"It's a question which needs thought, so I'll give you my response at a later date, when I've figured out an answer. I suspect you have already done that."

"Yes."

"And which way would you travel?"

"Huh, when I look into the future, I mean the England that our children are going to inherit, I don't like the way it's shaping up. I know London like the back of my hand, but it's changed so radically, just over my lifetime to date. It's certainly nothing like it was, when our parents brought Colin and me from Middlewich, to live in Kent, when we were both small children….and in cosmic terms, that was just yesterday."

"Yes, I suppose both of you were born in Cheshire, but bred in Kent."

"That's right, deep in the Sevenoaks, Tunbridge Wells, Maidstone delta. I read only recently that John Cleese doesn't recognise London anymore, and I've been hearing that viewpoint from work colleagues and friends, too often for my liking. The thing of it is, Barry, they are right, and we don't seem to have any recourse, to correct the huge imbalance which has developed."

"You can blame the politicians for that."

"Oh yes, I know….that is irrefutable."

"Traitorous bastards, aren't they?"

"For sure….but just to develop my theme, even at the microcosm level, you know the changes you see, in your own little universe. Some of these, I find disturbing."

"For example?"

"Charlotte….since starting arts and crafts studies at the local tech, she's got involved with this trendy New Age, neo-political set over the past year or so. I suppose I didn't notice at first. You know how easy it is to become blinkered, with a rose-tinted impression of someone?"

"Yes, I'm guilty of that, myself."

"I'm a-political, and the kids, thank God, can't even spell politics. Not even Wendy has any interest, and she will be 17 very soon. Charlotte used to follow her parents' right-of-centre views, nothing radical, just a belief in conserving what had sustained the sovereign state for over ten centuries. Usually, kids, certainly of our generation, reacted against their parents' views, as a matter of course. It was expected. But by their early-twenties, most had twigged the red, blue and yellow bullshit, seen it for what it truly is….there for the exclusive benefit of the chosen few, and their sacred cows. But Charlotte is only two years younger than me, and seems to be going through the rebellious trendy-lefty, politically-correct loving stage that should have happened when she was at university."

"Midlife crisis?"

"I thought that happened in your late-sixties, in this day and age, with life-cycles lasting much longer."

"True. Is that why, if you had the Tardis, you would travel back….I am right in thinking that for you, the past is more attractive?"

"Yes, but with the caveat I could take Charlotte and the kids back with me, as well."

"What would you do, if say you could go back as far as 1984?"

"Huh, the Orwellian watershed year….I suppose live in England, as it used to be." Roger quivered, unsure of his thoughts, unable to continue.

"Yes, what else?"

"Probably become an MP. Try and stop what London and the rest of the country has become."

"I thought you may say something like that, but what about doing it now?"

"Now….oh, I'm beyond all that, Barry….and I hate to admit it, but I think using the currently available institutions is already too late. The damage is irrevocable. That's why I am so concerned for the kids' futures. Oh, I don't say anything to worry Charlotte. Besides, with her current trendy-lefty, elitist hat on, she'd probably say I was being reactionary, anyway."

"It's called ostrich mentally, head-in-sand disbelief to an inconvenient truth."

"Yes, you are right….but it is real, and happening all around us, like a malignant tumour, slowly consuming the body. One of the consequential benefits I get, being a stock market analyst, is access to government demographics and projections. You see, it's these key factors which principally determine future needs, and thereby where investors place their bets. If I take my businessman's hat off, and look at the data from an English father's and husband's perspective, it makes terrifying, catastrophic reading, worse than any global-warming disaster movie that your pal, Al Gore, could come up with."

"I see. Maybe Beverley, the boys and myself will come with you."

They dozed off for a while, sucked into near-slumber by the tweeting bird serenade, and almond petit fours settling on the solar plexus, but only being a halfway-house state, fundamentally, they were still more awake than asleep.

"Giles is courting now," informed Barry, for no particular reason, other than to strike up another conversation.

"Anyone we know?"

"Some girl from Exeter, he's brought her back home, a couple of times. I say courting, but I don't think it's serious."

"Why's that?"

"Oh, I think he has his eye on the main chance. He's got other and bigger fish to fry, but she's a nice girl."

"Good. Nothing wrong with stretching your legs in the long grass."

"Ha, ha, ha…. yes." Barry broke off in thought, momentarily. "She has a strange, if not unfortunate name."

"Really?"

"Yes." Barry levered himself up on his elbow. "It's Sally Shelingham, which if you say it too quickly, comes out as 'Sally's shelling them'."

"Some parents have got no sense of the ridiculous, when it comes to naming their siblings. John Thomas is the archetypal example."

"I once knew a Leonora Knocker at Leeds….oh way before Beverley. She used the shortened form of her Christian name, so it became Nora Knocker, but of course it got changed to 'Nora Big Knockers', and she was a well-endowed girl."

"If you think that's bad, there used to be a fund manager at the firm called Richard Head, known as Dick. Can you begin to imagine the hilarity, when there was an outside call for him, and the group secretary shouted across the bullpen, 'Call for Dick Head, call for Dick Head'."

"Hhaa, ha….yes, as you say, some parents have got no common sense."

As the clouds continued to waltz overhead, forming recognisable face and body-part shapes, Barry and Roger outlined them, with up-thrust pointing fingers.

"What a beautiful day," Roger said, half in appreciation, half with regret. "I can't remember the last time I lay on God's green

Earth, and scrutinised the sky."

"Yes, I suppose we are so involved with family and career, that we rarely find the time to enjoy the aesthetic."

"Funny you should say that, Barry. I was having a similar conversation with Hector McIntyre, just a few days ago….but that was more about escapism."

"Ah, Roger, it's a long time since I've heard you in a philosophical mood; first the Tardis, now escapism."

"Yes, I suppose it's the holiday environment, combined with release from normal everyday life and responsibilities. It produces conditions for the mind to run wild, for imagination to boil up….or am I talking complete bollocks, like that over-optimistic trader I told you about?"

"No…not at all. I think it's healthy to let your mind wander, at times. Bask in the shady uplands of the impossible. Someone at the university, a Professor Galbraith, I think, told me that daydreaming has a positive effect on the psyche. It opens the valve, that keeps all our latent hopes and ambitions locked away, allows at least the emulation….yes, I think that's the correct word, the emulation of our deepest desires."

"Huh, I think your tilt at the philosophical and the unobtainable, is stronger than mine."

"Yes….you may be right."

"Mmmm, what a beautiful day."

They began to nod off again, lost in a facsimile of Aldous Huxley's lysergic, acid-opened world. Neither of them got to travel this path, very often. Barry's professor friend was right, thought Roger. It does have a positive effect.

In fact, he could have sworn he was floating, but then he heard, "Daddy."

Back from the land of dreams, he sat up. "Hello," he said to Heather, "my little bundle of froth and joy."

"Daddy, can I have a frog, when we get back home?"

"A frog….I thought it was a gerbil, then a cat you wanted?"

"Can I have all three?"

Time to employ the usual get-out clause, thought Roger. "You'll have to ask your mother, Heather. Look, she's over there, with your Auntie Beverley." He pointed to the remnants of the abbey nave.

Heather took off like a greyhound chasing a hare.

"Huh, frogs, hey?" said Barry.

"What about them?"

"Have you heard the one about the junior-school class, out on a nature ramble with their young enthusiastic schoolteacher?"

"No, but I'm sure you're going to tell me."

Barry raised himself up, and then sat crossed-legged, ready to tell the tale.

"Miss Pringle takes a bunch of eleven-year-olds, out into the countryside, instructing them to go out, and do something nature-related. Then come back in an hour, and show her their work. So, off they all go. After an hour, they start returning. Little Jerry is the first back. He's done a drawing of squirrels collecting nutmegs. 'Well done, little Jerry,' says Miss Pringle. Then little Mary comes back, with a book of pressed flowers, and she also gets the 'well done' treatment from Miss Pringle. Eventually, all the class are back and have received accolades, apart from the class troublemaker, little Johnny. Miss Pringle is starting to become very annoyed, when little Johnny suddenly appears out of the blue. She says to the errant schoolboy, 'And what have you been doing in nature, little Johnny?' Johnny says, 'Well, Miss, I've bin down the duck pond, sticking bangers up frogs' arses'. Now Miss Pringle is a stickler for correct anatomical terminology, so she says, 'Rectum, Johnny, rectum.' Johnny replies, 'Wrecked 'em, Miss? Blew their fuckin' heads off.''

Chortling away in appreciative laughter, the punch line left Roger rolling about the grass. Barry also descended into uncontrollable giggles. In their awry stumer, they failed to see 'The First Wives Club', approaching them from behind.

"What's the matter with you two, then?" asked Beverley.

Starting to control himself, Roger replied, "Your husband, my cousin, has just told me the most incredibly funny joke."

"Joke," repeated Charlotte. "Are you going to share it with us?"

"Yes, yes….of course," confirmed Barry. "Just give us a moment to stop our stomachs churning over, from laughter pangs." He caught his cousin's eye. "You tell it, Roger."

"Right, right….well, you see, there was this frog." He stopped, having seen Heather suddenly emerge, from round her mother's back.

"Yes," said the wives, together.

Clearing his throat, speech beginning to fail him, he spluttered, "Well, we er…. we were just talking about frogs, after Heather came up, and asked me if she could have a frog."

"A frog?" exclaimed Charlotte.

"Yes, yes….I said to ask you," he responded back, lamely. "Obviously, she's not got round to it yet."

"Can I have a frog, Mummy?" Heather bleated out, whilst jumping up and down on the spot with excitement.

Charlotte didn't answer. She just glowered at her husband in an ominous fashion. She tutted, and then murmured not for the first time, "Roger, you're absolutely hopeless."

***

When the family outing got back to Barry's house, they were still on the driveway, when he announced, "Oh, I forgot to mention, we've got a surprise event for you this evening."

"Don't tell me, a Twenty20 cricket match," suggested Roger.

Barry smiled. "If only, no….the local amateur dramatic society is performing *Whitehall Farce* at the Carriage Works. I've got tickets for everybody."

"Oh, that sounds wonderful, Barry," enthused Charlotte, always an avid supporter of the arts. "Wasn't that made into a film entitled *Don't Just Lie There, Say Something*, with Brian Rix, Leslie Phillips and Joanna Lumley?"

"Yes," confirmed Beverley, also a film and stage buff.

Joanna Lumley, Roger thought to himself. He'd always had a thing for the iconic actress, ever since his schooldays. If Charlotte hadn't snared him, all those years ago, he would have gone off on a pilgrimage to find Joanna, worshipped her to the point of distraction, and begged her to have his babies. He was a leg man, that's how Charlotte entrapped him. She had great legs, but before her, Joanna represented his ideal leg goddess. Joanna's sultry come-to-bed voice, coupled with her legs and film-star good looks, always made him go weak at the knees. He had sought out her films and TV appearances, drooling at every frame of the blonde goddess, with the same gusto that Sherlock Holmes tracked down Moriarty.

"Wonderful, Barry," he chipped in, "the last play we saw was *The Glass Menagerie*, at the Apollo in London. That was some time ago, so another excursion to see the treading of the boards would be very welcome. Thank you."

Already, he wondered if the actress playing Giselle Parkyn would look anything like Joanna, who had played the same role.

"We know some of the cast," Beverley said fervently, "so after the show, we may get a chance to meet with them."

Now, he built up his Joanna look-a-like fantasy even more, hoping he would not be disappointed.

After an early evening dinner, off they went to the Carriage Works in Leeds, finding themselves stage centre in the stalls, just three rows from the front.

Loosely speaking, the play revolves around a government minister, who presents a bill on porn to the House, but that doesn't stop him having an illicit affair with two women, without his fiancée's knowledge. It also involves hippies kidnapping his best friend and co-supporter, in an attempt to get the porn bill scuppered. Following a tip-off, the police raid the hippies' flat, where there's an orgy going on, which inexplicably includes the minister, who escapes before the police discover him. Then the whole thing descends into an array of subplots, detailing various affairs between the characters, before culminating in the traditional farcical end, with everyone engaging in another massive orgy.

A few minutes after curtain-up, Giselle Parkyn made her entrance. No Joanna Lumley, Roger thought to himself, but not bad. He planned to keep an eye on her, for the rest of the play. It all went spiffingly well until the second act, when a piece of stage gallery came loose, under the footsteps of one of the uniformed policemen, raiding the hippies' orgy. He crashed through the flimsy stage set, onto the actors below. The actor playing the minister collided with one of his lovers, who in turn pole-axed one of the hippies. Of course, most of the audience thought it was part of the play. Roger thought Charlotte knew better, but then wondered if perhaps she didn't.

Turning to her husband, she said, "Oh, I don't remember that bit, or maybe it's an innovation. Either way, it's very funny."

Looking around his family members, Roger noticed that everybody from Barry to Heather had become near to lockjaw, through belly-aching laughter. The rest of the audience had reached a similar state of amplified cheerfulness. With more mayhem happening, Roger spotted a man at left corner of the stage, who he later found out was the stage director. Appearing to be very alarmed, the director signalled frantically across the stage, for one of the stage hands to bring down the curtain.

The stage hand began pulling at a cord, presumably connected to the curtain, but the curtain appeared to be stuck. In desperation, the director climbed the steps leading to the stage, starting to wave at the stage hand, to hurry up. Frustrated by the disobedient curtain, the stage hand entered the fray from the right, gesticulating at the director. Of course, the whole audience thought their signal interchange was an integral part of the play, the laughter level increasing to new heights. Moving steadily closer to centre stage, the director tried to issue instructions to the stage hand, but the noise of audience amusement drowned out his words. The laughter level went through the roof.

Then, from stage left, an ambulance crew suddenly appeared. Later, Roger found out that another stage hand had called 999, when the gallery first gave way, on the basis that someone might be hurt.

Dashing to centre stage, the ambulance men tripped over the fallen bodies and scenery, scattered in their path, bringing a fresh burst of side-splitting mirth from viewers.

To cap it all, the persistent stage hand on the right finally succeeded, in dislodging the troublesome curtain. It came crashing down, on actors and ambulance men alike. Roger climbed to his feet, with the rest of the audience. Everyone applauded rapturously, and shouted 'encore, encore'.

Only when the applause died down, did the director stand stage centre, explaining that the stage collapse was unintentional. The audience twigged there had been a minor tragedy. No one had been seriously hurt, but a lot of egos had taken a battering.

The next day's Yorkshire Post proclaimed, 'Unexpected ad-libbing at the Carriage Works theatre leads to real-life farce'.

For once, a shocking debacle had happened, and Roger hadn't been part of it, so could not be blamed. He thought that it was much more enjoyable, being a spectator than a participant, and it had been a great way to round off their tour, before heading back south.

CHAPTER 11: THE AYATOLLAH'S FUNDRAISER

Not long after the Frasers returned from touring, the start of the celebration season began. Wendy's birthday and Charlotte and Roger's wedding anniversary were imminent, plus various social functions, including the firm's feted executive-sponsored jamboree.

Luther Bembridge, VP Investment Banking at the firm's London based operation, was to have a party at his audacious, up-market Cheyne Walk apartment, for departmental heads, wealth, mergers and acquisitions and fund managers, stock market analysts, traders, and ancillary brokerage staff. Charlotte and Roger were invited. Mick Jagger and Keith Richards were nearby neighbours of Bembridge, so for anyone hailing from the Sidcup-Beckenham-Dartford rhythm and blues enclave, such as Roger, the chance of even getting a glimpse of the Glimmer Twins would prompt a positive response.

In the days leading up to the event, the Equities Director, Toby, stupid name thought Roger, but only his parents can be blamed for that, Chalcroft, known as TC or Top Cat because he constantly basked in the cream created by others, gathered together those staff invited to the shindig to brief them on its purpose and do's and don'ts.

Bembridge came from an Establishment background. He was so rich that he indulged in philanthropy more as a vehicle to illustrate his wealth, rather than as a medium to demonstrate compassion. He launched the Bembridge Foundation a few years ago, no one really knowing its mission, but accepting it must do some good, because the Bembridge family had been society benefactors for generations. However, cynics claimed it probably represented nothing more than a 5 star retirement home for disabled, pox-ridden, brain-dead gaga bankers. Top Cat informed the invitees that the foundation would be on the agenda at the event. That meant Bembridge would be expecting contributions, commitments and pledges from those attending.

A finicky character by nature, the VP was subject to wide mood changes, and thereby difficult to read. Somebody once asked Roger, 'What's the right way to approach Bembridge?' He answered, 'When he's in a good mood, any way is the right way, but when he's in a bad mood, no way is the right way'. Those who knew Bembridge were convinced that the TV character Malcolm Tucker from *The Thick of It*, had been based on the sometimes terrifying VP, although the antagonistic, bad-language happy, truculent Tucker was a wuss in comparison. Known as The Ayatollah in trading circles, the moniker gained through his autocratic, no-nonsense, black and white decision making style, Bembridge cut an awesome figure, not to be trifled with or in the least bit taken lightly. Neutral towards him, Roger neither liked nor disliked him. He thought Bembridge had fish eyes, scaly skin, and probably a tail, concealed in his pants, though the imaginative stock analyst conceded his vision was most probably wishful thinking.

Mind you, Roger thought, as TC continued his briefing, compared to The Ayatollah, a player from the firms New York HQ, ex-U.S Army Lieutenant-General Benjamin Garrett Sygrove, VP worldwide sales strategy was some piece of work, and should have been called Psycho, not Sygrove. Though well-connected with the firm, going back three generations through family relationships, Roger understood his appointment had not been universally lauded by all at corporate board level. Apparently, Psycho's hiring became inevitable, some form of quid pro quo, the source of which remained a closely-guarded company secret, enforced by the firm's Praetorian Guard of security agents in Manhattan. However, the good news was that he had limited powers. A fail-safe on his authority ensured the firm could not be put at risk, meaning he acted virtually as a non-executive director, with a cosmetic brief.

Last quarter, Psycho came over to Blighty to chivvy up the bullpen traders. Invited to his team talk along with other analysts, purely to observe proceedings, and as Chalcroft put it, 'To let Sygrove's gold dust brush off on us', Fraser witnessed his resolute technique close up. Roger thought Top Cat would cosy up to anyone who he thought could move him up the greasy pole. Still in Army officer mode, Sygrove employed scorched-Earth rhetoric to inspire his charges. So bullish, way beyond upbeat and chipper, he sounded more like Colonel Kilgore from *Apocalypse Now!* Completely ignoring prevailing market conditions, he outlined explosive growth projections that would embarrass Hans Christian Anderson, in terms of the incredulity of the fairy tale. Roger could almost hear him ending his talk with, *I love the smell of napalm in the mornings....smells like.... victory.* The dumb traders, mainly those of Essex origin, lapped up the double-hard bastard, work me until I bleed, let's go out and kill them message. Immediately, they tried out their new-found skills on private investors, only to be met by rejection and severe reprimands from Ricky Henshaw, the trading floor sales manager. Ricky was hard, and always keen on adopting new ways to improve revenues, but he wasn't stupid.

TC went through the protocol part of his briefing, like those invited were being granted an audience with Howard Hughes. Bembridge had a penchant for cleanliness, so they were requested to make sure that every stitch of clothing was methodically cleansed to U.S National Aeronautics and Space Administration standards, and everyone took a Turkish bath, to ensure no nasty micro-organisms found their way into Cheyne Walk. The long and monotonous list had some nodding off, its soporific effect accentuated by Top Cat's drone detailing requirements to the nth degree. Charlotte could have composed it, in one of her more mind-numbing moments.

The final valedictory item was particularly sensitive. Despite the Bembridge cleanliness regime, it transpired that Missus Bembridge, not his wife but his mother, would be attending the party, and suffered from uncontrollable flatulence. In order to avoid embarrassment to Missus Bembridge, the pack drill demanded that whoever was nearest to the rectum-release challenged lady, would pretend they made the unfortunate noise, making abject apologies to those in the immediate vicinity. It caused much hilarity among the juvenile traders, who couldn't wait to play their parts in the charade.

* * *

"You must be joking," exclaimed Charlotte, when Roger replayed the rules of Cheyne Walk etiquette for her.

"No….no, no, I'm being perfectly serious," he whined, trying to sustain a valid serious expression.

Unsure of the veracity of his claim, her dismissive stance continued. "You're just trying to fool me, Roger, like with one of your rugby club rousts."

"No, no, no."

"Honestly, Roger," she said, staring out of the kitchen window to emphasise her indifferent attitude, "you must think I fell out of a tree yesterday."

Continuing his bleating, he pressed, "It's true, it's true I tell you, it's true."

She turned to face her husband, hands on hips, looking all authoritative and matronly. "You expect me to believe that if this….what's her name?"

"Missus Bembridge Senior."

"Missus Bembridge Senior inadvertently breaks wind through the back passage, that whoever is standing next to her has to take the blame?"

"Er….yes."

DOGHOUSE BLUES

Becoming cynical and contemptuous, she contested, "I always did think that the financial services sector was filled with flakes and fruitcakes, but this really takes the biscuit."

At least she is beginning to believe me, Roger thought.

* * *

On the night in question, the Frasers got togged out in formal evening wear; Charlotte looked gorgeous in a stunning black gown, Roger in his penguin suit.

Charlotte asked Michelle, who lived just a few doors away, to look after the kids. Wendy and James generally said they were old enough not to need a nanny, as they put it, but Roger knew James would certainly agree to this particular babysitter. Michelle was a turbo-babe, huge greeny-blue eyes and flyaway blonde locks, a young Gwyneth Paltrow in the making, who brought the Fraser son to a standstill, no matter what he was doing, if he saw her walking down the road. She had recently graduated from University College, so Wendy was also going to be agreeable to Michelle, able to take the opportunity to grill her, on the philosophy and economics course she took. Heather thought Michelle was great, even if she sometimes got the answers wrong on *The Weakest Link*. The youngest Fraser would say, 'Michelle, you are at university, but you still don't know who plays Hermione Granger in the Harry Potter films'.

Just before they were about to leave, Roger saw Michelle coming up the driveway. Then he noticed James, also looking at her from another window, his eyes already glazed over and his tongue hanging out.

"James."

No response.

"James!" he repeated, in a louder voice.

"Huh," James responded, without shifting his stare.

"Remember our discussion at the garden party?"

"What discussion?"

"The one in which I recommended that you not only look at

the girls, but talk to them as well."

"Talk….oh, yeah."

"Well, here is an ideal opportunity to practice your communication skills with Michelle….you know, 'hello', 'good evening', 'how are you'."

"Huh….oh, right."

"Now, go and answer the door to Michelle….and be courteous with her."

James moved forward when the doorbell rang, his father a few steps behind him. Opening the front door, he immediately became frozen at the sight of the awesome Michelle. Roger started to mouth 'good evening', in the hope that the real words were actually coming out of his son's mouth, but nothing happened. James just stood in the doorway, fixed to the spot, motionless.

Taking the initiative, Michelle said, "hello, James," her voice still girly for a 21-year-old, but with a touch of the sultry seductress.

James' mouth still struggled to open in response, Michelle dumbfounded at the sight of Roger's dummy-like son, who appeared to be spellbound. Eventually, James' north and south did open, but no words came out, just a low-frequency sigh.

"Aren't you going to invite me in?" ventured Michelle, but once again she was faced with the image of a guppy at feeding time.

"James," she enquired, beginning to look concerned. "Are you alright?"

Time for super-Dad to intervene, before Michelle thought she'd come to the house of the living dead.

Striding forward, Roger said, "Ah, Michelle, so good of you to come over, please come inside."

"Oh, hello, Mister Fraser."

"I think you're old enough now to call me Roger, now."

She smiled, like he had awarded her first prize in a school poetry competition. She followed him into the lounge, James still stationary, hanging on the door latch.

"Is James okay, Mister Fraser? I mean, Roger."

"Just a little bit of immobility," he assured her, "it will pass."

* * *

They took a taxi to the fabled Chelsea residential address. Not much sign of Mick 'n' Keef, as they scanned up and down Cheyne Walk, but the night was young, so maybe they would be surprise guests of the Bembridges later on, some hope.

A Jeeves-type butler, in penguin attire that P.G. Wodehouse would be proud of, ushered the Frasers into the Bembridge inner sanctum. Already, at least 50 firm employees and their partners were gorging themselves silly, on champers, fine wines, oysters and caviar.

After accepting a glass of Bollinger, Charlotte and Roger slid over to Dennis Passmore, a fellow analyst and astute businessman.

"Evening, Dennis, any sign of The Ayatollah yet?" Roger enquired.

"Oh, hello Roger, no, Bembridge is yet to appear. I suppose he's going to make a grand entrance."

"Dennis, you may remember my wife Charlotte, from previous social occasions."

"Yes, of course, hello Charlotte. Good to see you again, lovely dress you're wearing."

"Hello Dennis, thank you."

"I'd introduce you to Georgina again," Dennis said, turning to look into the crowd. "But she's disappeared into the throng."

Passmore had been with the firm forever. Some say he was born in the bullpen, not to parents, but to a huge Cray computer, which constantly monitored the world's stock markets. Apparently, he used to have a full dark thatch and pale-blue eyes, but over the decades, dark had turned grey and largely disappeared, and the pale blue now hid behind bifocals. He'd also developed a slight stoop, through too many hours bent double over a monitor, trying to work out market direction and stock movement. Whenever Roger came up against an unusual issue beyond his ken, he took it to Dennis. In terms of exposure to the volatility of the money markets, Dennis had just about seen everything, and nothing the financial services sector threw up surprised him.

"How many of those shindigs have you been to then, Dennis?" Roger asked, half-expecting he had been to a lot, but the answer came as a surprise.

"I think about as many as you, Roger. Bembridge doesn't hold them all that often, and the first I can remember was in 1997, about the time you joined the firm. In fact, I've probably been to less than you."

Fraser hadstarted his career with JP Morgan Chase before moving on to Merrill Lynch and finally 'the firm', as it was euphemistically called by investors and employees alike, though many of his rugby-playing pals jibed him saying, they thought he had also been hatched via the firm's supercomputer.

"Oh, I thought all invitations were by royal appointment, and not optional," observed Roger.

"They're not….but one of my little perks is being allowed to be selective, in which of the firm's social events I attend."

"How do you manage that, Dennis?"

Searching the immediate vicinity, Dennis made sure there were no prying ears, and then whispered in Roger's ear. "Sometimes, Georgina gets the most appalling migraines."

He winked, and touched his nose several times, smiling. Ah ha, Roger thought to himself. That could be a useful ploy, in the years to come.

"Oh, Dennis, before you go in search of Georgina, let me ask you something."

"Anything, dear boy, anything."

"Have you met Missus Bembridge Senior before?"

"No….I don't think anyone has."

"I wonder why The Ayatollah is rolling her out now," wondered Roger, "particularly in view of her embarrassing problem."

"Ah, I do know the answer to that one. She is chairman, or should I say chairperson of the Bembridge Foundation, and as such attends all the fund raisers."

"Let's trust she's in control this evening," Roger hoped, "and no one has to carry the can, for her gastric limitations."

"Quite," agreed Dennis, "see you later."

Charlotte raised her eyebrows, nodding slowly. She still didn't quite believe her husband.

Gliding around the gathering, the Frasers chatted to fellow guests. Some Charlotte had met on previous occasions, others were new. Roger could tell how she felt about them, by simply examining her facial expression. Nothing overtly insulting became displayed, just subtle nuances only her husband could interpret, in this company of wolves and hyenas, as Charlotte has described them, during previous Bembridge parties. In general, she thought people in the financial services sector were either rogues and criminals or feckless incompetents. She was kind of right, but Roger had countered this monochromatic appraisal in the past, by suggesting that all industries had their good and bad points and share of the talented, as well as the dopes. She would merely retort that for financial services, it was a case of criminals and dopes only. 'What about me?' Roger would ask. 'You're different,' she invariably replied, 'but you should be applying your talents in a worthwhile enterprise like charities or the public sector.' Roger would shake his head, and say, 'Any public sector fool can spend money, it takes talent to make money'. That's usually when it descended into a minor philosophical disagreement.

"Roger."

Turning to the sound of his name being spoken, Lawrence Springs came into Roger's view, his least favourite of the Essex trader brigade. Roger noticed he was still not standing close enough to the razor. The bum fluff he started a few weeks ago had blossomed, into a full-blown Captain Birdseye chin warmer.

"Hey Roger, baby," Lawrence drawled, "how they hangin',

pal?"

He was in neo-Wall Street voice mode again. Roger wondered if after a few glasses of bubbly, the façade would melt, Essex barrow-boy speech taking over. Roger thought it would be interesting if Lawrence went head-to-head with Bembridge, not sure that Luther's speech decoder had been fine-tuned, to interpret the sub-cultural visceral sounds of the London-Essex border region.

Forcing a smile, he said, "Lawrence, how are you? No, never mind. Let me introduce you to my wife, Charlotte."

Virtually grabbing Charlotte's hand, Lawrence pined, "Hi, honey. Say, you've got a really smart husband here."

"My, aren't I the lucky one," declared Charlotte, pressing her free hand to her chest in mock recognition.

"You sure are, honey."

Before Roger's better half could respond, Springs saw someone else.

"Hey, Max, Maximilian," Springs blurted, "Hey Max, buddy."

Max Schofield, business attorney, was already in escape mode, pretending he hadn't heard. Springs charged off after his quarry, intending to entrap him in trading conversation.

"What an odious, obnoxious, self-centred, discourteous little wart," exclaimed Charlotte.

"Yes, and they're his good points," Roger confirmed.

The guests had started to really chill out, when the gong sounded, courtesy of Jeeves, and the Luther Bembridge entourage made their grand entrance, including his fabled mother. Fraser wondered what gastronomic anomaly form she would be in tonight. Immediately, Toby Chalcroft made a beeline for the VP, shaking his hand warmly, whilst exchanging a few words. The two senior players made family introductions then TC called for silence. Bembridge was going to address everyone.

"Do we bow or curtsey?" asked Charlotte, sarcastically.

"Ssshh....my main man is about to speak," her husband intoned.

"Ladies and gentlemen," Bembridge began, "it is our great pleasure to welcome you all. During the course of the evening, I will be passing around you with my mother, Missus Bembridge Senior, together with my wife, Missus Bembridge junior, and our eldest daughter, Claire Marie. Please, if you have any questions about the Bembridge Foundation, don't hesitate to ask us." The Ayatollah paused to gauge reaction. Of course, everyone smiled, before he continued. "The firm has had a particularly good trading quarter. In fact, this is the fifth quarter in a row of continuing growth, despite a bears market and fierce competition from other investment houses. I know that in the process, you have all made a lot of money, and hope you can find it in your hearts, to support the Bembridge Foundation this evening."

"I hope you're not thinking of giving our hard-earned money," exclaimed Roger's wife, "to this whatever it is foundation."

Our, he thought, I earn it, you spend it.

"Just a nominal donation, darling....it's expected."

Milling around the partygoers, the Frasers gravitated to some, exchanging a few words, but steered away from others who like Springs, Roger knew would incur Charlotte's displeasure. Eventually, they ended up in a group of mainly stock analysts, mutual fund managers and underwriters, talking about investment banking, and the quality of the Bembridge spread.

"It's probably all come from Fortnum & Mason," suggested Kristen, wife of Henry Jacques, who was Roger's immediate boss, and one of his close colleagues.

"That pate de foix gras is absolutely exquisite," Henry replied.

"Bembridge probably had the unfortunate goose shot this morning," said Roger, much to Kristen's amusement, "to ensure its freshness."

Kristen had a bit of a reputation as someone who quickly lost her inhibitions, after only a few sips of champagne. She would have been a gas at the garden party, but firm colleagues had been classified strictly verboten by Charlotte. If Roger's wife had her way, rugby players would have also been forbidden. With Kristen already appearing merry, Henry's task became to make sure that any further sips were strictly non-alcoholic, 'or she might get a bit wild', as he often told people.

Henry was one of the very few people Roger liked, not only at the firm, but in the entire financial services industry. Unlike most of the Dalek-like robots Roger interfaced with, everyday of his working life, Jacques had amiable human qualities and was capable of great subtle humour, an attribute Roger always found very appealing. Old-school and slightly eccentric, Jacques wore red and yellow bow-ties in the office, and had an intellectual aura about him, much like a university professor. He even came near to donning a monocle.

By contrast, good-time girl Kristen had few hang-ups. Though in her late-forties, she had retained girly good looks, and invariably projected an effervescent aura at social outings. She enjoyed herself by abandoning protocol at the earliest opportunity, fulfilling the notion that opposites often attract, Henry and her making a fascinating couple.

Touring the gathering, the Bembridges bestowed beatific-like gratification, on all within their compass. Their disciples became deferential to the point of prostrating themselves. Like dedicated followers of a venerated shaman, Roger thought some might throw flowers in to their pathway.

"You'd think The Ayatollah was his holy reverence, the Pope, wouldn't you?" Henry observed.

"Yes, but at least the Pope looks human," insisted Roger.

Puzzled by the remark, Henry asked, "What do you mean, Roger?"

"Well, for some illogical reason, I've always had the impression that Bembridge is secretly an alien, transforming himself into human form for public appearances, but in actual fact is a slimy man-eating lizard from the planet Zog….or am I thinking about Alice Vaughn from human resources?"

"Oh, she is a man-eater, no doubt about that," confirmed Henry. "I've seen her lick her lips at new intakes, fresh meat I think she calls them, as she sucks her tongue and lips together, like Hannibal Lector about to devour someone's liver."

"Yes, quite right….but we digress," Roger said, "what about Bembridge?"

"Well, your lizard intuition has got me thinking. He certainly has that cold scaly exterior and wet-fish eyes look, associated with reptiles." Flashing a rakish grin at Kristen and Charlotte, Henry narrowed his eyes. "They can be very unnerving, you know."

Both women tilted their heads, smiling at his remark, whilst swivelling about the hips, glass firmly held in hand, trying not to break out into raucous laughter.

"Funny you should say 'scaly exterior and wet-fish eyes,'" remarked Roger. "That is precisely the descriptive term, which sticks in my mind."

Continuing the zoological sojourn, Henry offered, "Yes, I can just imagine him slithering around, fork tongue striking out, tasting possible prey, his tail swishing around, and despatching competitors to oblivion."

"Ha, ha, ha," Roger reacted, "that's a very good image, Henry, very graphic. Yes, I can almost see that incongruous head, transformed into a killing machine, once he metamorphoses into his natural state."

"Oh, that reminds me," added Henry. "Did you hear that Ricky Henshaw got carpeted by Bembridge last week?"

"No, no," Roger replied, "I didn't."

"Bembridge's PA, Marcia Knight," he said to the girls, "told April Harrington, our group PA, that when Ricky emerged from the boardroom, he had turned white, and she could swear there were two fang marks on his neck, though Ricky said they were gnat bites, later on."

"Jesus," exclaimed Roger, "the things I miss, when I am doing my job properly."

As fate would have it, the possibly blood-sucked trading floor sales manager loomed into view.

Henry beckoned him over. "Ricky. Over here, old boy."

Tall and well-groomed, Henshaw was a ladies' man, divorced three times, and still on the positive side of 40. His reputation for whipping the sales team into shape went before him. He didn't care if they were little Lord Fauntleroys or Essex barrow-boys, so long as they could consistently make the weekly sales quotas, preferably exceed them. He, like other line managers and board members, came from the old establishment. Whereas four decades ago, all the traders came from similar middle-class to old-establishment backgrounds, the markets had gone global, and investment banks were looking for street fighters and dam breakers, who could tear apart sales forecasts and exceed them many times over. It became an expectation that had no limits, so the firm scoured the dregs of society, to find the kind of beast needed to thrive in such a competitive environment, a convenient blind-eye being turned to their provincial accents, chimps' tea party table manners and plastic lifestyles. As long as they did the business, that was the only measure.

Henshaw made his way over. "Hello Henry, Roger."

"You've met Kristen and Charlotte before, haven't you?" asked Henry.

"Yes, good evening ladies."

The wives reciprocated.

Henry put his arm around Henshaw's shoulder. Roger initially thought this may be teasing the sales terror, but then he quickly fell out of reverential mode, knowing that Ricky, like all the sales team, knew without analysts such as Henry and himself, they would be dead in the water. So the analysts were allowed their little peccadilloes and the occasional effrontery, testing trader mettle to accept analyst impudence.

"Ricky," Henry queried, "is there any truth in the rumour

that The Ayatollah recently carpeted you?"

Pulling at his shirt collar, the normally double-hard bastard sales manager wilted under the question before answering. "As a matter of fact, I did have an interview with The Ayatollah, er, Mister Bembridge."

"Ricky," probed Henry, "we're not being nosey, and we certainly have no interest in the content of your discussion with, er, Mister Bembridge." He turned to glance at Roger and Charlotte. "But we hear that he drew blood."

Henshaw cleared his throat, totally unaccustomed to being interrogated. Usually the inquisitor, he would take pleasure in torturing the trading floor sales team. His sadistic technique had become legendary, way beyond Sir Alex Ferguson's famous hairdryer escapades to punish badly performing Manchester United players. Reputedly, MI5 came to Ricky for the latest psychological truth-finding tools. But Jacques and Fraser didn't chide him for that, in fact they applauded it. For indulging in their cheeky, over-familiar, often rude dialogue with other functionaries, principally analysts like Roger, the traders deserved every little sharp pointed knife thrust at them.

"Well, it's true to say that Mister Bembridge gave me a very rough time, but...."

"Did he change in appearance?" Roger enquired.

"What?" returned Henshaw, obviously finding the question incongruous.

"Did he become a raving reptile?" suggested Henry.

Jerking his head back in genuine surprise, Henshaw exclaimed, "Have you people been taking hallucinatory drugs, or something?"

Looking terse, Henry replied, "No, no, no, nothing like that, Ricky." He shook his head to add credence to the reply. "What happened?"

Unusual for him, Ricky considered for a moment. Generally, he acted first before engaging his brain, a trait that usually proved more effective, in terms of getting the optimum performance out of the sales team. "Well....he did become volatile," Ricky conceded, "not in the sense of shouting or losing control, but more in his manner, his body language. He looked menacing, possibly threatening."

"Did he change into a reptile, a lizard?" Roger demanded to know.

Henshaw recoiled back, a priceless expression of incredulity etched on his face. "What are you talking about?" He cocked his head to one side. "I think you people have either had too much alcohol, or some of my delinquent traders have really slipped mind-altering lysergic acid into your drinks."

Shaking his head, he walked off, muttering to himself about analysts with hyperactive imaginations.

Moving on, Charlotte and Roger looked in on various other groups, before it was their turn to be recipients of the Bembridge beatification. They were with some of the M&A and wealth managers, when Roger felt a tap on the shoulder.

"Roger."

It was the lizard king himself, complete with entourage. Roger suddenly got what he assumed were hot flushes, although they were only meant to affect the feminine variety of the species. Consumed with visions of spiky tongues exploring every orifice in his body, momentarily, he lost vocal chord control.

"Good evening, Mister Bembridge," he squealed out in a high pitched voice, before clearing his throat. "Sorry….a bit of quail went down the wrong way."

Smiling, the VP encouraged, "Luther, please."

Lex Luther, Roger suddenly thought. Does that make him Superman, come to arrest a lizard, for crimes against investment banking humanity. The thought evaporated in a microsecond. Roger continued with civilities.

"May I introduce you to my wife, Charlotte."

"Good evening, Missus Fraser," the lizard king virtually breathed. Examining her more closely, he added, "I think we have met before. I never forget a face."

"Oh, Charlotte, please," said Roger's wife, beaming back one of her magnetic smiles.

"May I introduce my wife, Antonia and our eldest daughter, Claire Marie, and my mother, Missus Bembridge."

They all exchanged salutations of 'delighted to meet you', 'wonderful party' and 'glad you could come'. Missus Bembridge Senior appeared to have her gastric problem in check. Either that, or she wore fully sealed soundproof underwear.

Bembridge engaged Fraser in a conversation about futures, a very important topic in investment banking. The VP wanted him to share his thoughts, regarding the best investments for the firm in 2012.

Meanwhile, Missus Bembridge Senior had engaged Charlotte, in a discussion about children's television programmes.

"Heather, our youngest," Charlotte began, "tends to watch the animated material, and programmes which centre directly on animals. She has quite a developed sense of care for them."

"Oh, that's so good to hear, my dear. I remember when Luther was a boy. We would watch children's television together. He liked programmes about animals, as well."

"That's interesting. What did you used to watch?"

"My memory is not what it was, but I seem to recall a programme called Badger Hunt."

"Badger Hunt," exclaimed Charlotte. "Oh, I don't remember that one."

"Ah, I think I may have that wrong. Now let me see….it may have been Squirrel Hunt."

"Squirrel Hunt," repeated Charlotte, even more stumped by the name.

"No, that sounds wrong as well." After a moment of further consideration, Missus Bembridge Senior said with jubilation, and in a slightly raised voice, "I know what it was. It was Beaver Hunt."

Conversation came to an abrupt stop. Sentences left incomplete, mouths open like James' guppy moment with

Michelle, body motion frozen, champagne glasses apparently stuck to lips, superficial masks preventing anyone from seeing that their owners were beginning to smirk.

Becoming bright red, Luther Bembridge turned to Missus Bembridge Senior and said, in a cold calculating voice, "I think it was Otter Watch, Mother, not Beaver Hunt."

He turned back to face the group. Only Roger remained. The rest had fled to find a quiet place, where they could let out unruly laughter at the *faux pas*. Fraser tried desperately not to explode from the mirth tidal wave building up inside him. If it had got out, he could be handed his P45 on the spot.

"Lovely party," Roger exulted, in a faltering voice.

A little later, after the Bembridge entourage had moved on, Charlotte told her husband that the encounter was quite a moving moment. He wondered what she meant, thinking she still may have visions of The Ayatollah changing into lizard form, before their very eyes.

"Never mind that," he said, "how on Earth did you keep a straight face, when Missus Bembridge Senior came out with Beaver Hunt?"

Charlotte stared at him, with a perplexed expression. My, he thought, she has led a sheltered life, thank God. If she had laughed, he might well have got his P45.

As the Frasers recharged their glasses, and helped themselves to some delicious Beluga caviar, Roger noticed that they were on the Essex trader radar again. Knowing Charlotte would be put out, if confronted by the etiquette-challenged Essex traders again, he took her to a place of refuge, with a group of analysts he considered to be from the socially acceptable side of investment banking.

"The Bembridge elder daughter is a bit of a stunner," observed Oscar Giddins, a pension fund manager with an aerated manner, contact lenses which made him constantly squint, and a flushed complexion. "What's her name again?"

"Claire Marie," confirmed Leonard Noakes, delicately named Tubby, because of his generous waist dimension. If a man's girth was a measure of his success, then Leonard had been extremely successful.

Still single, Oscar constantly watched the field in the filly stakes. Having played around for nearly 20 years, he was looking for a suitable mate, and the Bembridge eldest daughter could be his latest quarry.

"She's out of your league, Oscar," advised Tubby. "Anyway, I can't imagine Bembridge allowing a lowly mutual fund manager to ravish his eldest daughter."

"Well, therein lays the challenge," Oscar replied. Scoping the horizon, he fixed his infrared sensors on the target, smiled gregariously, pushed his hair back from his forehead, and walked away. "See you later."

Whilst continuing to make polite conversation with Tubby, the Frasers thought they had avoided further advances from the Essex trader set. Then Pierce Finlay, another trader in the mould of Lawrence Springs, decided to adopt the Frasers as party companions. Unlike Springs, Finlay had retained his London-Essex border accent, for all occasions.

"Allo you lot, great party innit. Cor look at the 'arris on that. Allo Roger, got any 'edge fund 'ot opportunities for me?"

Virtually feral, in the sense that his minimalist communication techniques were indicative of his untamed origins, Finlay had all the outward appearance of the archetypal East End barrow-boy, fresh of the stalls in Billingsgate Fish Market. Rough, uncouth, impolite and crude, were words Roger had often heard to describe him. However, on the plus side, being street-smart and book-wise, he had attained a level of market understanding, that many of his contemporaries were incapable of emulating. Remarkably, some of the firm's private investors thought his earthy banter was charming and oldie-worldy. Summoning up visions of the Artful Dodger, they were seduced into parting with their hard-earned cash by his 'lo-fi' honeyed tones. Going into 'Del Boy' mode, he would tell the punters that the investment decisions he made on their behalf were sound. He usually finished the sell with those immortal

Peckham-inspired words, 'you know it makes sense'. And he didn't even drive a three-wheel Reliant Robin. The little oik cruised the Basildon and Billericay chicks in a Porsche 911 Carrera GT, the ultimate status symbol for the successful Essex boy trader.

"You mean hedge fund," Roger corrected.

"Yea, 'edge fund."

Noticing Charlotte had adopted a derisory countenance, in response to the trader's arrival, Roger decided to go for the Dutch uncle approach. "Well, Pierce, this is neither the time nor the place to conduct trading business."

Finlay came over all perplexed or was he just being thick. "Yea, why's that then, Rog?"

Before he could answer, Springs joined the group, with an entourage of other Essex-based traders, their high-gloss, low-intellect girlfriends in tow.

"'Ere' Pierce, are you givin' Roger GBH of the ina ear?" asked Brendan Kirkman, a particularly virulent example of the garrulous, cockney rhyming slang trader.

"'ello', Brendan, my son, yes I am."

"Oh, Roger's open for business then, is he?" enquired Kirkman.

"Certainly not," Fraser replied.

"That's a pity, Rog," Kirkman said, "I could do with some extra bunce, 'cause Shirley 'ere. Say 'ello, Shirl."

"ello' Shirl," the giggly girl blurted out, in a high-pitched voice that would chip plasterwork 100 yards away, and would have her failing the Elisa Doolittle audition for being too coarse.

"Yea, as I wos sayin'," Kirkman continued, "Shirley 'ere 'as bin promised a new top set. She's a good lookin' gal, but she's got nothin' in front." Roger thought she had nothing on top, either. "Stand sideways, girl," Kirkman insisted. "So they can take a gander at you."

Shirley duly obliged and sure enough, though a very pretty girl, Twiggy had more between her neck and waist than the waif-like Essex lass.

"We're gonna give you somethin' that 'ill make Dolly Parton jealous," concluded Kirkman, "aren't we, girl?"

"That's right, Brenny."

Obviously her pet name for Brendan, thought Roger.

While this stimulating, high brow conversation continued, they were unaware that Missus Bembridge Senior talked to a group next to theirs. Suddenly, a terrific whoosh emanated from her nether regions. Both groups went conspicuously quiet.

Then remembering the instruction from Top Cat, Tubby Noakes said, "Oh, do excuse me, those Moroccan figs are starting to take effect."

Sideways eye motion revealed that Missus Bembridge Senior appeared relieved, carrying on the conversation within her group. A few moments passed, and then another blast boomed across the room. This time it was a monster, very loud, and accompanied by a pungent odour. Both groups started navel-gazing and clearing throats. Someone had to carry the can.

Finally, chivalrous Brendan Kirkman turned round and said, "Don't worry, Missus Bembridge....'ave this one on me!"

CHAPTER 12: STAG NIGHT

One of Roger's mates from the rugby club was getting married, and as a traditional consequence, intended to have his stag do at the clubhouse. Roger had arranged for a five-hour pass from Charlotte for the Friday evening, so he could attend the festivities, and looked forward to the event with great excitement. They were raucous, but good-natured affairs. The bridegroom usually lost his trouser at some stage during the evening, and threatened to inflict pain on those responsible, should he end up in Aberdeen the next day, en route for a North Sea oilrig, or became an unwilling crew member of a Shanghai-bound tramp steamer, just 24 hours before his expected pristine attendance at the wedding. Over the years, there had been some narrow margins for error, with bridegrooms still putting on their morning suits, as they were whisked up the aisle by their irate in-laws to be.

"You will behave yourself, won't you, Roger," urged his over-cautious wife.

"Of course, my sweet."

"Is Daddy going out, then?" asked their youngest daughter.

Smiling down at the bundle of froth and joy before him, he replied, "Yes, Heather, Mummy has issued Daddy with a five-hour pass. So Daddy is going to thoroughly enjoy his short stint of unadulterated freedom."

"What does 'una-doll-ta-rated' mean?"

"Unadulterated?" he clarified.

"That's what I said," intoned Heather, frowning, "you should learn to listen, Daddy."

"I was only….oh, never mind. It means untouched, untainted."

"It means highly conditional, as far as I'm concerned," warned Charlotte.

He cast a disparaging look at his wife, but she batted it back with twice the force.

Incisive as ever, Heather noticed the potential conflict. "Will you be sleeping in the spare room again, when you get home, Daddy?"

Not if I can help it, he thought.

"No, Heather, nothing like that."

"I wouldn't rule it out," advised strict disciplinarian Charlotte.

She's like that sometimes in the bedroom, Roger thought to himself, only in a good way, but that's another story.

Entering the debate, Wendy enquired, "Is Dad going out on the juice again?"

Raising his eyebrows to their eldest daughter, and near to astonishment, he said, "On the juice. Where on Earth did you pick up a term like that, Wendy?"

"Oh, Dad, I'm 16, 17 in a few weeks."

True, Roger thought to himself. Gone were his halcyon visions of her, being a cuddly innocuous little girl. She had been a young lady for some time, only he often chose not to see it, because he craved her formative years. He consoled himself with the knowledge that Heather was still in her harmless chaste years, though Fozzie Bear may give him an argument on that accolade, and there were still plenty of them left for him to play the doting father.

"Where are you going, Dad?" asked James, as he also joined the 'lets make Roger feel bad about going out' party.

"To a stag night at the rugby club, son and heir."

"Huh," James complained, "I'm never allowed to go to parties like that, and I'm a member of the rugby club."

Introduced into the rugby fraternity at a tender age, James had first participated in mini-sevens, and then played for his school in the junior 15. Now he turned out for the rugby club's Colts 15, and seemed to be a very promising player.

"It's for seniors only, James," Roger advised, with resolute conviction. "You're still a junior, and you're underage. Besides, it's not a conventional party….a stag do is more of a ritual, to be enacted with honour and solemnity."

"Huh," exclaimed Charlotte. "More like an excuse for grown men to act like juveniles, drink gallons of beer, and leer at half-naked women."

"Half-naked women," enthused James. "Oh, Dad, please let me come."

Before Roger could reply, his wife jumped in. "Certainly not….it's bad enough that your father goes to these debauched celebrations for renegades and vagabonds. I'm not having my son go, as well."

"Oohhh….I'm never allowed to do anything," James complained again in a sulky manner, whilst subconsciously kicking the point of his shoe into Charlotte's Persian carpet, in frustration.

"James," she threatened, "stop that, you'll ruin the carpet."

Laying a fatherly hand on his son's shoulder, Roger said, "Your time will come, James, before you know it. In a few years' time, you'll be…."

Suddenly, Roger felt Charlotte's X-ray eyes upon him.

"He'll be doing what?" she glared.

"About time I put my jacket on and left, isn't it?" he said quickly.

* * *

The rugby club was only a few miles away, so after Roger called for Steve and Gordon, they'd be walking it. It was a really balmy evening, conducive to striding out, and the exercise would definitely sharpen their appetites, for John Barleycorn and Harry Hop.

Established in 1923, Kappa Corinthians Rugby Football Club had become the epicentre of Roger's life outside the family and the firm. It provided the welcome antidote to all those trials and tribulations, and rigours and tremors, which impinged on his daily life. He had joined the club in his early-teens, and despite jumping ship to play university rugby for three years, he had been a member ever since.

Currently, he played for the over-forties veteran 15. His friend, Charlie Farley, had often asked him, 'How does an out-of-condition, fleshpot-gorging vulture like you even walk, let alone play rugby?' Roger would tell him, 'Well, it's strictly mind over matter; that and a lot of self-belief to compensate for the lack of speed I used to have, flying down the wing in my formative years'. These days, he played more at centre, using guile, cunning and slyness, to body swerve around oncoming opposition forwards. Failing that, he kicked them in the goolies, before throwing a try-making pass to Hugh 'Dusty' Maltman, who was two years older than him, but still built like a greyhound. If Dusty could hand off the first few tackles from ageing forwards, and then outsprint the backs, a try became a racing certainty. Steve played hooker, most appropriate for him, as he always fancied himself as a male prostitute. Gordon played in the half-backs, mainly at fly-half.

Bursting through the clubhouse doors, the cavaliering trio were greeted by the sight of grown men, most in positions of great responsibility to the nation, beginning to let loose. Noisy and boisterous, the sound level became raised further by the PA blasting out Roy Orbison, Chuck Berry and Ray Davis classics, not necessarily sung by them.

"Hey, the three stooges have arrived," said Evan McGinley, a Celt by birth, but an adopted and honorary Kentish Man.

When Roger had first met Evan, he asked him, 'What brings you south of the border?''Buds, Jimmy, buds', Evan replied. 'Buds,' Roger asked, looking mystified, 'what kind of buds?' His newfound Scots mate had seemed speechless, even offended, as if Roger had asked him an impolite question. Then Evan replied, 'Buds with big tits, of course, Jimmy.' 'Oh, I see, you mean birds?' Roger attempted to clarify. 'Aye,' confirmed Evan, 'that's what I said, buds....with big tits'.

Since then, like the rest of the club, Fraser had learnt to transpose Evan's Celtic tones into normal English. Now Evan and Roger understood each other, although they sometimes had to go round the buoy several times to confirm their understanding, a pleasant process often conducted with mutual good-natured Mickey-taking by both sides.

At their initial Anglo-Celtic summit, Roger also told Evan about a holiday, Charlotte and himself had in the Cairngorms. They came back to their family-run hotel one day, to find the owner had the floorboards up in the hallway. Roger had asked him what the problem was. He answered, 'There's a moose in the hoose'. 'A moose', Roger replied, trying to figure out how a large creature like a moose could possibly get under the floorboards. Finally, he said, 'Excuse me asking, but how big is this moose?' The owner peeped up from his work and said, 'He's only a wee fellow, could fit in the palm of my hand'. Roger suddenly twigged, 'You mean a mouse?' 'Aye' he confirmed, 'a moose.' All Evan could say in response to the tale was, 'Ah well, they don't speak properly, north of Glasgow.' Pots, kettles and black came to Roger's mind.

"Evan, how are you, my boy?" Fraser asked, whilst shaking his hand warmly. He felt predisposed to address him as my boy, because Evan was still on the right side of 40.

"Roger, I've been hearing some interesting things about your social life."

"Don't believe any of it," Roger retorted with put-on bluster. "It's all vicious rumour, put about by my legions of detractors, designed to undermine my high standing in the community."

Very well lubricated already, Evan burst into laughter.

"You're such a bull-shitter, Roger, but I love you anyway."

He got up off his stool, and planted a big wet kiss on Fraser's forehead. It wasn't that Evan was a whoopsie, or that rugby players were secretly effeminate pansies, it was just a way they had of expressing comradeship with each other. Leastways, that was what Roger had always been led to believe.

"You've heard about the garden party, then?"

"Heard about it? I've seen the video on YouTube. And got the tee shirt."

With the event beginning to boil up, Dusty Maltman entered the clubhouse. Roger waved and shouted for him, to come over and join them.

"Hello, Dusty, you old antipodean criminal," he said, slapping his shoulder.

"Roger, you pommy bastard," came the reply, as he firmly gripped the Englishman's hand.

From Down Under, and a Queenslander by birth, Dusty had a swarthy complexion, mainly resultant from sun worship, a Tony Curtis-style haircut, and a chiselled face with a granite jaw. Roger had winced at the sight of Dusty, getting clobbered by opposition forwards during wing runs, only to see him get up and carry on, like he had a mild bump in a wine bar. Failure was not in Dusty's vocabulary. There had been times when the veterans had been down and out in a match, and he turned it around with a flurry of great runs, resulting in tries between the posts. Typical of people Roger had worked or socialised with from the Southern hemisphere, there wasn't a more popular player in the entire club. They seemed to have a pioneering, never-say-die spirit, which according to Roger's mother-in-law, and she was probably right, had been bred out of the English in recent decades by politically-correct politics.

Another honorary Kentish Man, the Aussie had been with Kappa Corinthians for at least 20 years. Whilst backpacking through Europe, he came to Blighty to see the land of his forefathers. He fell in love with a local girl, Sylvia, married her, became a dual national, had a family, and only went back to Oz to get fresh supplies of sheep, and the real Fosters, as he called it.

"Say, Dusty," said Gordon, a wicked glint in his eye. "Is it true that you still need a criminal record to get into Australia?"

"Another cheeky pommy bastard, hello Gordon."

"Now don't take it personally," Steve added, "after all, you are meant to be a well-balanced Australian."

"A third pommy bastard….what do you mean by that,

Hunt?"

"Chip on both shoulders, of course," confirmed Steve, goading the genial gent.

Standing back, Dusty eyed the miscreants with censure in mind. "Same old pommy clichés about Australians, hey? Isn't it about time you lot admitted that you're descended from a bunch of lamebrain, degenerate, poof-pastry no-hopers, and that Australians can beat you at any sport you care to name."

"Er, chess," Roger suggested.

"What?" exclaimed their irascible chum.

"Backgammon," offered Gordon.

"I'm talking about real sport, you dopey pelicans," Dusty protested, "not namby-pamby, trendy, pinko frilly knickers, shirt-lifting girlie games."

"Oh....you must mean cricket," offered Steve, his grin brimming with pride, Australia having been demolished by England, in the summer Ashes Test series.

"Yes....no," Dusty backtracked.

"Could it possibly be no, because we whupped your criminal hides in the last two Ashes series?" suggested Roger, also unable to prevent the smile of winning satisfaction enveloping his boat race.

Considering for a moment, Dusty replied, "Well, you've got me there, but the Aussies will rise again, and we still haven't forgiven you poms for Jardine's bodyline bowling tactics against the great Don Bradman."

"Tisk, tisk," said Gordon, brushing at Dusty's shoulders.

"What are you doing, Anderson?" Dusty asked.

"Just brushing off those famous chips, dear boy."

Scanning them again with steely eyes, Dusty went for a counter-attack. "One day, I'm going to get you three on a tramp steamer to Botany Bay, and when we dock in the land of the golden throat charmer, I'm going to put you lot in yokes, and invite my Australian brothers to feed you to the sharks, off the Great Barrier Reef."

"You'd have to catch us first, Dusty," suggested Gordon,

DOGHOUSE BLUES

knowing the speedy wingman would beat all of them in an egg and spoon race, on one leg.

"Catch you....why, I could lasso and hogtie you lot, before you even knew what was happening."

"Okay, enough Aussie baiting for now, chaps," Roger said. "We have some serious drinking to do."

"Ah, Roger, now you're talking....lead me to it, boy," requested Dusty. "My throat is like an Abbo's armpit."

They launched into Shepherd Neame's finest, and explored more ways to wind up the dogged Aussie, a game enacted many times, but still providing pleasure to all participants. Despite being outnumbered, Dusty usually got the better of the poms.

"You fellas don't know the first thing about Aussie humour," insisted the antipodean. "Now let me tell you a real wallaby joke."

"Go ahead, Ned Kelly," encouraged Steve.

"Right....this is about Bruce and Sheila." He grinned nefariously, and then said, "You see, Bruce is driving over Sydney Harbour Bridge one day, and sees his girlfriend, Sheila, about to jump off. Bruce slams on the brakes and says, 'Sheila, what the hell do yer think yer doin?' Sheila turns around with a tear in her eye, and says, 'G'day, Bruce, ya got me pregnant, so I'm gonna kill myself'. Bruce gets a lump in his throat, when he hears this. 'Sheila,' he says, 'not only are you a great root, but you're a real sport too.'"

"Good one, Skippy," said Gordon, smiling.

"Aussie humour at its finest," Roger added.

Robert Westcott, known as Bob, the club's president, joined the Anglo-Aussie contingent. "Gentlemen, here to do some training, in preparation for the start of the new season?"

"Of course, Bob, of course," replied Steve. "Where else can an important social occasion like a stag night be combined with a strict and challenging training regime?"

Further horsing around and ribbing took place, whilst they got on with the serious business of drinking the clubhouse dry.

Then the bridegroom to be, Christian Bowcott, made his grand entrance, supported by his best man and his brother, to shouts of 'here comes the poor unsuspecting sucker,' implying Christian didn't know what he was in for, once he pushed that manacling ring onto his bride's third finger. Christian was 22, well built, blonde haired, blue eyed, and very innocent in the ways of the world. A really good open-side flanker for the first 15, and a good ol' boy to boot, everyone at the club liked him. Seasoned veterans of domesticity, like Roger, felt sorry that the impending doom-laden future he was about to set out on, would turn him overnight from a bright carefree young man, into a subdued, perpetually burdened hostage to fortune.

The groom to be, or victim, the title, dependent on who assessed Christian's predicament, made his way over to Bob Westcott, to pay his respects. It had become an expectation for the more junior players to honour their elders, at social occasions held at the club, quite rightly so in Roger's opinion, since he was rapidly becoming an elder himself. Age 65, Bob had retained a full head of dark hair, all his faculties, and was still as fit as players half his age. He had been with Kappa Corinthians for over 50 years, man and boy, had turned out occasionally for the veterans, well into his fifties, and was therefore considered more of a vintage player, according to some.

Shaking his hand warmly, the club president met the young lamb to the slaughter with a broad smile.

"Looks like you have had a few already, Christian," observed Bob, worldly in manner, and eternally diplomatic on these strident social occasions.

"Yes," replied the flanker, almost hiccupping, "just enough to take the edge off, and give me the courage to face whatever waits."

"You mean your forthcoming marriage," offered Steve.

Christian smiled. "Huh, no….whatever you reprobates have got planned for my stag night," he replied, hiccupping. "The marriage too," he added, almost as a flyaway comment.

DOGHOUSE BLUES

"Well, young Christian," Roger said, his tone implicit with reassurance, regarding his passage of rites, "you will not be disappointed."

"Roger, I didn't see you skulking behind Steve." Lolling, he turned his head more and saw the third member of their troupe. "Gordon, where were you hiding?"

"My, you do appear to be spaced out," Gordon told Christian.

Clearly, the first team flanker would not need too much more lubrication, to totally annihilate the last vestiges of his inhibitions.

The master of stag night ceremonies, John Hillenbrand, also known as John the Revelator, and Kappa Corinthians current first team tight-head prop, called for silence. Like most props, he was a walking mountain with a booming voice, ideal for the job he was about to perform. In a scrum, after the referee said 'crouch-touch-pause-engage', John normally let out a banshee-like war cry, scaring the living daylights out of the opposition. Very effective, it often resulted in hairs standing on end.

"Gentlemen," he thundered, "and those of you yet to accomplish that exulted title, may I have your attention." Remaining conversations died away. "We are gathered here this evening, in this hallowed cathedral-like clubhouse, set on this sacred turf, to help our friend and comrade, Mister Christian Bowcott, make that great transition from freedom to lifelong shackles." Cries of 'hear, hear' came from the assembly. "We wish him well in his future endeavours to get a pass, allowing him to enter this illustrious company again." Nods of encouragement from fallen warriors confirmed the challenge ahead for the bridegroom. "In the meantime, we have generously arranged some suitable entertainment for Christian..." Peering around the gathering, the Revelator's gregarious smile turned to a serious countenance. "...And the rest of us, to see him on his way to enduring domestic servitude, and give him some lasting memories of his former life."

Building up to the evening's main event, his voice ratcheted up a few octaves. "And now, without any further ado, may I present for your edification and enjoyment, the queen of the tease, the princess of posing, that slinky temptress of the night, that luscious lady from Armentieres, Mademoiselle Solange Desmarais."

A huge ripple of applause went up, and a sultry sorceress appeared from behind a curtain. She was a vision of blonde waves, pouting red lips, enticing near-to-chartreuse eyes, and a curvy five-nine, all decked out in seven-inch certified high heels, sheer 18-denier nylons and a cheeky little basque, barely covering her ample bosom and apple-shaped derriere. Not exactly in the first flush of youth, but still in lovely condition, as Roger would subsequently report to those not in attendance that evening, who had failed to acquire the necessary pass-outs from their loved ones. Later, he would recount the event to club secretary Daniel Hughes, who couldn't make the stag night, due to what he called unpredicted domestic circumstances. In other words he had a barny with his trouble and strife. Daniel would ask, 'How can you supply so much fine detail?' to which Roger would reply, 'Just put it down to, I'm a stickler for feature description when it comes to the female form'.

Male chins dropped and knees began to buckle. Roger heard Steve say 'hubba, hubba, hubba,' to no one in particular. As strains of *The Stripper* surged through the clubhouse sound system, Solange strutted her stuff like a well-practised stage actress, the graceful shapes and curves she made adding to the allure and fascination. Every man in the room only had eyes for the delight, thrusting and jerking before them. The Russians could have invaded at that moment, and every red-blooded male in the rugby club would have welcomed them with open arms, so long as they didn't interrupt concentration on Mademoiselle Desmarais. Finally, having teased her devotees to the point of distraction, she descended on Christian Bowcott, weaving her magic and entrancing him with her feminine allure. She sat him in a chair and went to work undressing him.

DOGHOUSE BLUES

When finally down to his boxer shorts and socks, she mounted him, and rode him into oblivion, the rest of the club cheering on the action, before she took a final bow and departed the wolf pack, to whistles and cheery requests for an encore.

Noticing the bridegroom's eyes had glazed over, and seeing him growling slightly, a concerned Roger asked, "You alright, Christian?"

"Just a little bit of stiffness coming on."

"Yes, we're all suffering from that," Roger assured him.

"I need a beer to put the flames out," Gordon announced.

"Make it two," Roger said.

"Three," added Steve.

Out of the blue, Garfield Truscott sidled up beside them. "Let me get these, boys," he offered.

So taken aback by the startling proposal, Steve, Gordon and Roger froze for a moment.

"Cor....you're not going to buy a round, are you, Garfield?" enquired Steve, huge metaphorical exclamation marks above his head.

"Certainly, I am."

"You mean....you intend to part with money?" suggested Roger.

"Of course," Truscott confirmed.

Amazed, the three friends exchanged shocked glances. Truscott had a reputation for being a tightwad, as had his pal, Mitchell Flowers. Gordon thought the two misers had contests to see how long they could sit at the bar, before one of them was shamed into coughing up for a round.

"Well, lads," he advised, "we'd better watch out for low-flying moths, when Garfield opens his wallet."

Sure enough, Truscott produced his flea-bitten wallet, not opened since 1993. He spun the wheels to the combination lock securing his readies, and hey presto, pristine 1993 onecers bearing the Queen's seal popped out.

"What's the occasion then, Garfield?" asked Roger, not really expecting a candid answer.

"I thought with young Bowcott getting hitched, this would be a worthwhile time to buy my old buddies a drink."

Steve almost fell off his stool, in disbelief. Gordon appeared visibly stunned.

Needing to unearth the real truth, Roger sceptically enquired, "Nothing more to it than that?"

Facing them with the body language of someone who wanted something, Truscott admitted, "Well....since you ask, there is, er, a matter you can help out with."

"I knew it," said Gordon, tossing his head upwards, the gesture confirming that the offer of refreshments would not be free of charge.

"Well, what is it, Garfield?" asked Steve, like Gordon suspecting a conditional response.

"I was wondering if you could possibly help me shift some flagstones next Sunday," he requested with a self-assumed winning smile, hoping to solicit cooperation from them. "If we start early, we should have it done by lunchtime."

Steve, Gordon and Roger exchanged questioning glances, so bemused by the overconfident request, that it took a few seconds to sink in.

"Let me understand this, Garfield," said Steve, "you want us to come over to your place, early next Sunday, and spend the morning humping flagstones. Is that right?"

"Yes, quite right."

"What about your mate, Flowers?" Steve wondered.

"Oh, I've asked him."

"And?" pressed Steve.

"He wants paying for it."

"And our reward?" asked Gordon.

"The drinks I'm about to buy you."

The three caballeros looked at each other, eyes wide open, in amazement. They couldn't figure out whether to merely punch Truscott's lights out for his breathtaking audacity, or take him outside and feed him to the juniors, who were still practising their scrum-downs under floodlight.

DOGHOUSE BLUES

Finally, Roger took the initiative. "Garfield, we would like to thank you for your offer, but the boys and I are churchgoers, and we never miss Sunday mornings."

Curling his upper lip in reaction to their devout religious calling, Truscott gave them a wry smile, and then scurried off in search of other potential suckers, his unsoiled 1993 currency still intact.

Roger ordered three pints of Shepherd Neame Master Brew. They all took large pulls on the beer, its cleansing of their palates, an attempt to disenfranchise themselves from the stingy Truscott.

Shaking his head, still recovering from the intended con, Steve advised, "I wouldn't give him the steam of my tea, as they say in Manchester."

Gordon and Roger agreed. They quickly moved on from the grubby encounter, as Terry Nicholson came their way.

"Way aye, bonny lad," Roger said in his best imitation Geordie accent, to their first team Number-5 lock, an 18-stoner made from carbide and ceramic, hailing from Newcastle, and yet another adopted Kentish Man to Kappa Corinthians.

"Way aye," returned the jovial Geordie.

"Terry, come and join us for a drink," offered Gordon.

Smiling at the invitation, the burly Newcastle man settled into a seat.

Assuming a critical deportment, Steve inspected him up and down, his eye mischievous and searching. Noticing the action, Terry scanned his own front, but remained mystified as to the purpose of Steve's inspection.

Finishing his scrutiny, Steve said, "Tell me, Terry, can you actually speak English, as well as Geordie?"

Now Terry was affable, but his temper rose quickly, especially when he had received a boot sandwich from an opposing forward, or his sub-cultural heritage was being brought into disrepute.

Slamming his pint glass down on the bar, he said, "What d'yer mean, man, I am English."

Supporting Steve's assertion, Gordon said, "No, you're not, you're a Geordie."

Snorting, a menacing look developed on Terry's enormous face. "Why, I ought to knock your block off."

Before he could rip into his fellow veterans, Roger said, "Relax, big man….Hunt and Anderson are just trying to wind you up."

After grunting and growling like a tearaway bull, Terry began to relax his posture, but not before putting the evil eye on Steve and Gordon, and wagging his finger, indicating the next time he might not be so forgiving.

Before things became more fractious, current first team captain, Martin Gayle, joined the happy band of strolling minstrels. Having played for Rosslyn Park and trialled for Harlequins in his early career, next to Bob Westcott, Martin was considered to be the club's most notable asset. Also a colossus, mainly built from steel superstructure joined together with carbon fibre, he played Number-4 lock, and was thus Terry's partner in the boiler house of scrum downs.

"Hey, Nicholson," he opined, "I hope you are not giving our mighty veterans a hard time."

"What me, capt'n?" The Geordie smiled expansively. "Naw."

"We were just debating if your lock partner is English," Steve advised Martin.

"Ah," said Martin, joining in the rib tickling, "he's definitely a Geordie….I have to sign his work permit, every time he turns out for Kappa Corinthians."

Rising to the bait, his fuse definitely getting shorter, Terry demanded, "What d'yer mean, man, I'm as English as yo are."

Beaming a warm, generous smile, Martin slipped his arm around Terry's shoulder, and hugged his teammate. "Of course you are, me old mucker, don't take any notice of us smart-arsed southerners."

"I never do," Terry exclaimed.

They all broke into hearty laughs, resultant from the mutual camaraderie. No longer about to blow the top off the clubhouse, Terry came down from Mount Etna, his temper quelled, his North-East heritage intact.

If you were going to be a rugby player, you had to get used to ribbing, an integral part of the culture, protocol expectation demanded that those on the receiving end took the jibes without resorting to fisticuffs. Everyone was subject to it, Roger included. In fact, because of being well-known for his self-inflicted domestic calamities, also being blamed for those not of his making, he had more ribbing than most. The trick being to play along, then it soon defused.

"Just one last question, Terry....if I may?" insisted Steve with a coy expression.

"Oh, aye," said the Number-5 lock, steam pressure building again.

"Tell me, is it true there are no women in Newcastle, and that's why everyone is called 'man', and that Geordie couples don't have children, they have some sort of alien beings called 'burns'."

"Ya cheeky bastard," exclaimed Terry, his quick temper back to boiling point.

"Take it easy, big man," advised Martin. "The veterans are just trying to wind you up. They don't mean any harm." He turned to face Roger and his pals, with raised eyebrows. "They love you really."

Effeminate gestures and Geordies didn't mix.

"What?" cried out the man mountain.

Catching on to the charade, Gordon put on a poofy Alan Carr or Graham Norton-type voice, and with a limp wrist extended said, "It's true, Terry, all us veterans fantasise about you."

"Ooohh, that's right, Terry," Steve added, fluttering his eyebrows.

Again, an outburst of manic vitriol erupted from the giant Geordie, club captain Gayle restraining Nicholson's advancing huge hands, from wrapping themselves around Steve's neck.

"Terry, it's okay," declared Martin. "They don't mean anything, they're still trying to goad you."

"Well, if they're not careful, I'll take 'em ootside, and fettle the lot of 'em."

"Don't worry, Terry," Martin said. He smiled wickedly. "If it gets too bad, I'll help you....what do you call it?"

"Fettle 'em," confirmed Terry, thrusting his weight forward, like a demented rogue elephant.

"Got a lovely tone of phrase, hasn't he?" mocked Steve.

News of the disastrous ending to the Fraser garden party had spread around the vicinity, like wildfire. Additional to Evan McKinley, many more at the rugby club had seen the offending YouTube video, Roger constantly bombarded with surreptitious remarks, questioning his ability to organise a piss up in a brewery. Martin wanted to know the gory details. Egged on by Steve and Gordon, Roger outlined events which led to the tipping point, including the fabled Chopper Read account, started by his cousin Peter.

"Do you know there's a U.S television series called *American Chopper*?" Martin asked.

"You're joking," Roger said.

"No, seriously," returned Martin.

Taking a glance at Steve and Gordon before continuing, Roger said, "I'd hate to think what that's all about."

"Probably a phallus erectus competition," suggested Steve.

They all began to snort and cackle louder, Gordon observing, "Can you imagine all those septics, comparing member size?"

With the stag night really getting into full swing, the first 15 assembled in the centre of the clubhouse for singing duty, including Christian Bowcott, still with a massive smile on his face, resultant from his tawdry encounter with the lovely Mademoiselle Solange Desmarais. They gave the audience a rendition of 'row, row, row your boat, gently down the stream, belts off, trousers down, isn't life a scream, oohhh'. Further traditional rugby club songs followed, accompanied with lewd enactments of *Do Your Balls Hang Low? Farmer's Daughter, Ivan Scavinsky Scavar, Dinah, Dinah Show Us your Leg* and *If I Were the Marrying Kind*, the latter, especially for Christian. During the gaiety, the participants approached their objective to drink the clubhouse dry, but with a lot of beer ending down shirt fronts, instead of passing into thirsty mouths.

After the raucous sing-song, Christian attempted to sink a yard of ale. Definitely looking worse for wear, his grasp on the glass container failed him, its contents mainly spilling into his left ear and jacket pocket, not that he was remotely aware that most of the beer had not connected with his mouth.

Putting his arm around the bridegroom-in-waiting's shoulder, John Hillenbrand said, "Hey, Christian, you really liked Solange, didn't you?"

Slithering to his feet from a semi-seated floor position, like he was under the control of a snake charmer, Christian attempted to achieve the perpendicular. Still in rowing mode from the songs, but didn't realise it, he nearly elbowed the Revelator in the nose, with his in-out action.

"John, John the Revelator," he said, as his eyes rolled upwards, "I really want to thank you. She, she....she's wonderful...." The sentence trailed away, as he slightly regurgitated beer with a hiccup.

"You really liked her, then?" asked John.

"If it wasn't for....for....what's her name?"

"Andrea."

"That's right, Andrea....my lovely bride to be." Christian hiccupped again. "I would have really gone for Solange."

"Is that right, then?"

"Oh....oh, yes."

"Christian....Mademoiselle Desmarais wasn't a woman."

"Wasn't a woman....what do you mean?"

"It was a man in drag, Christian, a man."

"Yeah....he was gorgeous."

Christian had really gone, John the Revelator joshing with

him but the bridegroom-to-be, was so far zonked and zapped, he would have bought into anything in his perished state.

After more bridegroom ribbing, various renditions of the club chant, and a lot more beer, Roger noticed Evan McGinley appeared to be in a disgruntled state. Evan punched the palm of his hand, like Robin does in the spoof Batman TV series, and appeared to be talking to himself. He seemed to be extremely annoyed, with someone or something.

"Hey, Evan, my main man," Roger said, laying his arm around the Scot's huge right shoulder, "what's up?"

"Huh, oh, Roger," the big forward half-snarled, "I've just had a set to with Devonport."

A good loosehead prop, Felix Devonport was also the ultimate wind-up merchant, one of the younger set, but his weather-beaten appearance made him seem older than his years. He liked to joust with the more senior players, just to bait them. He couldn't resist ceasing on some poor unfortunate's personal characteristics, or a tricky situation they found themselves in, maliciously exploiting it, to feed his own brand of tacit humour. He didn't do it in a jocular way, like say Steve Hunt. Consequently, few at the club gravitated towards him, for real friendship.

He'd already had a go at Fraser, having seen the garden party video on YouTube. Roger had managed to fend him off, by suggesting he had influence with the first team selection committee, partially true if not slightly stretching the claim, and told Felix that if he continued to incur his displeasure, he might find himself playing for the juniors, the ultimate indignation for a first-team squad player.

Of course, it was all done in the best possible taste, the semi-veiled threat tempered by subtlety, but Devonport got the message, backed off, and turned his venom on a fresh victim. Steve said that Roger should have eased the cheeky sod, but though well-built, Devonport had at least two stone on Roger, was 22 years younger, and very fit. Roger told Steve that discretion was the better part of valour. Besides, Roger didn't want to get back home blooded, and suffer an even more intense beating, mainly from Charlotte's tongue. But the bottom-line reason not to engage Devonport in a fistfight, came back to the earlier assertion. Ribbing was part and parcel of rugby club life. Turning on a fellow club mate or easing him to use Steve's vernacular, whether that person was liked or not, was viewed to be unacceptable, and possibly punishable by ex-communication from the club, which for some was worse than secession of bedroom rights.

"What's Devonport said this time?" asked Roger.

"He impugned the Scottish nation," Evan moaned, "cast doubt on our ability to perform at the 2011 Rugby World Cup. Said we'll get the wooden spoon, and we won't even beat Romania."

In rugby circles, that was a serious insult.

"Ah, I see," sympathised Roger.

"If he's not careful," Evan warned, "I'm going to give that mealy-mouthed Sassenach a Glasgow kiss."

"Don't rise to the bite, Evan," advised Roger, "remember our code, death before dishonour."

"He's taking it too far, Roger," Evan complained, "Devonport is not worthy of the code."

"You've never liked Felix anyway," observed Roger. "Why is that?"

"I don't like his face."

Recoiling back, astounded by the remark, Roger said, "Well, there's not an awful lot he can do about that."

"I can," resolved Evan.

The evening finished in the traditional way. Christian was de-bagged. In fact, he lost all his clothes, apart from his socks and shoes. His balls were blacked, and he was chained to a lamppost outside his bride-to-be's house, with an L-plate strapped around his chest. He got off quite lightly, compared to others in recent times. The rugby club members put one poor devil stitch-less on the Eurostar, who came to his senses in le gay Paris. A second found himself a willing passenger, in a 40-tonner bound for Inverness, replete with minimal clothing, and thinking he was going home to his mum. Things got a whole lot worse for that bridegroom, when the driver discovered he was sat on his Yorkie.

In Christian's drunken stupor, he actually thought he was standing at his intended's front door. As his comrades left him to his fate, he could be seen staring up at the streetlight, and was heard to say, hiccupping, "I know you're in….the light is on."

With all the stag night participants feeling worse for wear, a fleet of taxis were summoned, to take wanton warriors to their homes, loved ones, and a fish supper.

***

"Woman of the house," Roger shouted.

No response. He had managed to get the key in the front door lock, and let himself in. Am I in the right house, he thought. He took a cursory look around the hallway. He could see Miss Piggy and Kermit the Frog, their heads facing a corner, with dunce hats on their heads. They must have had a catastrophic round on 'The Weakest Link', Heather banishing them from her bedroom.

"Woman of the house," he said again, in a raised voice, losing slight control of his vocal chords, in an attempt to be heard.

The hallway was dark and he couldn't seem to find the light switch. Then he saw light, beginning to emanate from the lounge, as the silhouette of his lovely wife emerged.

"Hello, wonder woman," he extolled, smiling graciously, head bobbing up and down, resting his weight on his extended right arm, precariously holding the stairwell banister.

She had her arms folded. A bad sign, in fact a warning sign, verging on danger.

"Wonder woman," she repeated back to her husband. Her

foot tapped the polished oak wood floor, and her hand started to go for something behind her back, which Roger thought might be his shotgun.

"Yes...." he pleaded, "it's a compliment, darling."

Then the landing light went on.

"Daddy's home," said Heather, as she came racing down the stairs, and leapt into his arms.

"Hello, sweetheart," he said.

Heather pulled a critical face. "Daddy, you need some mouthwash."

"Enough to drown in," he was sure he heard his wife mutter.

"It got a bit out of control, Charlotte," he confessed.

"Oh, did it?" Charlotte said, coming a bit closer to inspect him. "What's that on your neck?"

"What's what on my neck?"

Making an examination, Heather remarked, "Daddy's got lipstick on his neck."

For a moment, Roger Fraser was nonplussed, then his memory kicked into recall.

"Ahh....I can explain that," he said, whilst suddenly realising his mouth felt very dry. "You see, when Mademoiselle Solange Desmarais had finished her act, she gave Christian....that's the guy who's getting manacled, sorry, I mean getting married, a big kiss. Then later....much later, after Christian had ignored our pleas to stop drinking, he got very friendly with me, thanked me for helping him develop into the rugby player he is today, and tried to kiss me." He stopped, noticing Charlotte appeared to be unconvinced. "Or was it Evan....no, he got me on the forehead, and wasn't wearing lipstick. No, it was Christian....but, but, but I managed to avoid his advance, and his kiss got planted on my neck."

Smiling at the end of the explanation, pleased with his near perfect recollection of events, he awaited his wife's response. That was a big mistake. Charlotte's foot tapping had increased, and she'd entered the red zone. Heather noticed as well.

"Is Daddy in trouble again, Mummy?"

"Oh, yes…Daddy's in very hot water, which is still coming to the boil."

Not thinking about the consequences, he let out a slight snigger, another big mistake.

"It's the spare room for you tonight, Roger," Charlotte told him, "and bread and water rations for the next week."

"Mummy, I've got a better idea. Put me down, Daddy."

He released their youngest. She ran over to her mother, and whispered something in her ear. *Et tu*, Heather, thought Roger, *et tu*. A few moments later, he found a dunce's hat had been placed on his head, and he was sat in the corner of the hallway, with Miss Piggy and Kermit the Frog, face to the wall doing penance.

"Goodnight, party boy," crooned his wife, with obvious glee.

"Goodnight, wonder woman," he said, looking to the top of the landing stairs, as the light went out. "Cruel bitch," he then uttered under his breath.

"What did you say, Roger?" she shouted down.

"Er….nothing, darling."

CHAPTER 13: GUATEMALA

Roger licked his wounds from the pasting he got, after returning home from the stag night more than slightly inebriated. Contrite and apologetic when he sobered up, it didn't prevent him from becoming the victim of forced labour. 'Penance will be good for your soul', Charlotte informed him. The following weekend, he wore a hair shirt, became confined to the spare room, and lived on prisoner rations. By the Sunday evening, after cleaning every square inch of the kitchen, and exterminating a forest of persistent back-garden weeds, she took his yoke off and allowed him some meagre comforts, in preparation for the working week ahead.

The same daily challenges faced Fraser on Monday morning; battle breakfast, the tiresome train journey and dealing with tedious traders. Then he got a call from Toby Chalcroft, the Equities Director, asking him to come to his office.

Dutifully he stomped off to the executive floor, wondering what TC had in store for him.

"Come in, Roger," Top Cat instructed, before Roger could even knock the door.

"Morning, Toby."

"Enjoy Bembridge's party, did you?"

"As a matter of fact, yes, Charlotte and I had a wonderful time."

"Good."

He expected Top Cat to get to the point after the pleasantries, but the exec went quiet, so Roger took the initiative. "Was it something in particular, Toby?"

He glanced up from his desk, but said nothing.

Toby Chalcroft was a chameleon-like creature, in the sense that his ultra-sensitive antennae could pick up subtle changes and nuances, resulting in him changing, according to what he perceived to be the best option for him. Whereas most people would be oblivious to what was staring them in the face, TC only seemed to need the briefest glimpse, to determine what was going on, and how to manage a situation to accomplish the optimum outcome.

He had what Roger called doll's eyes. Whether he was happy or sad, they never seemed to express the slightest emotion. Top Cat's body language rarely betrayed any reaction, but he was always ahead in the game, when it came to the understanding and subtleties required, to become successful in the maelstrom and volatility of investment banking. Though fast approaching rugby-ball shape, where once a slender frame stood, and his brushed-back dark hair was thinning on his forehead, Chalcroft had an uncanny knack to apparently change his physical state, particularly his voice tone, according to what he wanted to accomplish, the ploy amplifying the chameleon-like impression. Sometimes, he could appear to be larger than his actual physical dimensions, when evangelising about some strategy crusade or leading a corporate new business campaign. On other occasions, he could just as easily shrink into the background, when he wanted to avoid heat.

Top Cat could be friend or foe, ally or enemy, confidant or disciplinarian, all in the space of the same conversation. The mask he wore, fully interchangeable from a suite of options he had developed, during 30 years in the business. His victims, adversaries and colleagues never quite knew what camouflage he might be wearing, or what masquerade was really in play, behind the expressionless facade.

Fraser prompted him again. "Toby."

"Sorry, Roger, I was just mulling over the best way to address you, on a thorny situation which has only come to my attention, overnight."

"Oh, yes."

"You remember that mining investment in Guatemala, from 2008?"

"I should do. I constructed and helped barter the deal."
"Right."
"Has something happened?"
"You could say that, Roger, you could well say that."
"What?"
"We received an email, sent overnight from Guatemala City. The agent representing our interests in the Villa Nueva mining project has been shot."
"Dead?"
"Probably better if he was….but no, just a flesh wound in the leg. He's in hospital and the miners have come out on strike."
"But why?"
"Apparently, he was shot accidentally, by a Mexican surface worker. The Mexicans are not liked by the Guatemalans, because they are taking their jobs. So with the agent being shot, the Guatemalan miners have decided to make a stand."
"I see. So presumably our investors are getting very nervous."
"The stock is falling, like a stone. Our principals have demanded that we intervene. What makes it worse is that additional to the original cobalt and nickel deposits, silver has recently been discovered in one of the new workings, so the investors are losing out on the new potential, hand over fist. Before you came in, I checked the precious metals markets. Cobalt and nickel buy prices are rising, because word has gone round that Villa Nueva are in trouble. Further, the Hong Kong stock market closed, with silver at 40.75 Hong Kong Dollars per ounce and rising. So you see, it's bad all round."
"What's the firm going to do?"
TC got up from his executive-style chair, walked to his twentieth-storey office window overlooking Canary Wharf, then turned to face Roger. "You're going to Guatemala City, Roger, to sort it out."
"What?"
Chalcroft sat down at his desk, earnestly eyeing the stock

analyst. "I've talked to Bembridge, and we both agree that you have the necessary experience and tact, to sort this debacle out."

"But Toby, I'm an analyst, not a trouble-shooter," Fraser protested. "Surely one of the traders would be more appropriate." He paused, collecting thoughts. "What about Ricky Henshaw? This is his neck of the woods, isn't it?"

"Ricky is otherwise engaged. Besides, Bembridge liked the way you sorted out that mess in Lagos, and that even bigger mess in Ukraine."

"Yes, but those were commodities and equity securities issues….not open gang warfare in the pueblo."

Adopting a headmaster-like authoritarian stance, Top Cat said, "Nonetheless, Bembridge and I both think you have the necessary gravitas and interpersonal skills, to sort out this Guatemala issue. We have a lot of faith in you."

"Do I have a choice?"

"Let's just say, it would be a huge feather in your cap, if you were to succeed on this one."

Beginning to appreciate Jim Phelps predicament, when he accepted an assignment for his *Mission Impossible* team, Roger felt resigned to agree the task. Wincing at Top Cat, he said, "I guess I'd better tell Charlotte to pack an overnight bag."

"Good, you're booked on the 06:15 BA flight to Miami tomorrow. You will then take a UA flight from Miami to Guatemala City."

What's he going to say next, Roger thought to himself. 'Should you or any of your IM force be caught or captured, Luther Bembridge and I will disavow any of your actions on behalf of the firm'?

"Oh, and by the way," added Chalcroft, "Hoskyns is going with you."

"Hoskyns," exclaimed Fraser.

"Yes, you're going to need a contracts officer to support you with legal matters, and he is familiar with Central American business law."

Though an accomplished contracts expert, Walter Hoskyns,

the firm's commercial manager, had a reputation for dithering and being a wuss. Roger hadn't experienced many dealings with him, but he did know him to be quite a nervous fellow. Walter had a pointed nose, and always reminded Roger of Muskie the Muskrat, from the *Deputy Dawg* show. Hoskyns twitched, like his face had whiskers in place of a moustache, hence the approximation to the furry cartoon character.

"Are you sure Hoskyns is cut out for this?" Roger queried. "I mean, he's quite a jumpy chap, still takes Valium, doesn't he?"

"Quite, and we'll make sure he is well dosed up, before he climbs aboard that Miami-bound flight with you."

* * *

"Hello, Roger, had a good day at the office?" enquired Charlotte.

His nearest and dearest was preparing dinner, Italian by the smell of it, and the kids were bunched around the TV in the lounge, watching *Eggheads*, trying to second-guess the answers to Dermot Murnaghan's questions.

"Something unexpected came up," he replied.

"Don't tell me, someone's been caught watching internet porn, when they should have been making trades."

"No."

"Then it must be that one of those odious Essex boys has bankrupted the firm, with crippling debt."

"If only."

"Dinner won't be long. Why don't you join the kids and relax?"

Suddenly, he found himself standing right behind Charlotte, as she stirred the Bolognese sauce into the meat and vegetables, simmering nicely on the stove.

"Charlotte, I have something to tell you."

"What is it, my darling?"

She must be in a really good mood, Roger thought to

himself. She only called him my darling, when he had carried out all expressed wishes to her complete satisfaction, or when she had spent half his monthly salary on a Stella McCartney creation.

"I'm going to Guatemala tomorrow on business."

"Guatemala. That's in Central America, isn't it?"

"Yes, come and sit down at the kitchen table for a minute."

Relaying his mission to Charlotte, he left out no details.

"Oh, Roger, that all sounds dangerous….I mean, it's Central America; shootings, drug cartels, anacondas," she paused, "loose women."

"Charlotte, it's all very civilised, there are no shootings in commerce….well, apart from our agent, and that was unintentional, just an accident….I won't be in the jungle, so close encounters with giant snakes is unlikely."

"What about the loose women?"

"There'll be no time for that….not that I have any intentions in that direction," he assured her.

* * *

At four o'clock the next morning, a taxi whisked Fraser off to Heathrow Terminal 5. After check-in, he wandered round the BA lounge, looking for Hoskyns, finally finding him curled up on a sofa, looking really spaced out, obviously dosed up to the gills with Valium.

Beaming a generous smile at him, Roger cheerfully said, "Good morning, Walter."

Hearing Roger, his eyes rotated, revealing the look of dread, even impending doom. Roger thought there's no need to be sullen at the prospect of going to Guatemala. What will be, will be, had always been one of his maxims, best to assume a positive approach to the challenge ahead.

Starting to stir from his semi-anaesthetised state, Hoskyns said almost dreamily, "Oh, hello Roger."

"All set for the Villa Nueva caper?" asked Roger.

"Yeessss." Looking up, his head bounced about rhythmically, like one of those nodding dogs, placed on a car parcel shelf. Then he very slowly added, "I'm….really….looking….forward….to….it."

Waving his hands in front of the commercial manager's face, Roger noticed his eyes were glazed over, movement hardly registering. As well as being intrinsically nervous, Hoskyns hated flying. He believed the theory of flight to be an illusion, and that he would perish at the hands of a kamikaze aircrew. Hence the industrial-strength dose of the haze-inducing depressant, he took at Chalcroft's insistence.

Deciding to leave Hoskyns in his near to trance-like state, Roger started reading the morning papers, whilst they waited for the Miami flight to be called. Then the stock analyst saw what looked like at least 20 walking, talking man-mountains enter the lounge, and deposit themselves in the comfy chair area, next to the zonked commercial manager and him.

Judging by the mumbled conversations in the group, Roger concluded they were an American college football team. He noticed one guy, with the same hairstyle as *Predator* from the 1987 film of the same name and just as ugly, had a speech impediment causing him considerable trouble forming words. Further physical inspection revealed that with his upturned bog-brush hairstyle, he'd look great doing the haka with the All Blacks. What a character, Roger thought to himself, deciding to christen him 'Chummy'. Roger couldn't help feel a little sympathy for his predicament, acknowledging that without clear and articulate speech, his own job would be impossible. He watched him struggle to participate in conversations about gridiron football, sacking quarterbacks, and offence and defence tactics. Then someone accidentally spilled a full glass of orange juice into Chummy's lap. The conversations came to an abrupt halt, everyone staring at the orange juice, soaking its way through his custom-made Nike tracksuit bottoms.

Appearing to be extremely startled, the speech-affected player sucked in air. A swift decrease in temperature around his nether regions raised his hackles, ice still melting and turning to steam, as he inspected his ruined garb.

Glaring at the offending orange juice spiller, he then tried for control over his voice. Roger could see him struggling again, but Chummy's efforts eventually reached critical mass, and out came, 'Mmmmmmmmm….mmm….mo, moth, moth…. mother, motherfucker!"

The angry retort boomed around the lounge, everybody suddenly looking in the direction of the sound source, including the semi-conscious Hoskyns. Then they heard the click-click of a BA lounge attendant's high heels making their way in the American's direction. Fraser caught sight of her advancing on the 'offensive' football player and she was fuming.

Stopping short of the foul language creating culprit, the attendant forcefully said, "Sir, you can't use words like that in the BA lounge."

Seeming to partially recover full control of his vocal chords, Chummy retorted, "But this chintzy motherfucker spilled ice-cold orange juice on me."

"Sir," she cried, even more forcibly, "you can't use language like that in the BA lounge."

Two hefty BA security guards arrived on the scene, to support their female colleague.

With Chummy still bleating, Roger's initial sympathy for his communication deficiency waned. He wouldn't stop what his fellow ball-players called 'un-American blaspheming'. Managing to haul his ass out of his seat, the BA staff escorted him away, still blaspheming, still dripping wet and still steaming. He struggled during transit reminding the stock analyst of scenes from *Alien vs. Predator*. All the BA security guards needed were venomous scorpion-like tails and two sets of teeth, for the open-mouthed lounge passengers to witness a great early morning re-enactment of the movie.

* * *

They were about halfway across the pond, nicely chilling out in business class, when Hoskyns began to come out of his Valium cloud.

"Roger."

Busy banging his laptop keyboard, in preparation for Guatemala, Fraser replied, "Yes, Walter."

"Roger....I don't think I can go ahead with this visit."

Still consumed by his chosen task, Fraser glanced at him momentarily. "What....what do you mean?"

"I've never done this kind of thing before," Walter admitted with a dire expression, "I don't know why I agreed to do it."

"Probably because Top Cat said it would be in your best interests," nonchalantly replied Fraser.

"How could you possibly know that?" Walter wondered.

"Just a wild guess....anyway, what can't you do?"

Hoskyns gave him one of those confessional looks, more associated with misbehaving choirboys. "I don't actually know too much about Central American business law, Guatemalan in particular."

With a glare of consternation, Fraser abruptly stopped keystroke action, and faced in the commercial manager's direction. "So how come you were selected for this shindig?"

"Somehow, Bembridge got it into his mind that I had experience of Central American business contracting, when in actual fact, Alistair Uttley is the expert."

"You met with The Ayatollah?"

"Yes."

"Why didn't you tell him, that you were the wrong man?"

Walter grappled around, trying to find the right words to express his dismay. "You know what he's like. Once he has his course set, he's unshakeable....and he kept on looking at me with those eyes. You know....that icy stare which says, 'Don't cross me, or else you'll never work in investment banking again'."

Assuming a questioning countenance, Roger asked, "So exactly how much do you know about Guatemalan business law and practices?"

"Only what I picked up yesterday, reading the Villa Nueva contract and its terms of reference."

Sinking back into his seat, Roger said in a resigned voice, "One hell of a time to tell me, Walter, one hell of a time. Here we are, halfway to Miami, and you drop this bombshell."

Hoskyns became remorseful, looking at Fraser, all tense and fidgety. "What are we going to do, Roger?" he asked, his voice breaking, as if he hung over a precipice.

"For you, just make out like Harry Pearce."

"What? How do you mean?"

"Be cool, like the *Spooks* head of counter-terrorism. Let me think about what we are going to do."

Roger knew that turning around at Miami, and heading back to Blighty was not an option. The firm's hanging committee would be waiting for them at Heathrow, ready to administer swift justice, in the form of a torturous execution. There was only one thing to do. Bail out of the 787, then claim asylum with the U.S Federal Reserve. No, he couldn't do that either, no parachutes. Only one thing for it, they would have to wing it.

"Okay, Walter, here's what we are going to do," instructed Fraser. "You're going to bury your nose in that contract and learn it verbatim. No sleep, minimum rations. I'm going to construct an engagement plan, which steers us away from Guatemalan law, so we can conduct negotiations in international law." He paused, leaning towards the brittle-looking commercial manager."You do know international business law, don't you, Walter?"

"Yes, yes I do, Roger."

"Right, let's go to work."

They arrived at Miami International, 09:45 Eastern Standard Time, went through the transit procedure, and then climbed aboard a United Airlines flight, bound for Guatemala City.

They watched the senior flight attendant, going through the normal do's and don'ts routine, addressing the passengers through the plane's intercom system.

He finished with, "United Airlines wish you a pleasant flight," then turned to another male flight attendant and said, "Boy, I sure could do with a blowjob and a cup of coffee."

Unfortunately, he had left the intercom on. The whole passenger deck heard his plea. Walter and Roger were in the back row of business class. As Roger looked back into tourist class, he saw a stewardess, thundering along the cabin like a demented wildebeest, waving her hand forward furiously, trying to attract the senior flight attendant, before he blundered into another obscenity.

As she passed, Roger heard a guy in the next seat row to them say, "Hey, hon."

She stopped.

"Don't forget the coffee?"

* * *

Two hours and 35 minutes later, they touched down at La Aurora airport. After going through the usual torturous fiasco at passport control and customs, Roger and Walter jumped in a cab, its lack of adequate air conditioning, giving the pair their first taste of the sauna-like weather conditions in Central America. Arriving at the Real Guatemala Hotel, the intrepid expeditionaries were immediately struck by the colonial- like ambience in the lobby. Europeans were making final preparations for year-long treks into the Guatemalan jungle in search of Pre-Colombian civilisation traces, and dandy dudes dressed in safari suits and wielding fly squatters sat at the bar, drinking pink gins and munching on melon and prosciutto skewers. Fraser and Hoskyns felt like they should be wearing pith helmets and gators, rather than Giorgio Armani suits and

Bruno Magli shoes.

The local time was four p.m., ten p.m. back in Blighty. As soon as Roger got to his room, he called Charlotte, as promised the previous evening. Exchanging a few words, he assured her that an anaconda had not consumed him yet, and little gunfire was to be heard in the streets. He also advised, that in the furnace of extremely close atmospheric conditions, it was nearly 80 degrees Fahrenheit, with a relative humidity of 90 per cent.

After a wash and brush-up, Walter and Roger were back in powwow mode. They sat in the hotel restaurant, consuming traditional Maya cuisine, washed down with Ron Zacapa, whilst finalising their engagement strategy. Outside, a carnival atmosphere raged as the locals celebrated a Christian festival, replete with Carman Miranda impersonators, firecrackers and calypso music.

Several local ladies gave them the glad eye from the bar. It was like meat market central. A pimp dressed in a Kid Creole outfit hanging at the back, instructed his stable of pulsating pulchritude, to 'Put some pizzazz into it' and to 'Shake those butts'. Flashing their pearly gates, the sirens wriggled on their stools. Some were hounds, but others were the epitome of Central American allure. One wore a skirt so short, that she belted it around her neck. Further down the parade, a more elegant breed of femininity came into view. These weren't hookers, just Guatemala's finest, window-shopping for prospective husbands, preferably rich prospective husbands.

Out of pure courtesy, Roger returned one or two smiles, but that's as far as it went. Though some of the ladies were very tempting, he had quit wolfing around, after meeting Charlotte. If he strayed, she wouldn't divorce him, she'd put a bounty out on him, wanted dead or alive, preferably the former.

As the strains of the Latin pop died away, relative peace and tranquillity returning to the restaurant, the Englishmen turned their attention to matters in hand, recognising the task they faced would be challenging, and probably, infuriating.

***

Señor Ignacio Emilio Martinez Soto, or Iggy to his friends, the unfortunate agent who took the bullet, was the firm's representative, a kind of go-between, connecting the Villa Nueva mining company and associated principals with London. Early the next day, Walter had composed himself, and appeared to be Valium free. He accompanied Roger to the hospital, to visit Señor Martinez.

At his bedside, Iggy's wife, Señora de Martinez, fretted and tugged on her rosary beads, as if doing penance, for a crime she didn't commit. Probably a good-looking girl 30 years ago, traces of lost youth still remained in her huge maroon eyes, but like for most pueblo woman, the onset of middle-age had brought a rounded figure, and a moon-shaped face.

Roger vaguely remembered Iggy, from investment banking negotiations, back in 2008. Iggy had been on the Villa Nueva team in an observational role, taking little part in the final contract talks, but Roger did recall exchanging a few words with him, regarding his career background, and impressions of the mining company. Now approaching his mid-fifties, the agent was a small thin man with wavy jet-black hair, an equally wavy moustache which curled-up Salvador Dali style, and sad deep-brown eyes. In his prone state, the eyes were even sadder.

Iggy gave them the full SP on events, leading up to his unfortunate collision with lead. From his opening remarks and remorseful body language, Roger immediately detected that Martinez had a guilt complex as big as Barbados, presumably for what had happened. But Iggy had been merely an innocent bystander, used as pawn in the great chess game of employer-employee working relationships. To unblock the impasse, Roger sought cogent facts, not superfluous contrition.

"Always, we had an uneasy relationship, between the Guatemalan miners and the Mexican surface workers," advised Iggy. "The miners want all Villa Nueva jobs to go to Guatemalan workers, but the Mexican migrants will work for less, so the company management uses them where they can."

"Yes, we were aware of the potential labour disputes, back in 2008," Roger confirmed. "But we were given to understand that the argument was merely posturing."

"It was…." replied Iggy, "and perhaps this situation happened spontaneously, rather than through deliberate action. Either way, a few days ago, the miners and the surface workers were in the company cantina. Nearly always, they all go there for a beer after a shift. The two sides stay apart by keeping to different areas. The Mexicans were celebrating someone's birthday, so they were very excited. I was in the cantina with the works manager, Señor Salazar."

"Enrique Salazar?" Roger asked.

"Yes," confirmed Iggy.

"I remember him from the London negotiations," Roger verified. "How is he? Was he affected by the shooting?"

"He's well," advised Iggy, "but disturbed at what happened. Anyway, Salazar and I were discussing production schedules and yield rates. You know, the kind of data, I usually report back independently to the firm. The Mexicans were getting really loud. Then one of the Guatemalan miners asked them to lower the noise. They didn't, so a skirmish, that is the right word?"

"Yes," Fraser confirmed.

"A skirmish breaks out," continued Iggy. "Señor Salazar stops the fighting, and asks the Mexicans to conclude their party, as quickly as possible. The Mexican who is leading the merriment said a few further words to his compañeros, then they all whistle and shout, one of them firing a gun upwards in celebration, a traditional form of letting off steam, in this part of the world." He trailed off, as if recounting the incident was too horrendous, for him to continue.

"I see….please go on," Roger encouraged.

"I am standing just a few feet behind Salazar. The bullet ricochets off a metal pipe, going across the ceiling, narrowly misses him, and ends up in my leg. I am taken to hospital, and a few hours later, Salazar visits to say the miners are out on strike, because a fellow Guatemalan....me, has been shot by the Mexicans."

"I see," empathised Roger, "so what happened next?"

"That's when I got Señora de Martinez to email the firm, for the attention of Mister Toby Chalcroft."

"Right," Roger acknowledged.

"Señor Fraser," advised Iggy, "there is more."

"Go on," Roger replied.

"The miners have got their union involved, and the Ministry of Labour and Social Welfare. The union is insisting that the Mexicans are dismissed, but the ministry say that is not possible."

"Why is that?" asked Fraser.

"Something to do with American international employment laws. The terms of aid made by the U.S to the Guatemalan Government prohibit such action."

"I see," Fraser said, looking at Walter, who nodded a confirming agreement to Iggy's supposition.

"Also," advised Iggy, "the Villa Nueva management insist the Mexicans are necessary, for the raw metals to be competitively priced, on the worldwide precious metals markets."

As Fraser understood it, there appeared to be little scope for negotiation, to get the miners back to work, allowing the Villa Nueva stock price to recover, and thereby relieve corporate investor pressure on the firm. It didn't look good. He began to feel that he was flying by the seat of his pants, a familiar sensation that usually preceded domestic disasters. But he had to remain focused on the strike issue, and optimistic that a solution could be found. Above all, he couldn't let Walter know his feelings. The commercial manager might relapse into nervous frenzy, throw a wobbler, and be no use whatsoever.

"Who should we talk to," Fraser asked, "in the miners union and the ministry?"

"Manolito Rodrigo Ortega Rios is the union boss," answered

Iggy. "Ruben Zacarius Hernandez Perez is the man at the ministry. Hernandez is the liaison manager for the mining union."

"Okay," Roger said, "I have those names written down. Am I right in thinking that Leo Dias is the best man to talk to at Villa Nueva?"

"Leoncio Jacobo Dias Ruiz?" clarified Iggy.

"Yes," Roger confirmed, "I think he would be a good starting point."

Leoncio, known as Leo, was the man he worked with, to qualify the earnings potential for the Villa Nueva investment portfolio. Although they had not spoken for some time, the stock analyst had a pretty good relationship with him. He figured, if anyone can identify potential negotiating points to get all sides in the dispute satisfied, and the mine churning out precious metals again, its Leo Dias.

As they reached the end of their talk, Roger noticed Señora de Martinez had added a bowing action to her rosary stranglehold.

Thinking she was concerned for her ailing husband, he said, "It's alright, Señora Martinez, your husband will be back home with you very soon."

"It's not that, Señor Fraser, she assured. "This weekend, I have a tenpin bowling tournament, and I need Ignacio to look after the children."

That's a good one, Fraser thought to himself, imagining Charlotte using that one on him. It made him smile.

Clearly embarrassed by his wife's sporting declaration, Iggy rebuked her in Spanish. Equally discomforted by the dressing down in front of strangers, his wife vehemently countered the reprimand, setting off a minor set to - in Spanish.

It seemed to Roger that no matter where you were in the world, some things remained constant, domestic conflict amongst them.

* * *

Walter and Roger were in Leo Dias's office at Villa Nueva, engaged in exploring strike resolution possibilities. He had gone off to find contract papers, relating to the investment portfolio.

"How you feeling now, Walter?"

"Really good….I haven't had a Valium since Miami, and I'm finding this situation very stimulating now. I have a good grasp on Guatemalan business law, resultant from going over the contract with a fine toothcomb." He stopped, as if expecting Fraser to give him a medal for his efforts, like Muttley received in *Wacky Races*.

"What's your understanding?" asked Roger.

"Well, the terms appendix is the key. It's really a sub-set of generic Central American company and business laws and practices. These are also included as a reference point in the contract documents."

"I see, so what have you concluded?"

With an apparent new air of confidence, he fixed Roger full-on with a self-assured stare. "Now I've studied them, I find they are abstractions from New York and Spanish business law; both of which I know."

"So you're cool about it."

"Oh yes, I feel certain that from a company law and business practice viewpoint, I know where our liabilities and risks are in this dispute. All I need from you, Roger, is to get all the principals around the table. We can outline those parts of the contract contravened as a result of the strike, and thereby who is liable for liquidated and ascertained damages….and probably open-ended consequential damages, in a court of law."

Considering for a moment, Fraser was not inclined to go down the litigation path, sensing it would be fraught with danger, and maybe open up a further nest of vipers. "I would prefer we leave the litigation, as an absolute last course of action. Remember, any trial would be held in a Guatemalan court of law, not London. The outcome would not be as clear cut, as you might think. Local politics would bring pressure to bear, making sure the outcome went against the firm." He paused, his expression emanating a cautionary approach. "No, my preference is to barter a deal between the affected parties, with the firm and thereby our investors seen as affected non-combatants in the dispute."

"Well, that's why you're here, according to TC."

"What else did he tell you?"

"He agreed with Bembridge that a business negotiator was needed. Then something to the effect that you had a good track record, dealing with delicate situations, resolving them to the firm's satisfaction."

"Hhmmm, I think that's what is known as a back-handed compliment."

Leo came back to his office, carrying a thick wad of papers. "Sorry to keep you. I had to gather up some supplementary documents, relating to Guatemalan employment laws."

Leo was as Roger remembered him, tall and thin with a gaunt face, a mane of silver hair, and trademark Frank Zappa-like goatee beard with an imperial and moustache. Extremely likeable, Leo had an open attitude to problem solving, accompanied by astute business sense, and a keen eye for detail. That's why he had gone to the trouble of unearthing the supplementary contract papers, Fraser thought to himself.

"Let me attempt to précis what Guatemalan laws say," he began, "about the employment of foreign nationals, and their rights in an industrial dispute." He glanced up from the documents, as if seeking approval.

"Fine," agreed Roger, "lets hear what the book has to say on the matter."

"Well, in essence, to comply with the terms of U.S development aid given to the Guatemalan Government, the Mexicans' employment rights have to be observed. U.S employment law is subsumed in part, into Villa Nueva employment contracts, because the Guatemalan Government still has a stake in the company."

Roger turned his attention to Walter. The commercial manager nodded his agreement to the interpretation.

"What it boils down to, to use your English phrase" Leo continued, "is that we cannot sack the Mexican surface workers, just because the Guatemalan miners are on strike." Collecting more thoughts, he shot a grimace at the contract papers on his desk, thinking how best to deal with the firm's representatives. "We've been expecting a dispute between the two groups for some time. The shooting of the agent, er...."

He stopped, looking at Roger questioningly, expecting him to fill in the blanks.

"Ignacio Martinez," offered Roger.

"Yes, Ignacio Martinez," Leo agreed, "provided the tipping point, the excuse for an industrial dispute."

"Can the Mexicans be redeployed elsewhere?" the stock analyst enquired.

"Not within Villa Nueva," advised Leo, "the miners want them out of the company. Of course, in the normal run of such disputes, the miners would eventually concede in return for more pay, but that could take weeks."

"We haven't got weeks, Leo," Fraser warned, "we haven't even got days. With every hour that passes, the Villa Nueva stock value falls and our investors lose money."

"Yes, I know," replied Leo, in a very matter-of-fact manner.

Under the circumstances, it seemed odd, Fraser thinking that Dias should be fraught with apprehension, instead of measured and calm with his responses.

"You don't seem all that concerned," Roger suggested, squinting at him to indicate surprise. "It's the future of the Villa Nueva mining company at stake, as well as our investors, and as a consequence, the firm."

"Yes," agreed Leo, "but you see, Roger," he paused, "because the Guatemalan Government still has a stake in Villa Nueva, our company losses will be covered."

"Covered by U.S aid," Walter suggested.

"Yes, indeed, Señor Hoskyns," corroborated Leo, smiling with satisfaction, in the knowledge that Villa Nueva were fireproof, with cast-iron guarantees from Uncle Sam.

"So what you are saying," Fraser clarified, "is that Villa Nueva are commercially risk-free in this dispute?"

"Yes, Roger," confirmed Leo.

After leaving Villa Nueva, Walter and Roger returned to the hotel. Calling Toby Chalcroft in London, Roger explained that new factors had come to light, resultant from the Leoncio Dias meeting, adding multi-complexities to the affair. All Top Cat could say was, 'Well, sort it, Roger, that's why we sent you'. He was reminded of a certain 'm' word, used by that American footballer, masquerading as the 'Predator' in the BA lounge, but refrained from shouting it down the phone and hung up.

"What did Chalcroft say?" Walter enquired, while he still combed the Villa Nueva contract, looking for a legal way out of the barbed quarrel.

Directing a wry smile at the commercial manager, Roger said, "Top Cat has cut us adrift, Walter. We're on our own."

"Motherfucker."

Roger had never heard him swear before. Giving his unlikely companion a sideways look of astonishment, he said, "Yes, I agree with your acidic appraisal."

Their next appointment with Ruben Hernandez, at the Ministry of Labour and Social Welfare, would turn out to be an even more eye-opening affair.

His physical features resembled those of a film extra, in a Sergio Leone spaghetti western. His deeply tanned and lined face was almost half-covered by a huge moustache, challenging the lip-warmer grown by General Sir Anthony Cecil Hogmanay Melchett in *Blackadder Goes Forth*, for the winner of the facial fluff of the century grand title. The second grand snorter they'd seen in the past few hours, it had Fraser beginning to think that eccentric moustaches were a big distinguishing feature in

Guatemala.

Leo had previously advised that Hernandez was a career civil servant, well versed in standing on a very thin fence, and not falling either side of it. It formed the impression in Roger's mind that Hernandez would make all the right noises but do nothing.

Already, Fraser was thinking about watertight, squeaky-clean exit strategies to get the firm out of the debacle, and cast-iron agreements which would have investors licking their boots in appreciation. But it seemed there was no way that the miners would return to work, so long as the Mexicans were anywhere on Villa Nueva property. Bartering a monetary-based quid pro quo agreement became a non-starter.

"Señor Fraser," began Hernandez, "please be assured the ministry is doing everything within its power to resolve the dispute, but we do have our limitations."

"Limitations, Señor Hernandez?" Fraser questioned, frowning.

"Please call me Ruben….yes, limitations. We have to work within the boundaries of the employment laws."

"I see….Ruben," confirmed Roger. "So what you are saying is that the ministry does not condone the strike, but you are restricted from doing anything about the Mexican workers. Is that correct?"

"Yes, because as you know, Guatemala receives aid from Uncle Sam. One of the aid conditions is that we comply with U.S employment laws."

"Yes, I do know about the laws now," Roger confirmed, giving the civil servant a searching look. "By the way, you said that I would also know about the U.S aid."

"Yes."

"How?" probed Roger.

Hernandez settled back in his chair, the huge moustache nearly blotting out the Sun, as its silhouette came across the window line. "Roger….I may call you Roger?"

"Yes."

"Guatemala is a small country," Hernandez began to explain. "There are few Chinese walls, as I think you English call them, erected between government departments and commerce. Your friend, Leoncio Jacobo Dias Ruiz, called me to say you were on your way to see me. I am sure you can work out the rest."

Grimacing with the feeling that Walter and himself would eternally be playing catch-up throughout the encounter, Roger said, "Yes, I can."

They batted the issue to and fro across Hernandez's desk. For each resolving suggestion Roger made, he countered with cold water, immediately extinguishing the way forward as unworkable, due to employment law restrictions. With the pointless game petering out, Hernandez gently rocked in his chair with a contented smirk. Fraser appeared calm on the outside, but inwardly fumed that the convoluted state of affairs remained solution-less.

Walter took the opportunity to go through some employment-related items in the Villa Nueva contract terms and conditions with Señor Hernandez, whilst Roger mulled over further options, but came to no firm conclusion regarding a workable settlement.

Walter and Roger left the Ministry of Labour and Social Welfare, no further forward in terms of resolving the dispute, and with the reinforced feeling that all combatants would know their intentions, well ahead of any meeting.

Next up in the drawn-out campaign was Manolito Rodrigo Ortega Rios, the miners' union boss. Very dusty, he looked like he'd been in a loft, searching for old papers, or maybe had just returned from an onsite mineworkers meeting, where dust perpetually hung in the atmosphere, coating those who passed through it. A very large gent, in fact super-large, Ortega barely fitted into the chair he occupied. When Hoskyns and Fraser made their introductions, they heard the seat straining to support his bulk, as he first leaned forward to shake hands, and then returned his full weight back into it with a thud, making the floorboards shake. He reminded Roger of Signor Ferrari, actor Sydney Greenstreet's character in *Casablanca*. Ortega also sported a lip warmer that would make Lord Kitchener jealous.

"Señor Fraser," he began, "I've been expecting you."

"Don't tell me, you got a call from Leo Dias."

"Why, yes....how did you know?"

"I've become psychic, since arriving in Guatemala City."

"What?" spouted Ortega.

"Oh, it's not important," Roger assured him. "Tell me, Señor Ortega, what is your take on this dispute?"

Reviewing the background to the strike, Ortega went on to give them every excuse under the Sun, why the union couldn't do anything to get the miners back to work. He argued that terminating the Mexican workers' employment at Villa Nueva would contradict the adopted U.S employment laws, and thereby impact Uncle Sam's aid. Maintaining that the miners were acting within the laws, and that the apparent dichotomy was merely circumstantial, he exuded the same look of insularity Fraser had seen of the faces of Dias and Hernandez.

"It's what you English call a Mexican standoff, if you'll forgive the pun," he concluded, smiling away as if already immune from any fallout.

Perhaps he is immune, thought Roger, but why?

Giving the lard mountain a forced, frowned smile, Fraser said, "Quite, but surely there have been similar labour disputes in the past, which conflict with U.S requirements. How were they resolved?"

Tilting his head to the side, a knowing expression developed on Ortega's bulbous face, causing the Lord Kitchener tribute to curl, and flutter at its extremities. "For sure, there have been instances in the past, but this is unfortunately our first experience of conflict with Mexican workers....so you see, we are in what I believe the American's call, virgin territory."

Like with the ministry man, for each avenue they pursued, Ortega had a reason why it couldn't be made a reality. It became almost like he was reading from a memorised crib sheet, containing standard responses to any motion that could possibly be tabled. As with Hernandez, and maybe even Leo Dias, Ortega didn't appear to be motivated in the least, to find a way out of the impasse.

Again, Walter took the opportunity to go through the contract term's and condition's, hoping to find a clause, which could be used as a fulcrum and negotiating point, from which all parties could become satisfied. But for every possible action suggested by the commercial manager, Ortega had a 'ah yes, but we can't do that because' counter-argument.

It increasingly occurred to Fraser that a Machiavellian-style cartel operated. All proponents; Villa Nueva, the ministry and the miners union, were seemingly interlocked and well-rehearsed to demerit and reject any suggestion tabled. Clearly, they all wanted the firm to carry the can, and thereby take consequential heat from blue-chip investors, but Fraser couldn't let that happen.

* * *

Approaching midday, the firm's dynamic duo was feeling mentally challenged by the conundrum, and physically drained, the very hot and humid climate further zapping their energy levels. Back at the Real Guatemala, despite air conditioning, Walter and Roger fanned themselves with the contract papers to keep cool.

They still had no tangible resolution to the dispute, enabling mining to recommence, and the investment portfolio to recover, time for some lateral thinking.

"Walter, am I right in assuming that we have other investments in Guatemala, additional to Villa Nueva?"

"Yes, I think so, just let me check. Let's see if the local Wi-Fi works."

Whipping out his laptop, he fired it up. A few minutes later, having connected to London, he had the answer to Fraser's enquiry.

"At present, the firm has investment portfolios with three other companies, registered in Guatemala. Alvarez Romero, who produce coffee grinds. Miguel Las Anonas, a sugar beet producer. And Santa Sofia, who are a gold mining company." He peered up, his face full with a questioning countenance. "What are you thinking, Roger?"

"I'm thinking that instead of trying to break down the front door to solve this problem, why not go through the side, or even back door?"

The near to ex-Valium junkie appeared dumbstruck, lateral thinking not really within his palette. "Huh?"

"Walter, we don't have any realistic options to pursue with Villa Nueva, you agree?"

"Yes, on the face of it, I suppose so."

"So….what about if we were to cut a deal, with another company?" Speechlessness still furnished Walters, Chevy Chase, he wasn't catching on. Roger continued. "Tell me more about Santa Sofia."

The commercial manager banged the laptop keyboard again, and out popped their investment portfolio.

"They are really an up-and-coming investment, relatively small compared to Villa Nueva, in terms of precious metal revenues."

"Yes, but they're a gold mine. I wonder what the current UK market value of gold is?"

Turning on his laptop, he made some key strokes to discover the answer.

"Let's see if the Wi-Fi works for me," he said. Less than a minute later, Roger had the data. "£1,163 per Troy ounce," he advised, then scanned other precious metals in the live FTSE spreadsheet. "Cobalt, nickel and silver are considerably less. Hhmm, tell me Walter; what does it say in the Santa Sofia profile about futures?"

Hoskyns scrolled down the company's profile."Ah, as it happens, they are looking for inward investment, to modernise plant and scale up resources."

"When?"

"Within the next two fiscal quarters."

"Oh, really?" Roger enthused, breaking into a radiant smile. "How very, very fortunate....Walter, I think we may have found our first break."

"But Roger, I still don't understand."

"Never mind, let me make some calls, and all will be revealed."

Three hours later, they were in the offices of the Santa Sofia gold mining company, with Guillermo Rogerio Vasquez Morales, VP Business Development.

"Your name is Roger," observed Vasquez, as they made their introductions.

"Yes, Señor Vasquez."

"Ah, we have something in common," Vasquez explained. "My second name is Rogerio. It is a good start, a good omen for business discussions." Smiling warmly, he then clasped his hands together to make a clapping sound. "Now, what can I do for you, Roger? I can call you Roger, can't I?"

"Of course."

"Then you must call me Guillermo."

Fraser took to him immediately. Vasquez's body language was very open, eyes betraying his every emotion, his mouth a trustworthy shape, all good signs for congenial business.

"It is some time, since we had any dealings with your firm," confirmed the VP.

"September 2003," confirmed Walter.

"Yes, indeed," Vasquez acknowledged. "What, may I ask, now brings you back to Guatemala?"

Shooting a knowing smile at the amiable Guatemalan, Roger replied, "Business."

"I see….and, er, is your business going well?"

"There is always room for improvements," answered Roger.

"Mmmm, it's very hot today," Vasquez observed. "Would

DOGHOUSE BLUES

you care for some refreshments, gentlemen?"

"Oh, that would be most welcome," gushed Fraser.

They exchanged civilities over mineral water, Roger further weighing up Vasquez, before cutting to the chase.

"Guillermo, how would Santa Sofia respond to a further cash investment from my firm, to be used for modernising production plant, and in the process increasing precious metal yield, by ten times its current level?"

"Ah, Roger, you come straight to the point. I like that. I am a man of action, and I like swift, concise business proposals." Rising from his chair, he turned his back to them to make inward consideration, his vision set on the distant mine-heads, he could see through his office window. "Hhmm, and what would we have to do, to receive this cash injection?"

Detecting a bite, Fraser said, "Modernising the production plant to improve yield would also involve taking on more workers. You agree?"

"Why yes," he said, turning to confront them. Realising the cat and mouse negotiation game was afoot, his face brightened, and his body language changed into an up tempo beat. "Increased productivity will certainly need more miners, surface workers and ancillary support staff, in fact, a whole upgrading of our human resources."

Leaning back in his chair, Fraser said in a low-key, but self-assured voice, "I understand that Santa Sofia use Mexican workers."

"Yes….Mexican, Belizean, Costa Ricans, even a few Europeans, but mainly Guatemalan workers, as you will appreciate."

"And I further understand that in the gold mining industry, Guatemalan workers have no issues, working alongside Mexicans. Is that right?"

"Yes," he confirmed, as a smile grew on his face. His Little Richard-style, moustache, another Guatemalan boggy contender of the year Roger thought to himself, lifted at the edges as his perfect white teeth became exposed. "Unlike in the cobalt and nickel mines....like your Villa Nueva investment."

"You've heard then?" Fraser guessed.

"Of course, Roger. Guatemala is a small country, close communities, word goes around in commercial circles." Gesturing nonchalantly with his right hand, he added, "you're going to have to get used to these Guatemalan ways, my friend." He settled back into his chair, his confidence tangible. "Indeed, I am very aware of your troubles at Villa Nueva."

Who needs the internet in Guatemala, Roger thought, when the grapevine is ten times faster?

"Okay," he said. "So you are aware of the current problem, between the Guatemalan miners and the Mexican surface workers?"

Holding his hands up to shoulder level in a gesture of candour, Vasquez replied, "Of course."

"So it will come as no surprise," proposed Roger, "that the cash injection is contingent, on Santa Sofia taking on the Mexican workers from Villa Nueva."

"I was expecting it," the VP shrugged.

"And?" pressed Fraser.

"Roger, I think we have a basis for mutually agreeable business, dependent upon how much your firm is willing to invest in Santa Sofia."

"I see." Turning to face Walter, the stock analyst winked, then asked Vasquez, "Do you have an office with a secure landline, we can use for a few minutes?"

"We do have mobile communications in Guatemala, you know."

"Yes," Roger conceded. "But our dealings seem to have attracted a lot of interest. I don't want third parties knowing our intentions. Inter-continental mobile communications can be monitored."

"I take your point, Roger," agreed Vasquez. "Here, follow me to the boardroom. The landline is secure from there."

Vasquez discreetly left Walter and Roger in the boardroom, only accompanied by mineral water, and Guatemalan savouries which remained untouched, at that moment, adrenalin rush sufficient to fuel them.

"What are you going to do, Roger?"

"I'm going to call Chalcroft."

Glancing at his watch, still set on Greenwich Mean Time, Walter said advisedly, "But it's just coming up to midnight in London....he'll be in bed."

"Yeesssss," Roger said, with a hint of glee and wickedness. "If TC wants this sorting, he's going to have to get used to his beauty sleep being disturbed. We need to know the limits of our negotiating powers."

He made the call. "Top Cat."

"What?" he heard, on the other end of the line.

"Toby, it's Roger Fraser."

"Roger....do you know what time it is?"

"Yes. According to my watch, Big Ben should just about be striking midnight."

"That's right. What do you mean, by calling me at this late hour?"

"Toby, I think we may have a solution to the Villa Nueva problem, and at the same time can develop some explosive earnings from another investment."

The line went quiet.

"Okay, Roger, I'm just sitting up in bed and placating my wife. Now, what have you got for me?"

Going into chapter and verse, Roger told him where they were in the resolution process, and about the proposed quid pro quo offer with Santa Sofia. The only thing Vasquez wanted to know was, how much they can say the firm would invest and under what terms. TC seemed slightly reluctant, so Roger went for broke.

"Toby," he pressed forcefully, "Walter and I have gone through all the angles. It's a good way forward to solve our problem. If we are allowed to cut a deal with Santa Sofia, and as a consequence solve the Mexican problem at Villa Nueva, then Robert's your mother's brother."

"What?" blurted Chalcroft.

"Bob's your uncle," Roger explained. "Everyone's a winner." He suddenly realised he'd lapsed into Del Boy lingo. The Essex traders had definitely left their mark on him.

"Hhmmm," wondered Chalcroft, "what level of investment are you looking for?".

"Well, based on my previous dealings with precious metal companies, I would say that a cash injection of around £35 million would be a good starting point, for plant modernisation."

"Sterling?" Chalcroft asked.

"Yes."

"That exceeds my remit. When do you need to know by?"

"We need it now, Toby. Señor Vasquez is waiting on our offer. Remember, the sooner we get the Villa Nueva miners back to work, the sooner the stock price will recover, and I think we are talking about minutes after a public statement is issued saying the dispute is over."

"Very well, I'll have to call Bembridge. He won't like it, but still, if you succeed, he'll come out smelling of roses. Give me ten minutes, and I'll call you back."

"Done," concluded Roger, thinking TC would smell of roses too, "speak to you in ten."

Hoskyns and Fraser paced around the Santa Sofia boardroom on tenterhooks, awaiting Chalcroft's return call.

"What do you think is happening, Roger?"

"What, back in Blighty?"

"Yes."

"The Ayatollah will be giving Top Cat heat for disturbing his beauty sleep, like I disturbed his."

Just as the appointed time neared the ten minute mark the phone rung.

Fraser answered it. "Toby?"

"Yes, Roger, it's me."

"Do we have a go situation?" Fraser enquired; slight tension in his voice with expectation.

"Bembridge was still awake, tending to some problem with Missus Bembridge Senior."

More uncontrollable flatulence challenges, Roger thought to himself. "Her unfortunate rectum-release problem?" he posed.

"Huh," returned Chalcroft, "no, not on this occasion." Fraser could almost feel TC smiling at the suggestion back in London. "Something completely different, but I'm not going to go into that," he advised.

"What did he say about the proposed deal with Santa Sofia, Toby?"

A slight pause ensued before Chalcroft answered, heightening both Fraser's and Hoskyns' trepidation.

"Looks like you're on, Roger," confirmed Top Cat, "Bembridge has authorised you to go up to £35 million. You'll find a letter of confirmation in your email inbox from me with words to that effect. Now….go make it happen."

Hoskyns and Fraser returned to Vasquez's office. He had been joined by Santa Sofia President, Octavio Pepe Gutierrez Rios, and VP of Finance, Sebastian Esteban Vicente Sancho Domingo Gonzalo Frascuelo Delgado Flores. Most people of Iberian or South American extraction had two forenames, followed by their father's and mother's surname. Señor Delgado appeared to have sufficient names to cover half of the Guatemalan national football team.

Vasquez went through the introduction protocol and the group exchanged some small talk but Fraser sensed that the Guatemalans wanted to get down to business quickly.

Taking the initiative, he said, "Gentlemen, I'm authorised by the firm to offer the Santa Sofia mining company a cash injection of 25 million pounds sterling, over a 12-month period, with four equal quarterly payments, to cover the modernisation of production plant, and beef up the workforce."

Immediately, a discussion broke out in Spanish, between the board executives. Obviously, they were discussing the proposal, and mulling over what plant could be bought with the cash injection.

Señor Gutierrez cleared his throat. "Señor Fraser, what would be the terms of the investment?"

"My colleague will go through the full terms and conditions of the proposal, but we are looking at an interest rate of 6.9 percent over ten years, or 5.8 percent over five years."

"Hhmm….you expect the worldwide price of gold to keep rising?" asked Gutierrez.

"Señor Gutierrez," Roger assured, "I'm a stock market analyst by trade. With the crash and the Euro crisis, the market value of precious metals has been strengthening. Gold in particular has soared."

"So do you think," Gutierrez probed, "with this cash injection leading to increased productivity and thereby revenues, the rising gold price will enable us to pay back the capital in five years?"

"We have a similar investment, with a gold mine in South Africa. After plant modernisation, the yield increased by ten times its previous level. They are in year four of a five-year loan, and could have paid back the capital plus accumulated interest, after three years. We would be happy to put you in contact with them. It's a very good reference for the firm."

"Hhmmm," pondered Gutierrez, "I see….excuse us, Señor Fraser."

The execs merged into a huddle, reminding Roger of pre-match rugby pep talks, immediately prior to kickoff. Looking over at Walter, he gave him a wink and an assured nod. Seeming to be perfectly composed, Roger wondered what the commercial manager's legendary Valium consumption was all about. Sometimes, if a person is put on the other side of their comfort zone, they find new inner strength, and hidden personality characteristics are revealed. Roger began to think that Walter had spent the greater part of his life, rarely venturing outside his chosen rabbit-hutch security blanket.

Now he had been put in a situation which would challenge Bembridge and Chalcroft, he'd found he was up to the task. Walter Hoskyns was making the transition from office wimp, to mover and shaker.

As the Guatemalan huddle came to an end, smiling faces emerged, and the recognisable sound of happy businessmen filled the room.

Addressing the firm's representatives again, Gutierrez remarked, "I believe there is something else, you wish to table for our consideration, Señor Fraser."

Assuming a calculating demeanour, he replied, "as part of the bargain, we would like Santa Sofia to employ 85 Mexican surface workers, currently with the Villa Nueva mining company."

"How quickly can your firm make the cash injection?" enquired Delgado.

"Within the next 24 hours, Señor Delgado," Roger confirmed. "That will give Walter time to take you through our standard t's and c's, before signoff."

More discussion in Spanish took place, between the Santa Sofia executives. Roger knew the odd phrase of classic Castilian, but they appeared to be talking in some strange dialect of Central American Spanish.

Finishing the second debate, Gutierrez announced, "Alright, I think we have a provisional deal." Pausing, he glanced round his colleagues, as they nodded their heads in approval. "Let me sum up our understanding of the business proposal. One, we will take a loan of 25 million pounds sterling at 5.8 percent over five years. Two, we will employ 85 Mexican surface workers from Villa Nueva, once the initial funds have been cleared into our corporate bank account. Is that correct, Señor Fraser?"

"Absolutely correct, Señor Gutierrez."

"Then we have a deal."

***

Back at the Real Guatemala, with the adrenalin pump now on standby, Walter and Roger realised they hadn't eaten since breakfast, and consequently were extremely ravenous. After a delousing and a change of clothes, they met in the hotel restaurant, intent on consuming most of the gross national food and wine product of Guatemala.

Vibrant with the feeling of success, Roger said, "Do you know, Walter, we could have gone to 35 million, as part of the negotiation. I was fully expecting them to ask for more investment, in return for taking on the Mexicans."

"Yes," agreed the commercial manager, "it couldn't have come out better, if we'd planned it that way, back in London."

"The lower investment number lessens the firm's exposure, and even better, it's a double-bubble win for our investors. They get to see recovery of the Villa Nueva stock and also have the opportunity to invest in Santa Sofia, plus the global precious metals markets."

"The Ayatollah and Top Cat will be pleased."

"Yes, I think there will be a Villa Nueva press announcement by the firm, just after our corporate investors have placed their bets."

"And made a killing."

"Yes, I'd make an investment myself, but I don't relish the thought of being investigated for insider dealing."

"God, yes, the Villa Nueva stock will rocket after the announcement."

"It will, and in will come the Gordon-Gekko-type speculators, who make a quick buck, before selling to corporate investors."

"So it is, so it will always be," concluded the commercial manager.

"By the way," Fraser prompted. "I called Dias, Hernandez

and Ortega on their mobile numbers. Said we had a solution to the Mexican problem, and all of us should meet at Villa Nueva, at nine tomorrow. They all agreed. I also sent an email to Top Cat, copied to The Ayatollah, giving a status report on our negotiations."

"Great."

"Now....enough work for the time being, let's switch off and wreck this town."

The next day, they advised Villa Nueva, the Ministry of Labour and Social Welfare and the mine workers' union, that the Mexican surface workers could be moved to Santa Sofia, within the next few days. As a result, the Guatemalan mine workers returned to work.

Leo Dias brought up the subject of increased production costs incurred by Villa Nueva, using Guatemalan surface workers. Fraser had anticipated that minor objection in advance, and had suggested to Ruben Hernandez, during the previous evening's telecom, that a government supplement should be paid, to cover the 20 per cent increase in labour costs. Hernandez had agreed the supplement, as a short-term measure. Before the end of 2011, all Guatemala's mining industry unions would be seeking better remuneration packages for their members. He'd checked that out with Manolito Ortega, the larger than super-large union man.

Within hours, Villa Nueva made a public announcement, saying that the industrial dispute had been resolved. Their stock price soared on the worldwide precious metals markets. Meanwhile, Walter took Santa Sofia through the contract details for the 25 million pound cash injection. Later, Fraser joined him and by close of business, Santa Sofia had signed off the deal. Job done.

That evening, Walter and Roger climbed aboard a big silver bird for Miami, and an even bigger one to cross the pond back to Blighty.

CHAPTER 14: THE FORGOTTEN BIRTHDAY

Fraser couldn't sleep on aircraft, even when BA put him in those business class coffin seats, which nearly fold out flat. Arriving back in Hazelwood, mid-afternoon the following day, he felt tired but very content, when he called out, "Hello, I'm home, hello."

No reply. He checked his watch. It was just past 3:30. Charlotte must have gone to pick Heather up from school. Wendy and James returned from their schools by bus, and were usually back home by five. Mmmm, this is a rare event, he thought, I have the house to myself.

Despite his tiredness, he thought about what little joyful mischief he could get up to. Out came the Jameson, and on went the Rolling Stones.

Although an aficionado of the Clash and the Jam, by the time he'd reached James age, having raided cousin Peter's superb record collection, he'd moved on to the Rolling Stones, the Who, Cream, Hendrix, the Velvet Underground and 1950's jazz. He still followed late-seventies New Wave and avant-garde, but had started to look wider and deeper into other genres, including classical baroque, and especially post-1920's blues. He totally embraced Nirvana and the American grunge movement, even some nineties power-play Britpop, such as early Oasis, his range so eclectic, it encompassed sound-scapes from Jeff Beck, through to Moroccan jazz, Led Zeppelin to Indian raga and The White Stripes to Khachaturian.

After the sustained adrenalin rush of the last few days, coupled with over 22 hours air travel and little sleep, he came down from the trip. Already, his first big pull on the Irish relaxant had rushed through his body, sending its soporific message to every extremity. He began to float, losing contact with terra firma, and heading in the direction of blissful escapism for company.

Settling back on the lounge couch, he drifted away to the *Let it Bleed* album. Mick 'n' Keef strutted their fabled blues rock oeuvre as he took further long pulls on the Irish charmer. By the time the strains of *Midnight Rambler* started to filter into his sensory system, he'd passed through the threshold, and navigated towards distant fantasies. Half-dreams soon overtook Charlie's insistent drumbeat, and Bill's pumping basslines. Usually, Fraser's dreams were filled with scary women, like Jannette Spliff Snorter and Lady Macbeth, he would tell his rugby playing mates. Not quite true, he loved his monster-in-law, er, mother-in-law. The night after the visit to the Summer Exhibition, he had dreamt that Snorter, the vocal-chord challenged paragon of political correctness, had him by the short and curlies, parading him through the Royal Academy, making him lick modern art exhibits, until he conceded they were great.

He'd just about gone through the subconscious barrier, and taken his place in a backdrop, playing guitar alongside Keef at the Marquee, belting out *(I Can't Get No) Satisfaction*, when he felt his shoulder being pulled.

"Roger."

Mmmm, he thought, it's part of the dream. Ronnie Wood is getting uptight, because I'm upstaging him in Keef's affections.

"Roger, Roger," the shoulder-pulling voice persisted.

"Mmmm…." he mumbled, "it's no good, Ronnie, I'm the main man in the Strolling Bones now."

"Roger," screamed the voice.

The pulling on his shoulder intensified. Ronnie was being very persistent, he thought.

"It's too late, Ronnie….you're out and I'm in….'I can't get no….satisfaction. I can't get no….girly action. Cause I try and I try and I….'"

"Roger, wake up," the voice requested, "it's not Ronnie Wood. It's your wife."

"Mmmm," he purred. "Charlotte, have you joined the

Stones as well....Mick won't like that....he's not as pretty as you."

"Roger, wake up, for goodness sake," his wife implored.

Leaving the Marquee stage, Roger threw kisses to the crowd, who screamed for more.

"Charlotte, did you enjoy the gig?" he enquired, starting to surface again.

Opening his eyes, there in front of him, hands on hips and breathing fire, he thought he saw his nemesis; Jannette Spliff Snorter, or was it his lovely wife?

"Roger, you've drunk nearly half a bottle of Jameson's."

It's my wife, he concluded.

"What?" he blurted.

"Oh, come on," she said, like a domineering shrew, "let's get you showered, and to bed."

***

A few centuries later, or so it seemed, the latest member of the Rolling Stones awoke, to find his loving family gathered around him. They were all looking down at Roger, like they were at a wake. Maybe he'd croaked. Then he heard a few muttered words, being exchanged between Wendy and James. No, Keef's latest partner in guitar slinging still occupied the land of the living. His vision finally fell on Charlotte, sitting on their bed, appearing apprehensive. He thought she held his hand, her expression apparently concerned for his welfare.

"Daddy, have you had an accident?"

That's got to be Heather, he thought.

Starting to prop himself up, he answered, "Accident, no I don't think so.... although my head is thumping a bit, and my body feels like the colossus known as Steve Hunt, tripped and fell on it."

"Not surprising, after all that Irish whisky you drunk on an empty stomach."

DOGHOUSE BLUES

That's got to be Charlotte, he thought.

His eyes were beginning to focus, and he saw his family were all dressed up.

"Going somewhere?" he lamely enquired.

"Yes, Roger," informed Charlotte. "We are going somewhere. It's Wendy's birthday. We're going to Elizabeth's of Eastgate….or have you forgotten?"

Oh my God, he thought. In the aftermath of the Central American furore, he'd clean forgotten it was their eldest daughter's birthday, this Saturday. Saturday, he thought to himself!

"What day is it?"

"It's Saturday, Dad," informed James. "You've been asleep for nearly 24 hours."

Fixing his stare on his eldest daughter, Roger whimpered, "Oh, Wendy, I'm so sorry, I…." Starting to shake his head in disbelief, his brain rattled against the side of his skull, creating thunder in his ears.

"It's alright, Dad," assured Wendy, as she reached forward and grasped her father's other hand.

"Right," declared Charlotte, with an air of single-mindedness. "You've got precisely 45 minutes to shave, shower, and put your best suit on."

Managing a tortured smile, Roger's face felt like it would crack under sudden change, from inert facial muscles to full-blown extension, but it was worth it to see the Sun rise up on Wendy's gorgeous face. She seemed to get a little bit lovelier each day. Gone was the young girl, it was the young woman who now shone through.

As he started to rise, he felt a sudden jabbing pain. It wasn't Charlotte, poking him in the ribs, it was his right hand. He stared at her, questioningly.

"You cut your hand on your whisky glass," she told him, "when I helped you off the couch, yesterday. It had to be bandaged."

What, the whisky glass needed bandaging, he thought to

himself, but didn't say it, not in a position to indulge in fatuous remarks.

"That's right," agreed Heather. "Daddy's been in an accident."

"You're nearly as bad as James for cutting yourself," Charlotte informed him, with a less than amiable bedside manner.

"Oh, I'm not that bad," Roger countered, turning his attention to their son.

When James was younger, he entered a period when he made so many visits to the local A&E, that they nearly issued him a season ticket.

Roger hugged and kissed the female members of his family, and James shook him firmly by his good hand; no namby-pamby, male-on-male hugging from his son, thank God, thought Roger.

Charlotte handed her husband a large glass of Alka Seltzer, whilst he showered. He wolfed it down, the bubbling miracle starting to extinguish his aching head immediately. By the time his ever-loving wife had re-bandaged his fragile right hand, and he'd got his best whistle on, Roger felt a bit more human, and very, very hungry.

His hand was not that bad, but for some reason, his one-man party the day before appeared not to have incurred his wife's displeasure, so he decided to play the old soldier, if that was what she wanted.

* * *

Charlotte called for a taxi, so both adults could drink, not that he sought a great deal of alcohol at present. Wendy already had her birthday cards and presents from friends and relatives, apart from the presents her mother and father would give her at the Rochester restaurant. She knew that Charlotte had forged Roger's signature on the card from them, but remained cool about it, acknowledging that her father had experienced an even more testing week than usual.

Elizabeth's of Eastgate had been one of Charlotte and Roger's favourite restaurants for over 20 years, though Roger was a little surprised it became Wendy's choice.

During their taxi journey, he said to Wendy, "I thought you would plump for TGI Fridays at Bluewater."

She gave him one of those 'oh, brother' looks, like he had been comatose in a cryogenic chamber for the last decade, then she informed, "That was strictly last year, Dad, even the year before. I'm much more sophisticated now."

"Oh, I see," he replied, feeling he had been put securely in his place.

"How did the business go?" Charlotte asked him.

"Very well indeed, I'll tell you about it later. Suffice to say, I think I'll be getting an obscenely large bonus at the end of the quarter, for services above and beyond the call of duty."

"They're not going to knight you, are they?" she joked.

Sniggering a low-level laugh, he responded with, "I'm meant to be the sarcastic member of this family."

"Sorry, Roger," she said, "just couldn't resist it."

The Elizabeth's of Eastgate à la carte menu looked mouth-watering. Absolutely ravenous, Roger became tempted to order a double portion of everything, but not wishing to appear glutinous in front of his family, he restrained his gastric urges. Calling over the waiter, as he advanced towards him, Roger noticed he was a very strange looking fellow. His inspection revealed he wore exaggerated winkle-picker shoes, Trevor Evans style from the trading floor, which combined with an extremely hooked nose, made it appear that when he walked, he was going to pick his nose with the fancy foot gear, with every step. It reminded Roger of Batman's adversary, the Penguin. Yes, that's it, he thought, their garcon de café was a dead ringer for Meredith Burgess, playing the dastardly villain in the spoof TV series, except the waiter had a far larger beak. He also had on aftershave, which would challenge biological and chemical warfare devices for worldwide supremacy. All in all, quite a formidable attendant.

"Sir," he began.

"Oh, hello," chortled Roger, still self-amused by his comical assessment of the Penguin-like character, "we'd like to order, please."

"Very well."

Roger started to detect a French accent, but the waiter probably hailed from much further east of Paris. First ordering what everybody else desired, Roger left his own selection to last.

"The Dover Sole Meuniere."

"Yes, sir."

"Is it fresh?"

"Certainement, monsieur, certainement."

"Pardon, monsieur," Roger requested, *"quand a-t-il pris."*

"Ce matin, a Ramsgate."

"I see," confirmed Roger, happy that the fish had been caught that very day,

"I'll take the Dover sole with sautéed potatoes, asparagus and broccoli."

"Et le vin, monsieur?"

"Camille Villard Meursault AC, 2009, *et deux verres de jus d'orange.*"

"Certainement, monsieur, certainement. Un excellent choix du vin."

"Do you think we can dispense with *les Francais* for now, I'm just about at the limit of my capabilities."

"Certainement, monsieur, er, pardon, certainly, sir."

Waddling off to get the drinks order, the Penguin muttered to himself about the limitations of the foreign language challenged English, and how he had narrowly failed chef school due to his odd physical dimensions.

"Hhmm, that was impressive, Roger," complimented Charlotte, "I haven't heard you speak French, since that holiday we had in the Dordogne two years ago."

"Not sure our fastidious French language loving waiter would agree with you," he suggested, "but I did my best."

"Except Dad got the vowel sound wrong for *quand a-t-il pris*," advised James.

"No doubt I did, son, but I'm out of practice."

Despite James' penchant for *The Inbetweeners*, and other assorted juvenile non-entities, he had developed into quite a clever scholar. Taking to languages like a duck to water, he excelled in Latin and German, as well as French, amazing his parents to the point of incredulity. The last thing they expected was a gifted linguist to emerge from their normally intellectually challenged son. If only he could ally his precocious skills to a discernible ambition, he could have a great future. But at present, his horizons were set no higher than shotgun on a bread wagon, or deckhand on a submarine. All very fashionably staccato and peer-group hip, but next year he began GCSE's, and by then, he would need to have a career in mind. Roger had told him that auditioning for the next generation of *The Inbetweeners* would not be an option.

On the other hand, Wendy had really started to shape up. Keen on economics, especially after listening to Michelle about the course she had just completed at University College, she also exhibited good linguist skills, but Wendy's main strengths were mathematics and English, ideal precursors for a career as an economist.

Too young to really have any thoughts about a career, Heather had surprised her parents on several occasions by telling them, that she thought she could do better than Chris Tarrant or Anne Robinson, as a TV game show host.

"Before the starters arrive," announced a smiling Charlotte, "it's time for Wendy to receive her birthday gifts, from her father and myself."

Wendy got ready to receive, what she hoped would be her impression of heaven on Earth, or at least something which would exalt her to a position of high office, within her girl set.

As Charlotte handed over two packages, Wendy's eyes lit up. Slowly pulling away the wrapping paper on both items, the Fraser's eldest revealed a 22 carat gold necklace and pearl earrings.

"Oh Mum, Dad….thanks so much."

"Try them on, Wendy," suggested Charlotte.

Wendy was already wearing a necklace, so she quickly removed it, and James helped her with the new neckpiece. She then delicately put on the pearl earrings.

"You can pose as *Girl with a Pearl Earring* for your mother, now," Roger suggested, "and she can emulate Vermeer's famous painting."

"Oh, that's a good idea, Roger," declared Charlotte, turning to Wendy. "Will you pose for me, darling?"

"Yes, of course, Mother."

"If you like," James offered, "I'll take a photograph of Wendy with the earrings, and you can work from that, Mother."

"Oh, an even better idea," returned Charlotte, filled with pride for the children, "thank you, James."

"We've not quite finished yet," Roger said, handing over an embossed envelope to Wendy.

"Goodness," she wondered. "What can this be?"

She went into heavenly orbit even further, as she revealed a £250 French Connection gift voucher.

"Oh, I never expected this, as well as the jewellery….oh Mum, Dad."

She got up from her chair, and hugged and kissed Charlotte and Roger, leaving his wife close to tears, and himself clearing his throat, also trying to hold back a flood.

Arriving back in the Frasers' midst with their drinks order, the Penguin continued his servilities in French, almost as if goading Roger to respond again in broken *français* phrases.

After the expected wine-tasting ceremony, the Penguin looking-on expecting perfect protocol before leaving, Roger proposed, "A toast to Wendy, happy 17th birthday, darling."

Everyone joined in. Roger thought he'd never seen her

looking more beautiful. Certainly no longer a little girl, she had grown into an elegant young woman, taking after her mother.

They tucked into their dinner, the tastes delectable and sublime, the luscious food sliding down like Michelin chef Raymond Blanc, personally coaxed it in the direction of awaiting gastronomic systems. Roger had liked some of the Guatemalan dishes, but the family's lip-smacking and scrumptious appraisal, confirmed French cuisine took some beating. In a different world, and on another planet, no matter how much the French annoyed the English, with their cross-channel ferry lightning industrial strikes that turned the A20 into 40 miles of car park for foreign juggernauts, and insisted the UK conform to EU dictats which they ignored, without a doubt, France headed the pack for the title, best worldwide cuisine provider.

"What have you lot been up to this week, while I've been away?" Roger asked, between mouthfuls of brown butter sauce and lemon-tinged fillets.

"I went to see *Fast and Furious 5*, with Neville and Jeremy," replied James taking the initiative.

"Oh yes, what's that all about?" asked Roger.

"Oohhh," swooned their son, almost becoming breathless, "it's absolutely awesome." Using the same clichéd vocabulary as the firm's Essex traders, Roger thought his son had swallowed the urban dictionary. "The best film I've seen in years," James concluded.

Roger found it difficult to comprehend, why a lad with such obvious intelligence got sucked into such tripe. However, at his age, Roger watched the modern gothic *An American Werewolf in London*, which his parents and Aunt Jemina thought to be appalling.

"And?" pressed Roger.

"It's a series....*Fast and Furious 5* is the fifth."

"You do surprise me, James," Roger intoned dryly.

"It's about street racing and heists, plenty of action," expanded James. "Most of it CGI-enhanced, lots of gunfights."

"What," Roger enquired doubtingly, "a hail of bullets going off in a tiny enclosed room, and no one gets so much as a flesh wound?"

"Not even the heroes."

"Doesn't that strike you as odd?" probed Roger, then answered his own question. "How on Earth can a million rounds be shot off, and no one even gets scratched, whereas Humphrey Bogart used one bullet for the kill....and as for CGI...."

"What do you mean, Dad?" interrupted James, now not so sure his monumental acclaim of *Fast and Furious 5* held water.

Before Roger could answer, his intrepid wife intervened. "Your father means CGI is just a lazy director's way to make modern film. It compensates for poor storylines, lousy direction and wooden-top acting."

Do I? Roger thought to himself. He probably did.

Continuing in the vein of the eminent film reviewer, Barry Norman, Charlotte added, "You and your friends should check out great epics like *Vertigo*, *Sophie's Choice* and *The Fountainhead*, for example, instead of wasting money on crass, meaningless juvenile rubbish for lamebrains."

Yes, my wife has a point, Roger thought. Funny how she had been seduced by minimalist art, which fitted the meaningless, juvenile rubbish for lamebrains' mantle, as far as he was concerned, yet she still rigidly supported classic film.

"What about *Pulp Fiction*?" he asked.

"Ah," replied Charlotte, "that's a modern take on classic film noir, told in a very original and thought provoking way."

"But it's in colour," Roger retorted, "film *couleur*," he insisted, dropping back into French.

"A trifling detail, Roger," she chastised him.

Accepting his attempt at irony had failed, and wishing to continue his stay in her good books, he happily conceded, "Yes, you're quite right, darling."

"I've seen *Pulp Fiction*," announced James. "It was really good."

"So have I," added Wendy.

"Me too," blurted Heather.

"What?" Charlotte and Roger exclaimed in unison.

They gawped at each other, astounded.

"When did you see *Pulp Fiction*, Heather?" asked Charlotte, tension visible in her face.

Considering for a moment, their youngest replied, "I saw it on television."

"When?" repeated Charlotte, alarmed at the thought of the John Travolta and Samuel L. Jackson characters giving their daughter nightmares, and worse still, turning her into an Uma Thurman-like, coke-snorting, pill-popping moll.

Seeing Charlotte transforming into 'Witchfinder General' mode, Roger thought it was time for their darlings to put on their tin hats, probably him as well, as somehow, he would get the blame for the children's indiscretions, he always did.

"It was when you and Daddy where out at Daddy's rugby club dinner, last Easter, and Jasmine was looking after us."

One of Charlotte's recently acquired arts and crafts friends, Jasmine liked girl-on-girl action, and her personal god, Jannette Spliff Snorter, had of course become Roger's nemesis. Consequently, little empathy or convergence of view existed between Charlotte's friend and her husband. Extremely butch, Jasmine liked to be the dominant partner in her female relationships, and naturally, she hated men. Once, she came up to Roger in super-powered lesbian mode, after he had grown a temporary top-lip warmer, and sneeringly asked, 'How long have you had that moustache'? He replied, 'Since I was 18....how long have you had yours?' She didn't like that, especially when Wendy and James howled at the retort. Jasmine had a very liberal attitude, some said irresponsible, for exposing children to what she termed real-life scenarios, to help them acclimatise to the modern world. Roger considered it to be so much arty-farty, trendy liberal bull, but Charlotte had been a great supporter until now. He could see his wife looking aggrieved, but refrained from criticising her friend, in front of their little angels.

"Wait till I see that Jasmine again, I'll, I'll…" she said under her breath, beginning to look away from the children.

"Give her a piece of your mind," Roger suggested helpfully.

"Ggrrgghh….more than that."

Wow, thought Roger, I just gotta be around for that one. There's no better spectator sport, than seeing a trendy, pinko, politically correct, self-indulgent, hypocritical, 'do as I say, not as I do' liberal, being taken apart at the seams, and disembowelled by his wife. Its always best to wear plastic sheeting for such exorcisms, to ensure protection from blood spatter, Roger had frequently told viewers, with weak constitutions and an aversion to claret spillage. Usually, the gory event attracted a sell-out crowd from the rugby club. Some players said the inspirational sight reminded them of pagan rituals designed to stir warriors into battle, and was retained in the mind as a motivator, to ensure a win on match days.

Charlotte descended from thoughts of torturing the unfortunate Jasmine. She turned her attention to their two older children. They were about to come in for some motherly interrogation.

"And where were you two," she berated Wendy and James, "when this was going on?"

"That's when I saw *Pulp Fiction* as well," confessed James, as he gulped in air, his Adam's apple traversing rapidly, up and down his throat.

"And you didn't think," Charlotte pushed, "it would be unsuitable for your young sister?"

James' mouth opened, but he had entered guppy mode, inhibited from making a rational reply, through fear of further reprimand by his mother's lethal tongue. With her X-ray vision burning his vital organs, he finally regained volition, acknowledging that Heather was far too young to see the film.

"Sorry mum, I didn't realise….I should have said something

at the time."

"Hhmmm," threatened Charlotte, "your father and I will have to talk about a suitable penance."

Turning her attention to Wendy, she probed, "Okay, birthday girl, and where were you?"

"I think I must have been in my room, doing homework, because that's not when I saw *Pulp Fiction*."

"Oh yes," Charlotte spouted, "so when did you see it?"

"Oh, years ago, when I went to a slumber party at Roxanne Harrison's, and we raided her father's DVD collection."

Now Charlotte entered guppy mode, her eyes wide open, staring blankly ahead to infinity. Roger could see she intended to speak, because her mouth waggled up and down slightly, but nothing came forth for a few moments.

Finally, she said, "And how old were you, when you watched *Pulp Fiction*?"

Backtracking in her mind, Wendy replied, "Eleven, I think."

Charlotte sunk back in her chair, and muttered to herself, "Both my darling girls have been exposed to a vicious and perverted film. It's a wonder they've not turned evil, already."

Such an about turn around from her earlier view, Roger thought, that *Pulp Fiction* was a modern take on classic *film noir*. Of course, he said nothing, fearing imminent heat would come his way. Then he had a moment of what he considered to be sublime inspiration, to put the affair into perspective.

He whispered in her ear, "You're over-reacting, darling, I saw *Taxi Driver* when I was ten."

"Yes," she complained, "and look how you've turned out."

Whoops, big mistake. It's a spur of the moment reaction, or so Roger thought, reminding himself what Steve Hunt had once said to him, 'Women do that, you've probably noticed', so he remained calm, not reacting.

"Mummy."

So consumed in visions of their daughters in abject depravity, Charlotte had not heard their youngest.

"Mummy," Heather said again, in a louder voice.

Charlotte's hearing system came back online. "Yes, darling?"

"I didn't think *Pulp Fiction* was very scary, anyway. Ann Robinson is much scarier."

Charlotte's jaw descended south again, further perplexed about her youngest daughter's take on the world.

The high tension ceased, when Roger changed the subject, to what little tragedies had unfolded during Heather's week.

"I got into a fight with Adelaide Perrett," she announced, "because she said that I'd said to Zoey Harvey that she was a poor hockey player, but I didn't, and Miss Neilson said I had to apologise to Adelaide, anyway."

Roger shrugged his shoulders, and then looked at Charlotte with a bemused expression.

"They've started to play hockey this term," Charlotte explained, "and Miss Neilson is the sports mistress."

"Oh, I see," replied Roger, blankly.

Continuing with her James Joyce length dissertation, Heather recalled more interconnected sub-plots and characters to get a grip on, than in an Agatha Christie whodunnit. Whenever he said, 'Oh, that's bad', when it should have been, 'You were right to hit her', she told him off, and started the whole blessed story again. Finally, he got the *Ulysses* long monologue repeated back correctly, and she moved on.

"I've also had to punish Papa Smurf and Fozzie Bear."

"What have they done now, Heather?" he asked.

"I was trying to teach them how to sing *All About Tonight* by Pixie Lott, but they kept getting it wrong, so for the time being they are banned from being contestants on *Britain's Got Talent*."

I bet they're disappointed, thought her father.

"I see," he said, "so you've had some challenges this week."

"Yes, but I'm expecting better next week, because I've told Papa Smurf and Fozzie Bear that if they don't sing properly, they will be put though Mummy's meat grinder."

"What about Adelaide Perrett?" he asked.

"Her too."

DOGHOUSE BLUES

Whispering in his wife's ear, Roger said, "Maybe *Pulp Fiction* did affect her."

To finish the celebration, Wendy's parents had arranged for the restaurant to present her with a birthday cake, replete with 17 candles. The whole restaurant joined in the happy birthday anthem with the Fraser family, while Wendy blew out the candles to great applause.

They were just getting down to munching their way through the cake, when Roger heard, "Hello, Woger."

Turning round, he saw it was their ex-next-door neighbour, Raymond Russell, and his wife Lois.

Raymond had a problem pronouncing his 'r's, like that total arse, Jonathan Woss. Now he really was an odious little runt, thought Roger, to quote his Aunt Jemina. In fact, Roger vehemently detested him, and would rather sleep with pet-hate Jannette Spliff Snorter, whilst reading texts from *The Female Eunuch*, than piss on Woss, even if he had spontaneously combusted into fire. Fortunately, apart from the 'r' problem, Raymond was a good old boy and nothing like Woss.

When the Frasers first moved into their Hazelwood house, Raymond came around, and introduced himself as Waymond Wussell. It took them a while to get used to his 'walves' and 'waltages' in place of valves and voltages, and 'wegiment' and 'wisk' instead of regiment and risk, but they got there in the end. In fact, Charlotte composed a Waymond to English translations dictionary.

"Raymond, Lois," enthused Roger, "how the devil are you?"

"We're fine," confirmed Lois, "hello Charlotte, hello children." She inspected the Fraser siblings. "My, you've all grown so much."

"It must four, nearly five years since we last saw you," Roger said.

"I know, Woger," Raymond replied, "lot of wateh under the bwidge since then."

The Frasers had some macabre experiences over the years,

but their experiences were poultry, compared to what had happened to the Russells.

Raymond once told Roger that he ordered a Chinese takeaway, only to be faced on the doorstep, by a man in a Fu Manchu costume, who had come to determine the good and bad locations within their dwelling, using *Feng shui*. Raymond had pleaded, 'But we ordered chop suey'. Inadvertently, he had called the Chen House, a provider of Feng shui services, from a pamphlet advertising Chinese businesses. A poor telephone connection, combined with the misplaced call, had led to the confusion. Apparently, Fu Manchu hadn't seen the funny side.

For some unquantifiable reason, Lois had always reminded Roger of Missus Warboys from *One Foot in the Grave*, a lovely lady, but a bit of a scatterbrain. Once, she accidentally shut Raymond in the stairwell cupboard, whilst he was sorting out some old papers, using a torch for light. He had his Walkman on at time, so didn't hear the door shutting and being locked. Lois thought he had gone out for the morning paper. She promptly left the house for one of her Women's Institute meetings, not returning until late afternoon, when she heard a banging, coming from the said door. Incandescent when she let him out, he spent the next 22 minutes on the toilet, relieving a day's fluid build up.

On another occasion, he had been fixing some loose roof tiles, when the ladder he used to climb onto the roof was taken away, by washing-machine delivery men needing access to the kitchen door, which the ladder had blocked. He blissfully carried on with his work, unaware he had no means to get down. Meanwhile, the delivery men left, and Lois popped out via the front door to do some shopping. Returning a few hours later, she became faced by the sight of her irate husband, gesticulating from the roof top. It had been a baking-hot day, and whilst marooned aloft, he got severely sunburned, having to be taken to A&E for second-degree burns.

Roger used to think he got into some ghastly scrapes, but compared to the Russell's roster of ghoulish misfortunes, they were child's play.

The Frasers exchanged a few more words with the Russells, who were then shown to their table. Wendy's birthday contingent made for the door to an awaiting taxi, whilst Roger settled the bill.

* * *

Back home, when the Frasers were all splayed out in the lounge, feeling content and carefree, James raised the subject of comedians. Very much into Michael McIntyre, he insisted he gave the family his impression of the Celtic clown, doing various stand-up sketches. Not bad, James altered his voice to approximate that of the current king of TV comedy, sending Heather into stitches at his antics, whilst the rest afforded him considerate half-smiles.

After the next comedic icon in waiting took a bow, Roger said, "If you think McIntyre is good, you should have seen the irrepressible Dave Allen."

"Dave Allen, who's he?" asked James.

"He was a sit-down, not stand-up, comedian from Dublin," Roger began to explain, "who regularly poked fun at the Catholic Church and political hypocrisy....but in the nicest possible way. He'd sit on a bar stool facing the audience, next to a glass of scotch on a table, keeping him company. He dressed in an evening suit, looking more like James Bond than Jasper Carrot. He'd come out with the most hilarious recollections of his upbringing in Ireland, and the various encounters he'd had with real oddballs, throughout his life. His delivery was perfect. He had audiences in the palm of his hand, from the moment he walked on the stage, and sat on his famous bar stool."

Roger's other childhood heroes included Bill Beaumont and Tom Verlaine, but Dave Allen held a special place in his affections. Roger's father introduced him, and his brother Colin, to the Irish humorist. As kids, they would sit enthralled watching *The Dave Allen Show,* the effect everlasting. They didn't appreciate it at the time, but Dave really was the one-man-show equivalent of the great Morecambe and Wise, universally loved and adored by the entire English nation.

Becoming lost in his misty nostalgia, James brought his father back with, "Dad, you were saying."

"Oh….thank you, son, for a moment I became consumed in the past. Huh. Do you know, he'd always finish on a commending if not biblical note, with *Goodnight, and may your God go with you*. Your mother and I went to see Dave at the London Palladium, at least 20 years ago. He was magnificent. A one-man show which lasted at least three hours, with a few breaks, so that the stomach muscles could recover from unrelenting laughter."

"Oh yes, I remember that," confirmed Charlotte. "Your father's right, Dave Allen was the funniest comedian I've ever seen. A compelling storyteller, who took the absurdities of modern life as his theme, and developed exasperated commentaries about them."

"You should really check him out, James," Roger implored. "Modern stand-up just doesn't come close to Dave Allen's controversial but subtle repertoire."

"How can you say that, Dad?" protested James. *"Live at the Apollo* is great."

"Hhmm, let me see, *Live at the Apollo*. Isn't that where a bunch of second-rate comedians, who look and sound roughly the same, each have a five-minute set before the next one comes on, with exactly the same line in hypocritical, politically-correct friendly patter, just like a baton being handed on, runner to runner in a relay race?"

"There's more to it than that," suggested James. "It's, it's…."

Before he could finish, Charlotte made her grand entrance. "And what's wrong with politically-correct friendly patter?"

Having to be quick on his feet, or his wife would engage them, him in particular on the subject ad infinitum, Roger said, "Oh, ask Lady Macbeth, erm, sorry, ask Davina, she'll tell you."

Great bowling, Roger, he thought to himself, got her leg

before wicket, knowing she would not question her mother's views in front of the children. In a gesture of repentance, he pulled his lower face into a winning smile. She frowned back that look of 'I'll deal with you later,' making him think it was a reckless life-threatening statement he'd made.

"Daddy, what does 'hippo-crit-tee-cal' mean?" asked Heather.

Thank you, darling, he thought to himself. By the time they'd debated the word, and whatever it led onto, hopefully Charlotte would have forgotten his smartarse transgression.

"That's a very good question, Heather, now let me see."

"Does it mean someone who says something," Heather proposed, "but does another thing?"

"You're very nearly there," he confirmed. "In general, it means pretending to have beliefs, opinions, ideals….erm….virtues, thoughts, feelings, even qualities and standards that are false."

"It also involves the deception of others, and is thereby a kind of lie," added Wendy.

"Yes, quite right, thank you, Wendy," he said, proud of his eldest daughter's grasp of the English language.

The birthday girl then added, "We went through *Rambler No. 14* by Samuel Johnson, in an English class last term. Johnson said that hypocrisy is not simply failing to practice those virtues that one preaches, he said something like 'nothing is more damning than to charge with hypocrisy, him that expresses zeal for those virtues, which he neglects to practice,' or something like that."

"Precisely, Wendy, precisely," her father agreed, enthusiastically, "and of course the practice is at its most self-indulgent among the political classes."

"I suppose you're going to pick on poor Jon Pressbutton," exclaimed Charlotte.

"Poor Jon Pressbutton," Roger repeated back, with a look of wonderment. "More like extremely rich, pampered, insulated from reality Jon Pressbutton, at the taxpayer's expense."

Turning to face Heather, as if she was a full-grown adult, he continued, "The artist, er politician formerly known as Two Jags Pressbutton,"he was going to add Two Shags Pressbutton reflecting his infidelity to his wife but then thought better of it in the children's company, "is a prime example of unadulterated, deceitful hypocrisy. Here we have a Labour politician who penalises downtrodden motorists like me, trying to force us off the roads we paid for, with even further penalising taxes, all in the convenient name of climate change, which is yet to be proven to be man-made….and we are to be perpetually made to use public transport, while he swans around in two Jaguar XJ12s."

Heather just gawked at her father, as if spellbound.

"Oh, Roger, that's a little unfair," stated his wife, trying to excuse Two Jag's jet set, champagne slurping, caviar-crunching lifestyle - at the taxpayers expense.

Pressing home the point, confident that God stood at his side, that truth would insulate him from Charlotte's wrath, and that Pressbutton's lifestyle was indeed like the excesses of Bembridge's parties, Roger said, "I'm in complete agreement with Davina on this one. She has no time for Two Jags either."

He'd played the risky Davina card twice now. That was rash, very rash, he thought. He'd got too close to letting fate's edge tempt him further; Conrad's *Heart of Darkness*, or the Redux edition of *Apocalypse Now!*, which was even gorier than the original, came into his mind. Roger didn't look at Charlotte, but he could almost feel her long, sharp fingernails scraping at his tender skin, taking off layer after layer, as they searched for tasty flesh to feed on. Perhaps God and truth could be trumped. She would be coming after Roger, Colonel Kurtz style, and he may end up headless by the morning.

Risking a sideways glance at her, sure enough he saw those familiar tempestuous warning signs starting to rise. She'd be a natural for Katherine in Bill Shakespeare's *The Taming of the Shrew*. The crossed leg, going up and down on the static knee, became a further indication that the viper was about to strike.

DOGHOUSE BLUES

Time for an exit strategy into calmer waters, he thought.

"Erm, Wendy," he chanced.

"Yes, Dad."

"How do things look on the school front this term?"

"What are you thinking about in particular?"

"Oh, I thought now you're embarking on A-levels, there may be some extracurricular school activities, which your mother and I may have to build into our schedules."

"As it happens," advised Wendy, "there are some events coming up….and of course, there's another parent-teacher evening, next week."

Oh boy, thought Roger, as he remembered the last PT meeting. They met Wendy's business studies master, who looked so young, Roger mistakenly thought he was a grammar school boy, reconnoitring the girls' school for a raid. Worse still, conversation revealed he was still wet behind the ears, in terms of his understanding of how business really works.

"Roger," his wife chirped.

"Yes, darling."

"I know what you're up to….and I'll deal with you later."

"Don't know what you mean, darling," he replied, trying the innocent puppy dog character on for size.

"I think you do."

"Is Daddy in trouble again, Mummy?" asked Heather.

"Oh, yes, Daddy is in trouble again."

Coughing cosmetically, pretending to clear his throat, Roger asked, "Now, what were we talking about?"

"Hypocrisy, Dad," advised James.

"Ah, yes, Jon Pressbutton," he replied, noticing Charlotte starting to scowl again. "No, we'd finished on him, hadn't we?"

"There are other forms of hypocrisy," suggested Wendy, "in addition to badly-behaved politicians."

Roger settled back in his chair. With the topic re-engaged, perhaps Charlotte would forget his earlier misdemeanour. No, he thought, he kidded himself. Like Heather, Charlotte had the memory of an elephant, although he had noticed in the past, that the longer the time between the offence and the trial, the less painful the punishment.

"Can you give us some examples, Wendy?" chimed in Charlotte.

"Yes, there is the hypocrisy of parents, who prescribe one set of ethics to their children, then do not adhere to that same set of principles."

That's good, Roger thought. It will be a challenge to answer that one, and come out of it squeaky clean and still respected.

Exchanging glances, Charlotte and Roger began to appreciate that they were both in the dock, this time.

"Would you care to go first, darling?" he suggested.

Her eyes rolled upwards, dragging his vital organs with them.

"Yes….yes, I will answer Wendy's question." She took a deep breath. This was going to be a long one. "Well, we are all subject to the taunt of hypocrisy, at some stage during our lives. I freely admit I don't always do what I prescribe."

"Hear, hear," said Roger, knowing it would cost him, but thinking it was worth it.

"I'd like to think I suggest certain rules for you children to adhere to," Charlotte continued," because I think they will be in your best interests. Those same rules, I know I sometimes break….and I am not going to justify my actions, other than to say they are symptomatic of adult human frailty."

Roger thought that he should get out the anointing bowl for Saint Charlotte. Beautifully and skilfully put, her retort had just enough confession to warrant truth, and a corresponding amount of contrition to gain sympathy. He couldn't have done better himself.

"What about you, Dad?" asked James.

"Me," he said, in a tone suggesting he would claim immunity from hypocrisy, just like the tenor used by one of those holier-than-thou politicians, or the BBC. "I'm not sure I get the chance to be hypocritical. Before I can indulge in little lamentable acts of double standards, your mother usually arrives with a very long pointed hatpin, and bursts the bubble."

"Daddy," Heather said.

"Yes, sweetheart?"

"What about when you came back drunk from the rugby club last week? You are always telling Wendy and James, not to drink a lot of alcohol….isn't that 'hippo-crit-e-cal'?"

"Well, Roger," observed Charlotte, "how are you going to answer this one, and still come out smelling of roses?"

Feeling like a rabbit, mesmerised by oncoming car headlamps, he knew if he didn't say something, he'd be crushed. Beginning to open his mouth, he could again hear the accompanying soundtrack to his calamity-prone domestic life, rising with a swell in the background. Looking around his family, he saw they were all expecting a cogent and convincing answer. It was the evening's grand finale, a cliff-hanger with a few scenes from next week's episode, followed by some inane commercials for lamebrains. With Roger still grasping at straws, the boom came down on the final scene, just like at the end of *Spooks*, when the screen collapses from top and bottom to the middle, with a pounding ssssshhhhhh.

CHAPTER 15: THE PARENTS

The day after Wendy's birthday celebration, the entire Fraser clan travelled over to Tatsfield, not far from Biggin Hill, to see Roger's parents. His father, John, known as Jack to family and close friends, retired from over four decades in retail management, seven years ago, and now spent most of his time exploring overseas with Roger's mother, Amy.

As a young man, Jack had enjoyed a lissom body, which Roger inherited, as had James, but with the onset of middle age, Jack's figure had become fuller, and his full mane of wavy black hair turned from dark to silver. Roger's mother, on the other hand, had sustained her young woman looks, and had full control of her body weight. Both parents had vivid, clear maroon to burnt-sienna eyes, always appearing alert, tuned into life, and receptive to any stimulus, which could add experience and pleasure.

Set in woodland surroundings, their home had provided many opportunities for Wendy and James to explore in their formative years. Still a source of absorption for Heather, she remained intrigued about the wildlife inhabiting the glades and dells festooning the woodland. She would run back to the house, to tell her parents and grandparents about her latest badger or squirrel sightings.

They were having afternoon tea on the first-floor roof veranda, overlooking the back garden, its vista stretching away into mature oaks and larch, interwoven by harebell and meadow cranesbill patches, when Amy raised the question of the children's futures.

"What have Charlotte and yourself got planned, Roger?" she asked, with a hint of mild concern.

He left it to Charlotte to map some broad brush strokes, which seemed to relieve his mother's concerns, at least in the

DOGHOUSE BLUES

case of their son.

"James should meet few obstacles, if he chooses the right career," suggested Amy. "Times are very tough, but if he gets into one of the professions, that should insulate him from the melee of uncertainties, plaguing the country at present. What are his current thoughts, Roger?"

Shaking his head from side to side, he replied, "Well, Mother darling, at present he seems to have no ambition, other than becoming a member of the next-generation *Inbetweeners*."

"The what?" enquired Jack, appearing surprised, but already knowing about youth culture dreams, from when Colin and Roger were James' age.

Colin once had it in mind to become a deep-sea diver, working off a North Sea oil rig, whilst Roger had experienced a predilection for motorbikes, wanting to be the next Barry Sheene. Both much respected, but risky ventures. Of course, those early teenage ambitions were transitory, soon fading as passing fancies, much to their parent's relief.

"It's a juvenile comedy show on Channel 4, Jack," informed Charlotte.

"Ah, that's nothing more than normal teenage fantasy," insisted Jack. "It will pass, but if I was in James' shoes, I would be going for *Top Gear* presenter as a pipedream."

"Oh, now you're talking, Dad," Roger replied enthusiastically.

"I can't think of anything else," Jack confirmed, smiling gleefully, "I have seen in the past ten years that looks more fun….and those three presenters get paid for it as well. Boy, if I had my time over again, *Top Gear* presenter would be my ambition."

"Mine too," Roger agreed with the same expression.

"Do you know, Amy, all my family are *Top Gear* freaks?" advised Charlotte. "I just don't understand the attraction, particularly for Wendy and Heather."

She went on to recall the journey back from the Royal Academy, when Aunt Jemina, Jack's sister, also confessed her addiction to Messrs Clarkson, Hammond, and Captain Slow.

"Well, I must say," asserted Roger's mother, "it has more entertainment value than most of the inane, pointless rubbish the BBC broadcasts. Anyway, James is an intelligent boy. I think within the next 12 months, he will find real ambition."

"That's what we keep on telling him," her son confirmed, "because this time next year, he begins GCSE's."

"Anyway, it's the girls I am more concerned about," said Amy. "Opportunities for women are not what they used to be. I know Wendy is keen on economics, but surely that profession is already overcrowded."

"That is true," Roger confirmed. "But thinking ahead, maybe I can get her started at the firm."

"Oh, that would be good," replied Amy, with glowing warmth, her concern starting to melt.

"Well," Roger continued, "don't say anything to her, for two reasons. One, she's still thinking about a career, and two, if she does commit to economics, I want to be sure the firm will take her, before placing that opportunity in front of her."

"Hhmm, alright," granted Amy. "That leaves Heather."

"Oh, she's far too young to make plans for her career, Amy," pleaded Charlotte.

"Not necessarily so," interjected Roger's father. "Sometimes, even at an early age, if a child shows an aptitude or talent for a particular discipline, then that should be nurtured." He settled back in his chair. "I remember Mark Knightly, one of Colin and Roger's boyhood friends, showed a natural capacity for golf, and his family helped him develop that skill."

"Oh yes," Roger confirmed, "Colin and I lost contact with Mark long ago, when he became a professional, and joined the European Tour. I read in Golf World a few years ago that he would retire from the game at age 45. Of course, he is a multi-millionaire already, so that proves Dad's point."

"Hey, I'll tell you who I did see recently," informed Jack. "Kevin Tolstoy's sister, Amelia. We exchanged a few words in the high street."

"Who's he?" asked Charlotte.

"Well," Amy explained, "Colin used to be keen on Amelia in his late teens, but the younger Kevin was another of Roger's school friends."

"I wouldn't go as far as that, mother," her son declared. "I know him….but he has never been a friend, just an acquaintance."

"Didn't he play for Kappa Corinthians?" queried Jack.

"Long ago, Dad." answered Roger.

"He's no longer involved?" his father asked.

"No….he had a falling out," confirmed Roger, "with some of the players."

Kevin Tolstoy, also known as Kevin Tall-story for his unbelievable porkies, had always been difficult to like. If you had been to the dark side of the moon, he had been there first, and got the tee shirt to prove it. If you had a hushed audience with the Dalai Lama, he'd done it already, and they were best mates. If you had somehow managed to get top-tier tickets to Liverpool versus Manchester United, then he had his tickets personally embossed, and sent to him by Kenny Dalglish, with the compliments of LFC. Whatever someone said, Kevin would always top it with some incredulous yarn, in one-upmanship.

His excommunication from Kappa Corinthians rugby club became both a turgid and sordid affair. He claimed that he could get ten Twickenham stand tickets for the 2002 England versus Wales match, from a contact on the staff at the England Rugby Football Union. Roger and eight others duly signed up to the deal. A few days before the match, after they had all made arrangements for afternoon passes from wives and girlfriends, Kevin boldly announced that his contact had let him down, and he had no tickets.

It wasn't the first time Tall-story had exceeded his capabilities to deliver, so on that occasion, with all those affected furious, they decided on a course of retribution. A few weeks later, after a training session, he returned from his shower, to find all his clothes gone. He managed to beg a towel off one of the juniors, and made his way to the clubhouse bar, demanding the return of his high-value Lacoste and Benetton back warmers. Everyone just shrugged their shoulders, and someone suggested that a contact from the England Rugby Football Union had half-inched his branded goods. Tall-story threw a tantrum, an absolute no-no at a rugby club, no matter how humiliated you are. He then proceeded to verbally abuse, to use a modern politically correct term, those he thought responsible for his loss, an act making him subject to disciplinary procedures, resulting in his expulsion.

"I remember him coming to your ninth birthday party," reminisced Roger's mother, "when you and Steve left him tied up in the woods."

"Oh, yes," Roger remembered, "I'd quite forgotten about that episode."

"What did he do to incur your displeasure?" enquired Charlotte.

Even then, probably truth exaggeration, Roger thought.

"You know....I can't quite remember, but I bet Steve can."

"We've strayed off the subject," said Amy. "What is Heather good at?"

"Well, certainly not golf," Roger advised. "But she is good at disciplining stuffed animals, who fail her expectations as contestants on *The Weakest Link*."

"It's too early to have any real cogent views," added Charlotte.

His parents seemed satisfied that Charlotte and he were at least engaged in future career possibilities for the grandchildren. The conversation became more general and academic, as the group visited the usual inter-family related subjects, including his Guatemala trip, and Charlotte's arts and crafts studies.

Outwardly, she seemed to be a career housewife, but it wasn't true. An architect by profession, and still at Cambridge when she and Roger first met, they married within 12 months of her graduation, and a few years later, Wendy and James came along in quick succession. Charlotte went back to work again, with the young ones put into a crèche, but when Heather was born, she decided to devote her attentions to their youngest, without competing work distractions. She still had contacts in the architectural world, and over the years, took on some home-based work. Sometimes, Roger felt guilty that his career had been sustained, whereas hers became truncated due to domestic responsibilities. Occasionally, when they were alone, he would ask her if she missed the cut and thrust of full-time work, but never quite got a definitive answer in response. He didn't push it, sensing that she felt unfulfilled career-wise, but wouldn't swap the pleasure that child rearing had brought, even if she could outperform Norman Foster. She would be 49 when Heather embarked on her A-levels studies. Roger thought that would be the time Charlotte returned to the world of office-based architecture.

Amy used to be a film reviewer for the Evening Standard, and still had many friends and acquaintances associated with the former celluloid, now digital world of film. She loved to talk about the silver screen. Over the years it had become one of many common interest points she had with Charlotte. Jack and Roger had been known to leave them to it for hours, whilst they played snooker. That day, Charlotte asked Roger's mother about powerful actresses.

"Well, Bette Davis is arguably the gold standard," suggested Amy. She considered for a moment. "I would also put Hepburn, Katharine Hepburn up there with her. Certainly Streep, maybe Vivien Leigh, and of course Maggie Smith comes into the reckoning."

"Maggie Smith is an interesting choice," said Charlotte, "where would you position her, in the great pantheon of screen goddesses?"

"Oh, I wouldn't say any of them were screen goddesses. That's the domain of Rita Hayworth, Ava Gardner, Marilyn Monroe and Sophia Loren."

"Core, Rita Hayworth," remarked Jack, "now she really was

a looker."

"Just like Mother, hey Dad?" added Roger, smiling at his father's fond reminiscence.

"Oh, absolutely," opined Jack, casting an appreciative look at his wife.

"Yes, I used the wrong term," Charlotte apologised. "I meant to say, how would you assess Maggie Smith's acting qualities?"

"It's a good question, Charlotte, now let me see." Amy cogitated for a moment. "Let's take *The Prime of Miss Jean Brodie* as an example."

"That's one of my favourite films," advised Charlotte.

"Mine as well," added Roger, "I always thought Pamela Franklin looked very fetching as a schoolgirl, especially with those secretary-like spectacles she wore."

Charlotte coughed artificially, indicating to Roger, he had began to stray into one of his sexual fantasy domains. On occasion, when in her good books, she would don the schoolgirl uniform and secretary glasses outfit, to satisfy his desires.

Realising he had indeed lapsed into fantasia, Roger qualified, "But, er, you're quite right, Amy, Maggie Smith was the real star of the film."

Turning a blind eye to her son's apparent fondness for schoolgirls, Amy continued. "Brodie is such a multi-faceted character," she reviewed with verve. "I remember reading Muriel Spark's novel, and thinking this must surely become a film. Then Ronald Neame fulfilled my prediction in 1968, with a stellar cast including Maggie Smith in the title role."

"So what is it about Smith's performance, that attracts your acclaim?" asked Charlotte.

"Well, an actor can only work with what the writer has written," she explained. "Interpretation and compelling delivery sets apart a great enactment from a lesser performance. You see, personality flaws build interesting and engaging characters. We all think highly of Ghandi, in terms of his moral rectitude, and leadership by Spartan example. Incidentally, that's a lesson since lost on all world leaders. But beyond that, his character was monochromatic in outlook, hardly the stuff that makes engaging literary characters. In contrast, Jean Brodie is one of literature's most charismatic creatures, but she is fatally flawed. That's what makes her riveting. If she didn't have contradictions, our initial fascination would soon wane. When Maggie Smith played the title role, she brought out those contradictions, imperfections and misplaced loyalties, perfectly. The staggering performance quite rightly earned her an Oscar."

Adding to the lore, Jack recited, *"I'm in the business of putting old heads on young shoulders, and all my pupils are the crème de la crème. Give me a girl at an impressionable age, and she is mine for life."*

Smiling at her husband, Amy extolled, "Huh, classic lines, spoken with passion, even the hint of an Edinburgh accent."

Being a great mimic, Jack had kept Colin and Roger entertained for ages when they were kids, impersonating Brian Clough, Eric Morecambe, Harold Wilson and many others. Roger and his brother tried to emulate his feats over the years, but both of them were poor at taking off personalities, in comparison.

"You know the Teddy Lloyd line?" Roger asked. *"They flee from me, who once did seek me out."*

"Yes," confirmed Amy.

"Is that adapted from *They Flee from Me*," questioned Roger, "by Sir Thomas Wyatt?"

"Possibly," his mother concurred, "it's a good question, Roger. I would have to look it up."

The debate continued, mainly between Amy and Charlotte, with Jack and Roger rocking gently in their seats, and occasionally waving to the children, who had ventured into the woodland paradise.

"You know, Charlotte," began Amy, "there are very few challenging roles for women in film, in this day and age. Most go to Kristen Scott Thomas and Helen Mirren....Helen's portrayal of the monarch in *The Queen* was quite regal."

"Yes," Charlotte responded, "I couldn't agree with you

more."

"Oh, I liked that film as well," said Roger. "Especially, James Cromwell's portrayal of the gaff-prone Prince Phillip. He had him off to a tee. Surprised Cromwell didn't end up in the Tower for relentlessly lampooning, one. Wonderful stuff."

"Me too," added Jack, "I found it quite moving. That's rare in modern film."

"Quite," agreed Amy. "It's easy to conclude that actresses, and come to that actors, are not as good as they used to be, but they can only act out what is put in front of them."

"As can directors," Roger added, "only direct from the script."

"Yes," agreed Amy, "but whereas actors have some latitude for poor performance, directors should know better, and refuse to even consider poor scripts, dealing with done-to- death themes."

"Why do you think that is, Amy?" Charlotte asked. "I mean why in general, has film excellence declined in recent times?"

"Yes, I'd like to know that," supplemented Roger. "It just seems to me that in general, apart from obvious gems like *The Queen*, what is on offer these days is in the main poor compared to the films Colin and I would go to see in our youth."

"Oh, there are many varied opinions," explained Amy. "Some have said that the rise of television was the start of dumbing down film, with studios trying to compete for the majority banal audience. That may have been partially true in the mid-1950's, but I would suggest that as many truly great films were made, in the two decades leading up to the 1980's, as were made before 1960. What really killed quality films being produced in large numbers, was further competition from de-regulated television worldwide, and the perpetual rise of personal computing, as a media for entertainment. That, coupled with accountants running the studios, in place of great pioneering producers, like Jack Warner, Selznick and Powell. Put these combustible factors together, and Hollywood and Pinewood both output dross, designed to compete for the affections of dumb television and computer audiences."

"Your mother is talking about the rise of the blockbuster, Roger," offered his father.

"Absolutely right, Jack," confirmed Amy. "From *Star Wars* through to *Pirates of the Caribbean*, those dreadful Tolkien adaptations and the endlessly ubiquitous Harry Potter, the public have been force fed mindless dribble. It has got to the point, whereby when they are confronted with a really good movie, like *The Devil Wears Prada* or *Infamous*, they are unable to see these films are potentially great, and the experience just fades, as further product into the pap maelstrom they usually watch."

"Strong but true words, mother," Roger agreed.

"There's nothing beats a good human story," injected his father. "I can remember my parents taking me to see *Casablanca*, when my father was home on leave during the War. Though I was very young, it left a lasting impression. *The Big Sleep* was another, and much later after I'd met your mother, *Bridge on the River Kwai* and *Lawrence of Arabia*."

"Ahh, well," intoned Amy. "With those last two epics, you are talking about the master director, David Lean. I once interviewed Lean, whilst he was making *Ryan's Daughter*. The Evening Standard sent me to Ireland, where the film was being shot on location. It became the most challenging task I ever faced. Lean's reputation went before him, as someone who had scant regard for the press, so I expected the worst, but he was a perfect gentleman; kind, courteous and very open, at least with me."

"Perhaps you caught him on a good day, Amy?" Roger suggested.

"Perhaps....maybe you are right. I've heard about journalists who were roasted by Lean." She stopped for a moment, backtracking in her memory. "I got to meet John Mills and Sarah Miles at the same time. Mills gave one of his greatest ever performances as Michael, the retarded village idiot." She leaned forward. "It was remarkable, because here was a leading man, used to playing hearts-of-oak Englishmen for decades, who Lean persuaded to take on this unglamorous supporting role….but Mills' performance was extraordinary. In my view, it rescued a film, which in the end became over-produced, and compensated for the possible miscasting of Robert Mitchum, and the lack-lustre acting of Sarah Miles. It won Sir John a much-deserved Oscar, for best actor in a supporting role."

"Did you get to review *Ryan's Daughter* for the Evening Standard?" asked Charlotte.

"No, they published my on-location interview, but someone else, whose name I can't quite remember, reviewed it. If memory serves, at that time I got *Zabriskie Point*."

"The Michelangelo Antonioni film?" Roger surmised.

"Yes, that's right, Roger…huh, couldn't make head or tail of it. That's the trouble with art-house films. They are intentionally staccato and obtuse, which on the one hand provokes thought, but not necessarily good entertainment. I much preferred his earlier avant-garde effort made in London called Blow-Up, starring David Hemmings. But I remember writing in the review of *Zabriskie Point*, words to the effect that neither of those art-house films compared with his Italian period. I think I cited *La Notte* and *L'eclisse*, as recommendations for Antonioni lovers to check out."

"You'd be appalled at what James considers to be a good film," said Roger.

"Well," Amy concluded, "I don't necessarily blame the audience. They can only appreciate what is on offer, like in any cultural medium, for example music, literature or film. If roles were reversed, and James was a young man in the mid-sixties watching *In the Heat of the Night*, and I was his age in 2011 watching the latest Spiderman movie, then we both may have juxtaposed views."

CHAPTER 16: THE BOYFRIEND

In addition to his normal analyst duties, Roger had been given a new leftfield challenge at the firm. Chalcroft asked him to take care of a visitor from the New York office. Not meaning wipe him out Mafia hit-man style, on the contrary, ensure his visit became a roaring success, and he went back to the Big Apple, glowing about the London operation.

Dan Lebowski would be the gentleman in question. Normally on the buy side of the U.S business, he had been tasked with assessing investment banking performance across the firm's international operations, and wanted to see how the Brits made out across their markets. Roger had previously experienced a similar conversation with Top Cat, before departing for Guatemala. The stock analyst maintained that Ricky Henshaw would be far better suited to looking after Lebowski, but apparently Ricky had crossed the septic over some double-bubble deal, and was persona non grata.

"Besides, Roger," assured TC, "at present, your currency is riding high in New York, and Bembridge wants Lebowski to take back the message stateside, that London is the firms' top trading centre."

"You're referring to the Guatemala job again?"

"Yes," TC confirmed, delivering a genial smile. "You exceeded our wildest expectations, with Villa Nueva and Santa Sofia. The big enchiladas at HQ were very impressed. This is collateral we can dine out on for months."

"So what exactly are Dan Lebowski's expectations?"

Chalcroft grinned one of those 'I know something you don't, and I'm not going to tell you' expressions. "Roger, let me ask you a question." He eyed him intently. "Where do you see yourself, in say the next three to five years?"

"Doing what I'm doing now with the firm, only further up

the ladder."

Top Cat came around to Roger's side of his huge executive desk, and slipped an arm across his shoulder. "We have some other ideas, for your future career with the firm."

Aye, aye, the buttering process has been unleashed, Roger thought.

"Oh yes, what are they?"

"You've rescued three very tricky situations recently. Obviously Guatemala, but also those businesses in Lagos and Ukraine, as well." "Yes."

"Roger, that called for skills, well beyond those of a stock market analyst, especially Guatemala." He returned to his seated position, and gaped at Fraser, as if about to bestow some sacred firm honour on him, the air of cavalier flamboyance in his manner suggesting more butter was about to be spread. "To recover our position over there, needed inventiveness, coupled with negotiating skills, way beyond that of your present remit. It was a brilliant bit of innovative business. I know of few people, worldwide in the investment banking sector, who could have accomplished that, achieving the result in such a short time, and in such a convincing way."

Wondering whether TC would ever hold him in such high esteem, if he ever got to know about the garden party debacle, Roger deduced that Chalcroft was definitely in sell mode. What did he want now?

"Bembridge and I think you are very well suited, to this kind of trouble-shooter work."

He stopped to gauge signs of a reaction, but Roger's face remained unchanged, neither betraying a sense of professional satisfaction at the accolade, nor any indication the trouble-shooter work gave him any particular thrills. Of course it did, but this wasn't the time to show that. When it came to selling, it took one to know one. Roger would be doing his level best to retain control of the situation, without committing himself further, until he knew what was being tabled.

Continuing the butter spreading, Top Cat added, "We also

think this is where your long-term future is, with the firm."

"But Toby, I'm an analyst. Any skills I have, which were used to resolve those three investments, I drew from deep inside my locker." He paused, letting his modesty sink in with the VP. "Not certain if I knew they were there to begin with....I'm not a qualified trouble-shooter."

"No one is, Roger. There is no business administration course centred on trouble-shooting. Such skills emerge through experience and maturity."

"Do I have a choice, Toby?"

"Of course....talk it over with Charlotte....let me know your decision, early tomorrow morning."

That's code for take the job, thought Roger, if you want to stay with the firm.

"We've wandered off track, haven't we?" he said.

"What?"

"Dan Lebowski."

"Oh yes....well, just let's say he'll be part of your brief. We'll finish up on that, tomorrow."

Starting to leave Chalcroft's office, Roger suddenly turned and asked, "This trouble-shooter brief."

"Yes?"

"If I did take it, presumably my baseline job will still be as a senior market analyst, reporting to Henry Jacques?"

"No," TC advised, as he advanced forward to where Fraser stood. "You will be director of market analysis, still reporting to Henry, but with a dotted line directly to my office. Your day job will remain as is, but with more responsibilities, and your night job, metaphorically speaking, will be on hot standby, ready to tackle any investments which are going tits up, within the working brief of the London office."

"Right." Fraser shot a questioning look at the Equities Director, intended to solicit more detail, but like his own earlier non-committal stance, Chalcroft too could play that stony-faced game, his expression revealing nothing. "See you in the morning, Toby."

"Goodnight, Roger."

***

Before Fraser left for Canary Wharf tube station, he called in to see Henry Jacques.

"Henry."

"I know why you here, Roger."

"You do?"

"Chalcroft came to see me this afternoon."

"And?"

"He asked me if I thought you were up to this trouble-shooter role, as well as your day job....I told him that in my opinion, you were up to anything."

"You mean...."

"I mean, Roger, that Top Cat paid me the courtesy of consideration....the decision had already been made."

"Henry, I hope you don't think I...."

"Roger, I don't think anything....I'm just pleased you are receiving some recognition, for your efforts on behalf of the firm."

"Should I...."

"Should you take the job? Well that's up to you....either way, I will be pleased for you."

Although Henry had seemed cool about it, as Roger made his way across Cabot Square, and past the Bang & Olufsen retail outlet, a feeling of abject guilt began to consume him. Irrational maybe, since Henry had always been his biggest supporter at the firm, genuinely wanting to see him succeed, but the seemingly quantum jump career progression still nagged at him.

He had little time for those merciless grinders on Ricky's team, or those in corporate mergers and acquisitions, who trampled on people, in their relentless quest to become the next Luther Bembridge or Toby Chalcroft. Roger prided himself that his career successes had been achieved on the basis of results, without hurting anyone in the process. Now he was developing an innate fear of being ring-fenced, with the very people he despised.

Later, he talked to Charlotte about the job offer. She, like Henry, seemed nonchalant, even encouraging about it. He confessed his reservation, regarding becoming pigeonholed with the firm's serpents, but she dismissed her husband's concerns as being representative of his high ethical standards, as she called them, telling him not to overly self-chastise himself.

"Roger, you've earned the recognition," Charlotte insisted, looking at her husband with pride. "You're one of the good guys. I know I give you a lot of heat for working in investment banking, but I know you are as honest as the day is long, and would never exploit anyone to further your career. Take the job, you deserve it."

So overwhelmed by his wife's sincere praise, he became flushed, not far from blubbing, and had to excuse himself briefly, on the pretext of needing to take off his new Bally brogues, because they were hurting his tootsies.

Returning to the kitchen, where Charlotte prepared dinner, Roger said, "It may mean more international travel, you know," trying to spell out, what he perceived to be one of the downsides of their family life.

"Good," replied Charlotte, "that means I'll have more opportunity to pursue my arts and crafts studies." His wife's face cracked into a grin. "Didn't mean that in a negative way, darling." She put her arms around his neck, drawing his face down, into her mass of gorgeous blonde hair, its aroma intoxicating. "I'm pleased for you, if this trouble-shooter job is what you want."

Is it what I want? he still thought to himself. Why aren't I seizing this opportunity with both hands? If a trouble-shooter role had been offered to him in his twenties, he would have taken it in a heartbeat. But there's the juxtaposition, leading to the inevitable corollary. Then, he had not the experience or the gravitas to do the job. Now apparently, he has both, and did admit to himself that he found the Guatemala episode stimulating and challenging. Maybe I've just become too set in my professional ways, he thought, the change the aspect which gnawed at him, not to press the go button.

Feeling more like a schoolboy seeking guidance from his mother, Roger said, "Charlotte, putting personal bias aside, do you really think I can do this combined analyst trouble-shooter job?"

Charlotte held his head in both hands, kissed him on the lips, then looking at him earnestly reassured, "Roger, I think you can do anything you set your mind on."

That's the thing about women, thought Roger. They are inspirational, in ways that the male of the species cannot hope to equal. Often, over the past 20 years, he had come to Charlotte with some kind of change or challenge, not knowing if he was up to the task, and filled with self doubt, only to go away believing he could float like a butterfly, sting like a bee, after digesting her encouraging and motivating words.

"You really wouldn't mind then?"

"No," she confirmed, not taking his remark at face value, "just don't get yourself killed in some back-of-beyond hellhole, the firm has chosen to invest in."

Responding with his best smile, heavily tongue-in-cheek, Roger said, "Oh, don't worry, there are sufficient insurances, to ensure you and kids will always live in the lap of luxury."

"Right," she said with a final rousing smile, "now go get yourself cleaned up, we have a guest this evening."

"Oh, who?"

"Wendy is bringing home a boy."

"What, to eat?"

"No, silly....to introduce him to us."

* * *

This would be a whole new challenging territory for Roger. The thought of some spotty oik, side-by-side with his gorgeous daughter, troubled him. Being a boy, it was different for James. His father could certainly handle him having girlfriends. A few years ago, Charlotte had asked Roger to do the birds and bees bit with their son, but James had already done it at school. It ended up with James telling his father things he didn't know, reminding Roger of when his father took him aside and said, 'Okay son, I'd like to talk to you about sex'. Being a smart-arsed nascent teenager, he replied, 'Certainly, Father, what do you want to know?' Of course, these traditionally embarrassing rights-of-passage moments were more of a problem for the parent, than the young person.

However, since both Roger and his father were at school, society had deemed it fit to authorise teachers, to in effect, instruct in the ways of procreation from junior school onwards. Not in the least bit red faced, during his fathers farcical 'birds and bees' discussion, James had felt quite relaxed talking about sex. That same semi-humorous, albeit life-changing event could not be applied to Wendy, at least not in her father's eyes.

He thought maybe he had better get the shotgun down from the loft, and dispense with the trouble before it began. He made the bold proposal to Charlotte, but she reminded him that it was still illegal to shoot schoolboys, at least before a trial. Jesus, he thought, I may have been able to handle Lagos, Ukraine and Guatemala, but I'm sure I can't handle the sight of some Neanderthal, pawing my little girl. The break point called for a few shots of Jameson to calm the nerves, before prehistoric man arrived.

Charlotte, Heather, James and Roger were in the lounge, when they heard the front door being opened. Moments later, Wendy was among them with her new friend.

"Hello, everybody," she chimed out.

"Hello, darling," replied Charlotte.

"Mum, Dad, this is Sylvester."

That's a cat's name, Roger thought, as he scanned the callow youth. He had two arms and two legs on a narrow frame, a head appearing to be too big to be supported by his disproportionately smaller body, and appeared to be glowing. He was also slightly shorter than Wendy, though she wore high heels. High heels, Roger thought. That's a bit of a come on, isn't it? His pulse rate began to race.

Holding out his hand to the macabre pulsating alien, Roger said, "Hello, Sylvester."

"It's Sly actually, Mister Fraser."

"What?"

"Sly."

Sly, Roger thought, hardly conducive to trust, is it?

"Come and sit down, you two," cordially invited Charlotte, taking the initiative, after detecting her husband's eyes looking upwards, towards the loft.

"And where did you meet my daughter?" Roger enquired, in the manner of a Victorian poorhouse superintendent, about to raise a whip, and flail the interloper's skin.

Sly became dumbstruck. Maybe he was having flash-forwards of exposed skinless flesh, resultant from incurring Roger's displeasure.

Instead, Wendy answered. "At the school debating society last term....Sly and some of his friends were visiting from West Kingsdown."

"I see," acknowledged Roger, ruefully, his sense of outrage heightening, "and where does Sly go to school?"

"I don't go to school anymore, Mister Fraser."

Oh my God, thought Roger, he's a dropout, probably a pornographer and drug baron to boot.

"I start at the LSE next week." Sly confirmed.

Even worse, Roger thought, his daughter was seeing an anarchist in waiting, who intends to burn down the London financial district, whilst her father was still working in it.

"I see," he said, "so you must be 18."

"19 in October."

Good grief, thought Roger, he's nearly two years older than

Wendy! He's a baby snatcher. Again, Roger gazed towards the loft, almost feeling his fingers on the shotgun triggers, about to give this drug-pushing, baby-kissing old man both barrels.

Charlotte saw her husband's growing consternation. "Would you care for some refreshments, Sly?"

If the baby snatcher asks for a light and bitter, Roger thought, that's it, he can look forward to a meeting with a few hundred lead pellets.

"Oh, that's very kind, Missus Fraser, a cup of tea would be nice."

He's worse than a baby snatcher, thought Roger, he's a pansy. He saw James sniggering slightly at Sly's effeminate request, as his son lost concentration playing an IPhone application.Son, Roger thought, you can help me bury this Svengali, this sinister seducer of young girls. Dispensing with a sneaky child molester, with a reputation lower than a crocodile's belly, would make for good father-son bonding as well.

Charlotte went off to the kitchen, tea making the only thing on her mind.

Still conjuring up excruciating methods to waste this demon from hell, or alternatively offering him a one way ticket to Kabul, with a hungry rottweiler for company, Roger heard Heather say, "Why do you use a name, which my teacher told me means underhand?"

Oh good, Roger thought, no one ever escapes from Heather's interrogations, him included. Roger looked forward to seeing the object of his new found abhorrence, squirm and shuffle in his seat, until he evaporated.

"It's just a shortened form of Sylvester….a kind of nickname."

"But you must like being called Sly."

"Yes."

"Is that because you are sly?"

Jumping in, Wendy admonished her younger sister. "Heather, you are being rude to Sly."

Damn, Roger thought.

"I just wanted to know if he behaves like his name," confirmed the youngest Fraser, accompanied with her most innocent of facial expressions. Roger could swear if she told him he had just left the room, he would believe her, she was that convincing.

Keep going you little beauty, thought Roger.

"Erm….no….I'm not in the least bit sly," answered the boyfriend, now suspecting Heather's jaws may prove to be more difficult to remove from his throat, than he first thought.

"Don't you think you should change your name" Heather continued, "to something like….trustworthy?" She paused looking all worldly like an enlightened seer, near to the philosophical. "Yes, that's it. If you change your name to trustworthy, you can shorten it to trust. Then you won't give the impression you are sly….then my daddy won't shoot you."

CHAPTER 17: THE BIG LEBOWSKI

Fraser took the combined job of trouble-shooter, and director of market analysis. What the hell else was he going to do, resign on principle?

Extremely pleased when they met the next morning, Top Cat virtually glowed with satisfaction, his trademark unreadable mask temporarily slipping to reveal his contentment.

"Excellent, Roger" he said vigorously, while almost draining the blood from the newly-appointed trouble-shooter's right hand, in a handshake which seemed to go on forever. "I knew we could rely on you." He sat down, continuing to look very pleased with himself. "Now, a new contract should be winging its way to you from HR. It will include 80 per cent uplift in your present salary to accommodate the dual role, plus the usual incentive factors and bonus accelerators." Chalcroft shot off a rich, gleeful smirk. "You're going to earn a lot of money, Roger, certainly as much as some of Henshaw's bullpen team, maybe more, dependent on the nature of the trouble-shooting tasks."

Roger was not exactly poor on his present remuneration package, enjoying a lifestyle that would be the envy of most.He did however become immediately sure that Charlotte would have plans for any increase. Their current six bedroom house, set in nearly two acres at Hazelwood, had always been her pride and joy, but despite her recently acquired social conscience, Charlotte's ambitions remained in the upwardly-mobile direction, including visions of an even larger property in the Weald. Roger had tried to scupper the idea, on the basis of impracticality for the children's education, and possible lack of a nearby rail station to get him into London Bridge. However, the overriding reason for his reluctance to move, laid in his desire to remain near to Kappa Corinthians, and his stalwart pals like Charlie Farley, Steve and Gordon. Roger would probably compromise, if Charlotte insisted on the larger property. It would be somewhere within the current locale, where there was a plethora of large houses with abundant land.

"What about Dan Lebowski?" Roger asked.

"Right, I've got your brief on that one."

Top Cat handed Roger a dossier, making him feel more like Jim Phelps than ever, especially now that the Equities Director appeared to have a further hold on his career at the firm. He wondered what little schemes Chalcroft would conjure up in the future to challenge his trouble shooter credentials.

Back in his office, Roger digested the file, mentally noting its key points, best to be forearmed, when it came to tricky, potentially volatile septics. The file revealed The Big Lebowski to be a shrewd New York operator, apparently a risk taker, who juggles tarantulas for fun. Coming up to 60, he'd been with the firm since 1976, had successfully met the target requirements of a whole raft of jobs on the buy-side, and still made the revenue numbers ahead of most when it came to stock trading. In the light of recent worldwide banking disasters caused by toxic debt, he'd been assigned a new remit, planning for robust futures, a brief to challenge the best minds in financial services. He'd already been across the Americas and Asia Pacific, now he was coming to Europe, England his first stopover, and he wanted a no holds-barred, plain-speaking, de-coloured view of futures from London's perspective.

Unlike those in the bullpen, Ricky Henshaw in particular, Roger didn't have to accomplish any weekly revenue targets, which could falsely inflate reality, the key reason why Bembridge and TC had chosen him to be the American's guardian.

**

Dan Lebowski's arrival at the firm's London office, in the guise of a latter-day Freddie Kruger, caused some consternation on the trading floor. Word had gone around that whatever

Lebowski eventually recommended to the firm's New York corporate executive board, may result in changes to bullpen personnel, so both the old-school and Essex boys were on their mettle and best behaviour. Of course, they would be pestering Roger every five minutes to check their status, both during and after the vengeful serial killer's visit. It all offered a mouth-watering opportunity for Roger, to make those who had tested his patience in the past, sweat a little more. Smiling to himself about the sadistic prospect, he wondered if he could resist the temptation, and concluded that he probably couldn't. Despite Charlotte's choirboy, butter wouldn't melt like accolade about his integrity, he wasn't that virtuous, and may not get another opportunity to wreak vengeance, whilst at the same time have tremendous fun at their expense.

As soon as they met, Fraser could see The Big Lebowski would be also out to take revenge, on those who had irritated him or caused annoyance over the years. A formidable looking gent with a square jaw, penetrating eyes, the build of a bull terrier, and an imposing demeanour coupled with a gravely voice, he probably took few prisoners, and would have done justice to the Freddy Krueger role in *A Nightmare on Elm Street*.

"What we considered to be questionable yesterday," Lebowski announced, "is considered commonplace today. And common sense tomorrow. Adapt or die....that's the way forward."

"Well, we're on the same page there, Dan. It's something that all analysts have been preaching, even before the Lehman's catastrophe, solid and reproducible business process, in place of the twin impostors of temporary triumph and suicidal despair."

Shooting a knowing grin at him, the New Yorker said, "You know, Roger, I've been waiting for an opportunity to be playmaker at the firm, for decades."

"Oh, why is that?"

Producing an incendiary smile, he replied, "I don't mind telling you, I've had to put up with a ton of shit from pesky fund managers and *prima donna* traders, worldwide to the point of distraction. I've got to where I'm going with the firm. The corporate layer knows it, and I know it. I've ruffled too many feathers in rarefied atmospheres to hit the executive level, but they know I can do a job for them, and I think they are well aware of my history of chastising delinquent buy-side players and asshole traders. So....as a reward to compensate for career flat-lining, they've authorised me to be the scalp hunter, the BSD." That's big swinging dick in civilian talk, Roger thought to himself. "And to root out, these BPM...." That's bullshit per minute, he thought. "....fly by night, jerk by the seat of their pants, stock raiding jockeys in the bullpen and deal them a dose of razor-sharp steel."

"I see, so, er, as well as futures, you're also on a kind of cleansing mission."

"That's right, Roger. I've been lopping off heads in the Americas and Asia Pacific, for the past few weeks. Now, it's the Europeans' turn. As far as I'm concerned, it's open season on asshole traders, and anyone else who has crossed me in the past."

"I can empathise with your history and bent-up frustrations, Dan, but I don't think you'll find too many buy-side players and traders in the London office, willing to put their foot in the way of progress."

As new master of the universe Lebowski rocked back on his heels, his grin widened.

"They told me you were diplomatic, back in the Big Apple. Well, keep it up Roger, and you and I are going to get along just fine. Now, let me take you through some of my projections, and see how they stack up against your futures figures for London."

The pair launched into Dan's material, and on first sight Fraser concluded, it did have that essential reality quality about it. Gone were the fanciful projections, the stock analyst used to receive a few years back, at the height of the derivatives explosion, which resulted in near-calamity for banking worldwide, through irresistible short-selling dalliance. Dan's qualified forecasts had the mark of the U.S Federal Reserve and the World Bank seal of approval stamped on them. They formed the basis of a very solid-looking futures forecast, over the next two to five years. To consolidate Dan's findings from the Americas and Asia Pacific, Henry Jacques and Roger had compiled the London futures forecast, using the same harsh reality checks. Colleagues in Frankfurt, Zurich, and other European firm hubs also had their numbers ready for Dan's inspection, andlike the London traders, the Europeans would be harassing Fraser, seeking guidance regarding their forecasts, as soon as The Big Lebowski left London, en route to the continent.

Now all that remained was to double-check their numbers, with those from the trading floor, to ensure no latency in the forecast, and discuss market strategy and operational implementation tactics. The latter had the bullpen traders far more concerned than the former. Would their skills sets meet the new go-to-market approach, they wondered? Dan and Roger discussed operational implementation over the next few days with Toby Chalcroft. Even Bembridge joined them in several meetings, indicative that with change, nobody remained safe, even at the executive level. The meetings with the traders became particularly gruesome or fun, dependent on which side of the table you were sitting.

Dan, the harbinger of doom, indeed had some old scores to settle, and began delivering on his promise, of making those who had offended him sweat most. Set to be particularly fretful, the review with Ricky Henshaw, the trading floor sales manager, became the pinnacle of Lebowski's wrath. Apparently, Henshaw had reneged on some double-bubble, Anglo-American deal with Lebowski, who had owned the New York end, and suffered fiscal downside as a consequence.

Before the meeting, Dan said, "Boy, I'd love to give that son of a bitch, Henshaw a one-way ticket to Tehran, with a rottweiler for company."

Yes, Roger thought, he could keep Wendy's friend Sly company at my expense, until his flight ticket gave out in Kabul.

"What's the problem between Ricky and you?" Fraser asked.

"It's got to be more than just a double-bubble disagreement."

The Big Lebowski half-grunted, the very mention of tricky Ricky bringing his temper to the boil. "Henshaw dealt me a bad hand, over a private equity deal which turned sour. Then he got involved in a mergers and acquisitions opportunity, on my side of the pond, which went tits up. Since then, I've viewed him as toxic, and I vowed, if I ever got the chance, I would inflict vengeance upon him."

"Not one for forgive and forget, then?"

"No….to screw me once, may have been an act of misfortune. To do it three times is tantamount to war."

Diplomatically, Roger offered to leave the meeting, out of respect for Ricky, but Dan insisted he stayed. Like Mickey and Mallory in *Natural Born Killers*, Dan wanted a witness left, to tell the tale. It would act as a deterrent to any would-be future perpetrator, thinking of messing with The Big Lebowski. Whatever Luther Bembridge did to Ricky at their much vaunted meeting, that drew so many comments at the Bembridge Cheyne Walk social, it paled into insignificance compared to the subtle dissection he received from Dan. Nothing gratuitous, no actual bloodletting, but Ricky got the heavily syntaxed message, loud and clear. Roger cringed throughout the gory process, almost offering Ricky a handkerchief to mop his brow, at the conclusion of the verbal assault.

Both physically and mentally drained, metaphorically speaking, Roger could see the gaping battle wounds spilling from Ricky's body, leaving a trail of regret as the meeting finished. In contrast, Dan beamed, appearing wholly satisfied with his own inflammatory performance, purring like Ernst Stavro Blofeld's cat, when it ate human entrails in *You Only Live Twice*. Fraser began to wonder if the American really worked for the CIA, out of Guantanamo Bay, and whether his true profession was inquisitor supreme. He made a mental note, never to cross The Big Lebowski, ever.

* * *

Dan and Roger went out on the town after one particularly long and taxing session. Some mergers and acquisitions operators and buy-side players challenged the New Yorker, only to find themselves skewered by a superior player. Though the combat had been swift leaving the end result in no doubt, Fraser could tell that Lebowski needed some r'n'r. To help grow the relationship further, and ensure Dan carried a positive message about the London operation, back to the Big Apple, the firm had reserved Fraser a room at the Hilton Waldorf on Aldwych, where Dan was staying. Consequently, there were none of the usual clockwatching distractions, when Fraser had to catch the last train back to Saint Mary Cray.

Roger had booked them into Langans Brassiere at the Mayfair Hotel, launched by Michael Caine, way back in the mists of time. Charlotte and Roger, plus some other friends, once saw the famous actor, dining at Langans with Michael Parkinson, Jimmy Tarbuck and the late, great George Best. The Big Lebowski was duly impressed, though only familiar with Caine.

A bit of an Anglophile, Dan could trace his family tree, on his mother's side, back four generations, to find his English ancestors hailed from Shropshire. He told Roger more about his background, his family and their New England lifestyle. On his second marriage, he had four offspring, two from each liaison. His latest family had a house at Cove Neck, Oyster Bay, on Long Island, and spent their summers in an ocean-facing beach house at Cape Cod.

As Lebowski outlined his chronicle, his lord high executioner mode became replaced by a gentler regime, so different; it served to illustrate the often unforeseen complexities of the human condition. Judging by his light-voice tone and homely countenance, Fraser thought Dan was probably a real pussycat, domestically.

Reciprocating, Roger gave him a thumbnail sketch of his own story, deliberately pulling out the odd highlight, which judging by Dan's account, would ring a common chord, drawing them closer. Then they showed each other wallet-sized family photographs; the 'ah's' and 'oooh's' cuddly-toy-like exchange further cementing Anglo-American relations.

It had been nearly 33 years since Fraser's new found colonial friend last visited London. He could not believe how much it had changed. The impressions of the capital he had captured in memory, had been virtually eradiated through social engineering, and, as he put it, he felt just as isolated as an Anglo-American on London's streets, as he had in Hong Kong during the Asia Pacific section of his evangelising tour.

That remark reminded Roger of a business trip he made to Hong Kong, very early in his JP Morgan Chase career, to check out a joint venture with a local investment house. Coming out of the Conrad Hotel onto Queensway, not far from the recently rebuilt HSBC headquarters building, he had literally waded into a sea of Chinese people, all at least 12 to 20 inches shorter than himself. As he had scanned around, whilst trying to navigate a straight course, he got the distinct feeling he would be enveloped, and drown in the endless human sea, its wave motion surrounding and jockeying him around in every direction.Quite overwhelmed by the experience, he had likened it to wading into the sea at Broadstairs, the power of the English Channel's incoming waves pushing swimmers aside.

While attending a social at the Royal Hong Kong Jockey Club, Roger had relayed the startling impression to the local Europeans and Americans, whom he dealt with on the joint venture. They responded, saying that overpopulation caused by people fleeing from the mainland communist regime, since Mao took power in 1949, had filled the British protectorate to breaking point, but that the same overpopulation would be seen in European countries over the next three decades, caused by similarly unrestrained, Third World inward migrations.

The wading impression stayed with Roger and like for Dan Lebowski, often when out on the streets of London now, he did feel isolated and disenfranchised, the sole Englishman in a sea of foreign faces, the prediction made at the Royal Hong Kong Jockey Club proving to be real.

"I remember most of the classic buildings," Lebowski eulogised, "way before Canary Wharf or the Broadgate were built. They haven't changed, it's the people. Where are all the English people, Roger?"

"Oh, don't even go there. I had the same conversation with my cousin, Barry, just a few months ago." Knowing he must look perturbed, he paused, but with Dan on the same page of the hymn book, he felt predisposed to continue. "It's something that has gone so far, it seems irreversible, least ways without a revolution."

"Jees, that sounds bad." Recoiling back, the American harvested more impressions from his stay, before he added, "You know, since I arrived, all I seem to see on the streets are non-English people. Most of them look like crooks and villains. It wasn't like that back in 1978. London is more like Detroit or Chicago now, and that's not good."

Trying to bring the conversation back into the realms of levity, the newly appointed trouble-shooter said jokingly, "Maybe the U.S military will create an LZ at Camber Sands, and liberate us, huh?"

Lebowski's eyes narrowed. "Roger," he said, earnestly, "the firm can arrange anything. We even have contacts and influence in the White House. If you would like me to set up...."

Realising his attempt at black humour had backfired, Lebowski taking him literally, Fraser put his hand on the American's shoulder, cutting his remark short. "As I intimated Dan....don't let's go there. It's just too painful."

Giving him a wry look, the New Yorker intoned, "Okay, buddy, it's your town."

"Best we keep to non-controversial subjects."

"Why, are we being recorded?" Dan offered, as he broke out into laughter, and slapped Roger's back in a friendly gesture.

Grinning in response, Fraser wondered if that was not as far-fetched, as it sounded.

"Let's stay talking about the business or our families, or our hopes and dreams, but not about London's demography....it's just too depressing, and I want you to leave the capital with some good impressions."

"Okay, Roger, anything you say, you're the playmaker here."

"Thanks, Dan."

"Come on, the Red Coats are coming. Let's make like John Wayne with the Welsh shepherds, and get the flock out of here."

"Wanna go to Ronnie Scott's?"

"You're damned tootin'."

***

Early the following day, Fraser was all set to resume on the futures campaign with Dan, when he got an urgent message from Benedict Noone, also known as Benedict No-one, because of his tendency to evaporate when the going got tough.

Noone was an old school trader, but in terms of making Roger's life difficult, just as bad as those darned Essex-boy traders. He certainly looked the part with his Hugo Boss suits, red braces, and Yves Saint Laurent designer shoes, but Fraser learnt long ago that impressions do not always equate with assumed performance expectations. No-one hadn't got that innate sense of market shape and direction that a good nose brings, to the best of the best traders. Consequently, he never topped the daily trading revenue stakes, and made unforced errors.

Excusing himself, Fraser headed off for the trading floor. As usual, it bustled with traders screaming buy and sell numbers at each other, and support staff scurrying between computer terminals with fresh market information. Fraser found a glum-faced Noone in Ricky Henshaw's office, the sales manager also appearing downcast and a bit agitated.

"Got your message, Benedict," Roger said. "Only got a few

minutes. What is it?"

Ricky Henshaw supplied the answer. "Benedict has overexposed the firm, on that asset management real estate opportunity which came in yesterday."

"It's a hedge fund, isn't it?" suggested Fraser.

"Yes, Roger, it is," Ricky confirmed, his tone conciliatory, but with a tinge of burgeoning annoyance.

"Well," Fraser assured, "with the current governance and compliance conditions, our trader threshold must have come into play, to limit exposure."

"I kind of overrode the system, Roger," confessed No-one.

"Nonsense, that's impossible," Fraser retorted. "To exceed trader limit, you would need an authorisation code from a delegated company officer....and correct me if I am wrong, Ricky, but that's you in the first instance, then TC, then The Ayatollah."

"Someone in the CIO's office owed me a favour," informed the mistake-prone No-one, "and I got the authorisation code from them."

"Why?" Fraser questioned. "What on Earth possessed you?"

Sucking in breath and clearly embarrassed by his misdemeanour, Benedict informed, "one of our private investors, Hilton Investments, was going ape, to buy up the fund. The stock looked absolutely safe, so with Ricky and Chalcroft out of the office....I called in my favour."

"Why didn't you go to Bembridge?" asked Fraser.

"He doesn't like me."

"He doesn't like anyone," Fraser insisted. "Since when has that been an excuse?" Then realisation hit him. Holding his hands up in front of him, he said, "Don't tell me, the market price fell and Hilton pulled the plug, leaving the firm with the stock."

"It all happened in seconds, Roger," advised No-one. "One moment, the stock was sky rocketing, then one of the corporate investors starting selling, and it plummeted. Hilton also sold, leaving us with a big hole in the day's trading numbers."

"I'm afraid Benedict has got a habit of taking the literal and implementing it, independent of the consequences," added Henshaw, meaning he took directives, but exceeded his brief to accomplish them.

Emitting a shrivelling look Charlotte-style at No-one, Fraser asked, "And why are you telling me this? It's a sales matter, strictly Ricky's domain."

"It will impact the immediate futures forecast, you are preparing with Lebowski," informed Henshaw, in a very matter-of-fact way, considering he still burnt from his roasting with The Big Lebowski. "If he gets wind that London has a hole in the day's trading numbers, albeit temporary....heads will roll...maybe even yours."

"What are you expecting me to do?" Fraser asked.

"You're the trouble-shooter, Roger," replied Henshaw. "Keep that over-sized son of a bitch out of the bullpen, until equilibrium is restored."

Though intended to be outward-looking from the London office, not inward to shore-up failing traders, Roger didn't argue the point regarding trouble-shooter direction. His motivation became to keep the bombshell under wraps, until Dan safely boarded his flight to Frankfurt.

"Does Chalcroft know about the exposure?" he asked.

"No," advised Ricky, "he doesn't return from Zurich until tomorrow."

"What about The Ayatollah?" Fraser queried.

"In an exec board meeting all day," answered Henshaw.

"Okay," Fraser agreed, "I'll keep Lebowski occupied, but text me, as soon as you have recovery."

"Will do, Roger," confirmed Ricky.

"One last thing, Roger," said Noone, as Fraser was about to leave.

"Yes."

Looking like a sourpuss, Noone turned his attention to Henshaw, then to Fraser. "Got anything in the hopper, to help make the balance?"

"Jesus, what am I....the patron saint of traders!"

"Sorry to have to ask you, Roger," No-one bleated, the breathless look of contrition fused into his repentant expression.

"Put it down to teamwork," added Henshaw, with a silky smile.

"Teamwork," repeated Fraser, shaking his head and glaring at them. "Come with me, Benedict."

Of course, Roger knew why Ricky didn't sack Noone on the spot. By virtue of his line management role, Henshaw was implicated as well. Still licking his wounds, from his meeting with The Big Lebowski, he didn't want a return bout. Dan would love to skin tricky Ricky some more. Ricky knew it, so the last thing he needed by association, was putting the firm in hock. Since the Lehman Brothers meltdown, over-trading into the red had become strictly verboten, simply not allowed under any circumstances, unavoidable or otherwise.

The previous day, Fraser had received notification that a fresh tranche of gilts; bonds issued by national governments, Italian in this case, would be released at ten the next day. He went back to his office with No-one in tow. Checking the bond release status on his computer, he found it to be tracking as forecast. Normally, the firm would buy low, with perhaps a single trader, then if the price started rising through market confidence, would put more traders into play, to meet investor expectations. With the time at 9:15, they had 45 minutes to firm up their buy strategy. Getting on the horn to Ricky, Roger suggested they take the market by storm, and buy as much of the gilt as possible, when trading opened at ten. Then, as the price increased, sell sufficient of the stock to make up Benedict's losses. Henshaw agreed the strategy, and Fraser raced off to join Dan Lebowski again.

With the trouble-shooter doing everything he could to keep the New Yorker engaged, it became another heart-stopping next few hours in the life of Roger Fraser. At noon, he got a text from Ricky, saying the firm's position had been recovered. Of course, all the American had to do if he got wind of the debacle, was look at the daily stock watch trades, but Fraser hoped he would be more consumed by the futures strategy, than playing scalp hunter that day.

Lebowski and Fraser had lunch at Le Relais de Venise, then Dan left him in one of those God-awful coffee houses in Old Broad Street, whilst he went off to get some cash from an ATM.

Roger entered the establishment, in no mood to be tested further, and still smarting from the Benedict No-one induced white-knuckle ride.

Going up to the counter, he said, "Cup of coffee, please."

Some strange looking nondescript, with one of those multi-coloured, sculptured haircuts, and sounding more effeminate than a barrel-full of current talk show hosts, said, "We have some specials today; espresso deluxe, espresso con panna and caffé latte."

"Just coffee."

"Americano, cappuccino, caffé mocha."

"Just coffee," Roger confirmed in a louder voice.

"How about caramel macchiato, espresso macchiato or crème brûlée macchiato?"

"Just a cup of fucking coffee."

"We also have iced skinny-flavoured latte, iced caramel macchiato and iced caffè Americano."

"Look, fella, I'm not getting through to you, am I? I just want a cup of fucking coffee. You dig?"

"Would you like something with that? Antipasti bistro box, cheese and oat cake bistro box, or perhaps falafel mezze bistro box?"

"Aaaarrrrgggghhhhhhhhhh!"

By mid-afternoon, Fraser could see light at the end of the tunnel, Benedict No-one's debacle still off the American's radar. They were getting down to the short strokes, thought Roger. Dan only had a few more traders to interrogate, then that Frankfurt flight would beckon, and his focus would be on a swift exit for London City Airport.Roger used the word interrogate because discussion, or even dialogue, seemed so inadequate and lame to describe The Big Lebowski's encounters with bullpen staff.

Jasper Gilham and Todd Charnock, otherwise known as Beavis and Butthead because they look like dorks, or Gilbert and George because they seem to constantly work together, and tend to wear matching clothing, were on their way up to see Lebowski and Fraser.

"Why are we seeing these guys together, Roger?" asked Dan, "They're not faggots or pussies, are they?"

"That's a good question, but no....I don't think so. It's just they work well together and that seems to have led to a close friendship. They are known colloquially as the sisters."

"But they are married, I mean to women, or at least have girlfriends?"

"Couldn't confirm that either, Dan, but the other traders feel safe with them, if they happen to be in the gents' at the same time."

"All the same, it does sound suspicious. What does that halfwit, not fit for fucking sales manager think?"

"Ricky?"

"Yes."

"Well, Ricky is a red-blooded alpha male. I think if he even suspected they were rear gunners, he would have found some artificial excuse, to can them before now."

"What about Toby?"

"Oh, such mundane matters are beneath Top Cat."

"Top Cat....is that what you call him?"

"Just keep that to yourself, Dan."

Smiling at the insistent remark, The Big Lebowski said, "Roger that, Roger."

They heard a knock-knock at the door.

"Come in," said the New Yorker, in his deep brusque voice, obviously keen to have more fun at the traders' expense.

Beavis and Butthead entered, and advanced towards them

like twin matchstick men.

"Jesus," declared Dan, "you two look like a pair of tin soldiers, marching in step."

"We do everything together, Mister Lebowski," replied Jasper.

"Everything?" questioned Dan, while turning to glance at Roger.

"Yes, Mister Lebowski," assured Todd.

Turning their attention to Fraser, together they said, "Hello, Roger."

"Good afternoon, Jasper, Todd," he replied, trying not to smirk at Lebowski's obvious initial hostility to the pair.

Resting his elbows on the table, and leaning forward with the intention of becoming even more intimidating, Dan took the initiative. "Okay, gents, we haven't got a whole lot of time, so let's get down to business. As that note from Toby Chalcroft explains, I'm here to build London's futures figures into the global forecast, and implement the corporate go-to-market strategy. Roger is here to help me." He stopped, widening his eyes at the comic characters before him. "So….what you got for me?"

Answering, Gilham began, "Well, Mister Lebowski…"

"Call me Dan."

"Well, Dan," continued Gilham, "Todd and I have worked through our portfolios, and we have put together some interesting proposals, we think will turn into explosive earnings."

"You don't say," observed Dan, half-mockingly.

"Yes," Todd continued. "What we have avoids all the bear traps of leveraged commitment and downside risk. Better still, it is liquidity-crisis foolproof. It may be contrary to the standard consensus, but what we are proposing is a coherent set of brokerage assets that will…."

Holding up his right hand, like a judge stopping council for the defence, Lebowski cut Charnock off in mid-sentence. "Gentlemen, gentlemen….let's not be disingenuous. I'm not here to listen to abstract concepts." He grimaced at the sisters. "Just cut to the bottom line, and tell me what's in the fuckin' futures hopper, nothing extraneous or visceral, please."

Decoded, that meant the forecast futures dollar numbers, and be quick about it.

Beavis and Butthead cut to the chase, delivered the goodies to please The Big Lebowski, and ensured they kept their jobs, at least for the time being. The no-thrills process being fast and effective, the sisters soon caught on producing the goods, right on the money.

Within 30 minutes, the baptism was complete, and just like their entrance, the two toy soldiers made their exit in unison, with Lebowski saying, "Outstanding gentleman, that'll get you a case of beer."

When the door closed behind them, he turned to Fraser and said, "Jesus, Roger, you limeys sure got some strange folk working for you. I thought they were going to be feeble-minded idiots, but they got on track very quickly. Once I'd focused them, they nailed it. Their numbers are very much in line, with those you and Henry Jacques produced. I didn't know whether to shake their hands, or kiss them."

CHAPTER 18: THE HAPPENING

The night of the parent-teacher meeting at Wendy's school became a more problematical affair than Roger expected. Charlotte and he did the usual thing of listening to teachers' opinions, about their daughter's potential A-level performance, whilst Wendy waited discreetly in the wings. After a few 'hello, how are you' small-talk interludes with other parents, and whilst Wendy went off to chat with some school pals, they settled down in front of Mister Bryant, the business studies master, the one Roger assumed to be a grammar school boy, when they met him at the last PT event. Seeming a little older, perhaps because the girls had been giving him heat, he still had that wet-behind-the-ears look, appearing more like a fluffy puppy dog of Heather's liking, than a robust educator, capable of dealing with teenage girls, testing his mastery of the subject matter.

Whilst they were talking, the headmistress, Missus Greenwood joined them.

"Mister and Missus Fraser, so glad you could come," she said, brightly displaying a winning smile, clearly in sell mode, and having Roger wondering if she was related to Toby Chalcroft.

"Good evening, Missus Greenwood," returned Charlotte.

"I wonder if Mister Bryant and I could have a word with you in private?"

Whoops, thought Roger, what's Wendy been up to, that she's not told her parents about?

"Certainly, Missus Greenwood," confirmed his wife, now starting to look concerned.

The group retired to the headmistress's study. Charlotte and Roger sat there like two lower-sixth formers, speculating what they had done wrong, and how they were going to be punished.

It was always the same, when people were confined within the inner sanctum of authority. Conjecture about the possible cause ran wild, the unknown factor driving the assumed need to be ready for contrition. Whether it be the doctors', police station or a headmistress's study, miscreants or those completely innocent naturally thought the worst, and that they were in for a pasting. Roger and Charlotte glanced at each other, their slight nervousness surfacing, as Missus Greenwood made ready her opening gambit.

"Mister Fraser, I understand you are from the world of commerce."

"Yes, I work in investment banking."

"Good," Missus Greenwood continued. "As you know, Mister Bryant has not been with us very long. In fact, he is just starting his second year as business studies master."

"I see," Roger acknowledged.

"Mister Fraser," continued Missus Greenwood, "I'll come straight to the point. Would you be interested in supplementing the A-level business studies course, by using your business experience to help the girls better understand the subtleties of the business world in practice?"

Just about to give his response in the negative, he heard Charlotte say, "Yes, my husband would be delighted to help out the school."

"Oh," Missus Greenwood replied quickly, "I'm so glad you said that, Missus Fraser. Aren't you, Mister Bryant?"

"Very much so," he confirmed. "I think that if the curriculum could be complemented with a set of business examples and realistic experiences, it would help the students to better understand the subject, and gain high grades."

Cutting in, the headmistress explained, "Mister Fraser, you understand that for Wendy, and the other girls taking business studies to achieve high grades, textbook answers are no longer sufficient. What the examination boards are looking for is insight, originality, and challenge to accepted concepts. It is only through our students differentiating themselves with let's call it 'delta plus innovative answers', they will accomplish the treasured A* grade." She stopped momentarily, as if already thinking she had requested too much, then persisted with renewed resolve. "We were thinking if Mister Fraser could devote say four two-hour sessions over the next few weeks, that should focus the girls in the right direction."

"Oh, I'm sure Roger, er, Mister Fraser can do that," confirmed Charlotte.

Appearing relieved, Missus Greenwood replied, "Good….well, I will leave it with Mister Bryant to discuss the matter further with Mister Fraser. Now, I'm going to have to get back to the PT event. Thank you so much for your help, Mister Fraser."

"Oh, it's our pleasure," Charlotte extolled.

Roger thought he must be imagining the turn of events that had just taken place. Since confirming he worked in investment banking, he hadn't spoken once. It stayed that way until he was on the way out of the headmistress's study. Extremely pleased at the prospect of her husband helping the school, and thereby gaining reflected kudos, earned amongst her friends, Charlotte proudly looped arms with him. Worse still, Mister Bryant bent his ear further, about the need to supplement the course with pragmatic approaches, to understanding the exciting entrepreneurial and innovative techniques, currently used throughout the world of business, Roger still coming to terms with his enforced commitment.

Breaking the arm-loop with his wife, and leaving Bryant talking to himself, Roger charged off after the headmistress, in an attempt to clarify his position.He hailed, "Missus Greenwood." She turned to face him. "You do realise the Rugby World Cup finals will be concluding over the next few weeks?"

"Oh, don't worry about that, Mister Fraser," came the reply, as she patted his arm. "I don't think the girls have much interest in rugby."

Smiling assuredly, she strode off, leaving him in a James-like guppy-feeding moment, his mouth wide open.

As his equally content wife caught up with him, he turned to face her imploringly.

"Charlotte…."

"Later, Roger, much later," she replied, her smile now challenging the Sun for luminescent intensity.

* * *

Towards the end of September, the South East basked in a heat wave, summer finally arriving, three months after its scheduled seasonal slot. Maybe a black hole was pulling our Sun out of position by few millimetres, from its original geo-planetary position, Roger thought, causing the seasons to change. He could milk that one with Caroline Lucas and the climate-change lobby, until they had kittens.

Charlotte had booked them in to a New Age event for the weekend, at the Spa Hotel, Tunbridge Wells. It wasn't really Roger's thing, but his wife insisted it would provide a forum, to find more 'deep and meaningful insight into their marriage', as she put it. Aunt Jemina would be coming over to look after their offspring for the duration, so they felt assured the roof would still be on the house, when they returned.

For once, he left the office early, back in the bosom of his family by 5:30, and the Tunbridge Wells bound pair were on the road before six, after Heather insisted they both wore crucifixes for the weekend. Somehow, Heather had got it into her head that her parents were attending some life-changing ceremony, and if they weren't careful, would return as werewolves and vampires. She may have a point, he thought, reading the literature that the New Age organisers had sent to his wife, concluding that some of it seemed sinister, even ghoulish. However, he contented himself that the organisers had a license to practice, issued by Kent County Council, if that held any water in the risk-aversion stakes.

Earlier in the week, Charlotte boldly announced that she would be going veggie, in preparation for the iconoclastic happening, and as a consequence, he also would be going voluntary veggie as well, just for the weekend.

It wasn't often they went out without the kids, thought Roger, so best to make the most of it when the opportunity came along, even if it happened to be something not particularly to his liking.

With the weather forecast favourable, and since it was just the two of them, they took the beamer. Whereas driving the slow-to-respond MPV took sustained concentration, particularly with six up, the slinky, powerful road-hugging BMW M3 was a driver's dream, responsive, extremely quick, and more fun than being locked in the Pan's People dressing room, a boyhood fantasy for him. They had the hard-top down, so blasting along the M25 and the Sevenoaks bypass added to the zest of the drive. By the time they pulled into the Spa Hotel car park, fully charged up with vim and vigour, Charlotte looked sparkling, whilst Roger positively beamed with satisfaction. He loved piloting, as he called it, the M3, the nearest he got to his vision of heaven on Earth, outside the realms of sex games in the bedroom.

* * *

The New Age happening centred on exploring holistic ways to connect the mind and body to the spirit. Of course, Roger thought it was so much mumbo jumbo, self-induced, hocus-pocus hokum, but he said nothing to upset Charlotte, and played along with the sham. There were about 30 attendees, a mixture of stargazers, occultists, wisdom seekers, green worshippers, and spare parts like Roger, brought along for the ride. A meeting room had been laid out at the back of the hotel, with Persian rugs, coloured lights, healing crystals, and tumble stones, whatever they were. Dowsing rods for water divining, tarot cards and other New Age enhancement paraphernalia, including crystal runes, presumably there to ward off evil spirits, added to the regalia. Incense dominated the pervading physical atmosphere, the smell of amber, jasmine and musk joss sticks still diffused into the rugs and other soft furnishing from previous sessions.

A couple of New Age women ran the show. Head-priestess Jacquenetta Underdown, known as Kali, after the Indian goddess, the protector of abused women, had teamed up with Daina Kirkbride, known as Fortuna, after the Roman goddess of fate, who acted as Kali's second in charge. Together they provided the necessary elucidation and stagecraft needed convert mere mortals into New Age converts. The twin deities appeared to have been spawned by the same super-gods, on the shores of Atlantis or the dizzying heights of Mount Olympus. Both had large greeny-blue eyes, a mass of corkscrew auburn hair which would outsize that of Stevie Nicks at her witchy-woman best, and sallow lavender blush skin, drawn over thin frames and high cheekbones.

"Is it Halloween night?" Roger quipped to Charlotte, when they first saw the deities.

She just elbowed him in the ribs, and marched forward to make their introductions.

"Hello, I'm Charlotte Fraser and this is my husband, Roger."

"Greetings, my children," said Kali.

"May the wind always blow your worries away," added Fortuna.

Both the goddesses approached them, taking turns to wrap themselves around their bodies, and explore their faces, like Colin's cat Morpheus did, when he stalked prey. The deities felt bony and flat-chested. Roger's immediately thought was that they were men in drag with high-pitched voices. Naw, Charlotte would never fall for that, would she?

For every gathering, the curtains stayed closed, only candles allowed to create light, and all timepieces had to remain in bedrooms. The idea to create a time and space-free domain, in which thought processes could be concentrated on the New Age agenda without any distraction, apparently needed absolute silence apart from the deities yakking, and dimensionless surroundings.

Most of the sessions were a variation on fatuous, transcendental meditation, without the pain of the sustained I Ching position, for weeks on end. Old hippie, left-hand bollocks doctrine, brought up to date with New Age trendy leftie, everything that's green is good, nonsense. It mainly sent Roger into soporific spasms, but one of the love-ins became worthwhile reporting, because one, it was most unexpected, and two, delightfully controversial.

Kali said everyone needed to cleanse their minds and souls of all aggression and tension, if they were to connect with the soul and find true karma. Apparently, one method for accomplishing that aim was to channel all negative energy into one particular person, who wound you up. She had them sit cross-legged on the Persian rugs, to form a massive circle, the session being started with a Buddhist prayer and an 'om'.

Naturally for Roger, at least ten traders came to mind immediately as candidates. However, he resisted the temptation to air the firm's dirty linen in public. Instead, he went for his local MP, an absolutely useless waste of his mother and father coming together in joyful union, whilst Gordon Ramsey became the source of Charlotte's pent-up grievances. Poor Gordo, thought Roger, he always seemed to be the butt of someone's hate. Others that were tabled for the voodoo doll treatment included Boris Johnson, Roger could have had 'Doris' as well, Mark Thompson, vastly overpaid DG of the BBC, David Cameron, logically, Nick Clegg, inevitably, Gordon Brown, obviously, Mehdi Hasan, apparently a right little bundle of agenda-loaded, liberal elite posturing, Kelvin Mackenzie, Lenny Henry, David Starkey and Sir Fred Goodwin, who everyone could have picked, Roger included.

But the one candidate who received the most vitriol from a lady called Renata Lapham, New Age name Cassandra, meaning purveyor of predictions that no one believes, became the LBC radio host James O'Nobrain.

DOGHOUSE BLUES

Roger didn't know much about the guy, apart from the fact that he was a limp-wristed, 'do as I say, not as I do and have done', halfway up his own rectum, ultra-trendy lefty, who used his show to push social engineering and positive discrimination, for his own chosen set of holy cows. O'Nobrain had misread *Animal Farm*, really thinking all animals were equal, but some animals of his choosing were more equal than others.

Cassandra's destruction of the politically correct zealot became something to behold. Sitting two places away from the Frasers, her assault was quite measured at first, the predictions princess citing that his anti-Englishness, and pro-anything else, to be the source of her abject fury.

"He's a treacherous bastard," she maintained, "out to destroy England and superimpose his multicultural utopia on the nation."

She then went on to say that she had called the James O'Nobrain show many times, over the past six to eight years. On every occasion, the talk show host had annoyed her, to the point whereby she threw dishes at her pet rabbit. Apparently, when she did get on the air, O'Nobrain used his broadcast inhibit control to cut her off, superimposing his own views over the airwaves on whatever subject he supported, and Cassandra staunchly opposed.

On the last occasion she called the show, O'Nobrain had just discovered that we were in a severe recession, and advocated we buy British goods, whereas just a year earlier, when we were also in severe recession, he thought that supporting the country which had fed, housed, clothed and educated him was xenophobic and protectionist. This inflamed the predictions princess so much that she picked up her DAB radio, flung it to the floor, and jumped all over it, until his charlatan tones disappeared.

During the conclusion of her Persian rug polemic, she went absolutely Tonto, becoming progressively more agitated, her arms flailing about to emphasise the points she made, as to why O'Nobrain qualified as the source of her hate, and why he should be hung, drawn, quartered and disemboweled in public, presumably by her.

A very scary woman indeed, Roger thought that she would give Jannette Spliff Snorter a run for her money.

When Cassandra finished breathless and perspiring, he leaned to his right and said, "Excuse me, you don't happen to know my mother-in-law, do you?"

"Roger," he heard his wife say in a reproving voice, followed by the customary dig in the ribs.

Over the weekend, Roger nearly died of starvation, the New Age veggie food disagreeing with his palate. As fast as Charlotte stuffed it down his throat, it quickly made the return journey. Of course, the hotel dining room and bar were out of bounds to the New Age participants, all their food having been brought in by the goddesses.

He thought about a Colditz-style tunneling escape, or hiding in a laundry trolley, in a bid to find meat and alcohol, but his wife thwarted his every attempt to return to normality. She maintained that if they were going to get the full benefit of the New Age experience, they both had to stay the course.

He raised the subject of allowing an alternative diet with the goddesses, but none of his protestations cut any mustard, with the brown rice and armpit hair brigade.

"Roger, you're beginning to cleanse your body," Fortuna advised, "of all the fats and toxins that have been building up for decades."

"But I haven't been able to keep anything down since we arrived," he bleated in vain.

Joining the covenant, Kali put a reassuring hand on Roger's arm and said, "You will get used to New Age food, Roger. I know Charlotte is extremely enthusiastic to carry on the vegetarian diet, when you return home."

Gulping, he had thoughts about *Rosemary's Baby*, with him cast in the Mia Farrow role, trying to ward off devils, whilst his wife showed them the way to his tender loins. Perhaps Heather's concerns were not as far-fetched as he first thought. And it was still only mid-afternoon on the Saturday.

After lunch, the goddesses instructed the group to prepare for the next session. Making his way to the New Age room, Roger thought the term lunch stretched a descriptive point to the limit, because what had been placed in front of the enlightenment seekers resembled thick, slimy mulch, which upon inquiry turned out to be created from natural ingredients, reduced to the evil-looking concoction in a blender. He knew dozens of fellow rugby players who could consume gallons of beer without the slightest impediment to their cast-iron constitutions, but doubted that any of them would be able to keep down even a thimble of the witches brew, he had just been force fed.

Kali informed them that they were about to be transformed, by the power of positivism and ancient crystals. The participants sat to form a large circle again, the room quietening, as they focused on her. Standing in the circle centre, she held a chlorite healing stone in one hand, and a large fluorite crystal in the other. Apparently, they were good for absorbing stress, and enhancing spiritual mood.

"My children….our New Age movement are based on Western spiritualism and Eastern mysticism. We draw on these metaphysical traditions, then infuse them with influences such as self-help, which you experienced in this morning's session, motivational psychology, holistic health, quantum physics, consciousness research and parapsychology."

Ay, ay, parapsychology, Roger thought. Dennis Wheatley is suddenly going to materialise out of thin air, replete with a goat and human sacrifice, in the five pointed witches' circle we have inadvertently created.

"Our discipline is dogma-free," she continued, "inclusive and pluralistic. A world view emphasising that the mind, body and soul are interrelated, and that there is a form of monism and unity, throughout the universe."

"Isn't that a type of pseudoscience?" asked an attention-grabbing, if not anomalous looking gentleman, on the other side of the circle from where Roger sat.

"According to our great forefathers," she answered, "who include Neville Drury, Emanuel Swedenborg and Helena Blavatsky, the foundation of New Age philosophy is indeed attributed to pseudoscience….but children, do not be alarmed by the term 'pseudo'. In the context of our doctrine, it has no negative connotations, such as imitation, counterfeit or bogus, it is merely a term used to grammatically connect the sciences and philosophies which form our beliefs."

Continuing his qualification, the erudite disciple, approximating a Hare Krishna monk in appearance, largely through his chosen garb and shaven head, enquired, "Would you say that your adopted New Age beliefs also contain elements of older spiritual and religious traditions?"

"Yes, my brother," she assured him, "everything from the Gaia philosophies onwards, including ecology, environmentalism and archaeoastronomy."

Wondering what archaeoastronomy meant, Roger whispered a question in Charlotte's ear. She did her best to explain, leaving him with visions of astral invaders raiding ancient tombs. He put the interpretation to his wife, asking if they would be looking for Lara Croft but all he got back were half-uttered threats about slicing off his wedding tackle, if he didn't take Kali seriously.

"Thank you for answering my questions," said the blessed brother, as he bowed his head and clasped his hands, in prayer-like motion.

"You are very welcome," confirmed Kali, returning a complementary bow.

Deciding that he wished to preserve his manhood, Roger

turned off satirical cynicism, and opened the inquisitive valve. If not for feeling so near to starvation, he would be quite enjoying the session, finding its content to be both informative and stimulating.

More insight followed, with him trying to observe his wife's instruction. As they dived deeper into the thought-provoking material, he began to conjure up a malevolent, but highly practical scheme. Hhmm, he thought, the firm's traders could learn a thing or two, in terms of refining interpersonal skills, from that exchange between Kali and the monk. Perhaps I should suggest to Top Cat that the entire team, including Ricky Henshaw, do the gruel and water trip with the learned goddesses.

Handed the crystals by Kali, Fortuna took over the elucidation. She talked about the influence of Eastern and Western religions on modern New Age thinking, in addition to its Buddhism baseline. She then went on to say how Universalism and Western esotericism had also impacted current New Age wisdom.

Fortuna finished with, "The term 'New Age' refers to the coming astrological age of Aquarius. My children, you should welcome its arrival and celebrate." She paused. "It's the time of the season, when love runs high."

"Isn't that a line from *Time of the Season* by the Zombies," Roger suggested to Charlotte.

At first she gave him a disparaging glare, then recognising he may be right, relaxed her initial hostility to his assumed mocking and said, "Yes, I think I recognise that line."

"So glad you twigged," he told her, "I thought the proverbial dig in the ribs was coming my way again."

When they returned to the near normality of their room, Charlotte imbued with a sense of kismet, recognising the material which prompted her interest she had seen quite by chance, Roger thankful for the brief but welcome sanctuary, they decided to discuss the session.

"I suppose you still have reservations about New Age philosophies," prompted Charlotte.

"On the contrary, that last talk I found to be very enlightening, if not a trifle bombastic."

"You mean you agree with what Kali and Fortuna were saying?"

"Some of it hit the spot, much more so than I would have imagined."

"Hhmmm." She turned to face the window, overlooking the room where the sessions took place. "When I picked up the course information at the tech, I never imagined it would lead to such a profound experience. I'm not saying I could keep this up continuously, but it is something I would like to re-visit, from time to time."

"I could go along with that, if only the food was more agreeable. I haven't felt this hungry since Colin and I got lost in Snowdonia on a hiking expedition, when we were in our mid-teens. We misjudged the location of a youth hostel, ending up going a whole day without food, apart from a continental breakfast."

"Yes, I must say the food is difficult."

"I thought you told the goddesses that you would be sustaining the New Age food regime at home."

"Yes, I did, but I think I got caught up in my enthusiasm for the event." Facing him before continuing, she added, "I'm not sure I could eat New Age, every day for the rest of my life."

"Even though it is the dawning of the Age of Aquarius?"

Half-smiling at the acceptable side of his satire, she said, "Now you're being facetious again, but no, not even the approach of Aquarius could help sustain a New Age diet every day. I'm not even sure I can keep up the veggie routine."

Thank God for that, thought Roger.

* * *

By Sunday evening, when the New Age weekend trippers

returned home, Roger must have lost at least half-a-stone in weight, and felt close to fainting through lack of sustenance. After saying hello to the children, and seeing Aunt Jemina to her taxi, he attacked the larder and fridge like a swarm of locusts, devouring anything in sight, including solid meat, sweet or savoury, washed down with a few glasses of Chambolle-Musigny. It was the first time his constitution had felt near to normal, since the previous Friday, when he lunched at the Battery Club, courtesy of member Henry Jacques. He basked in the aftermath of consumption, patting his blossoming stomach and feeling satisfied.

Left with the impression that New Age philosophy was a catch-all for any spiritual and metaphysical doctrine, on reflection, Roger thought loosely speaking, it had succeeded in connecting his mind and body with his soul. Fascinating in the sense of an alternative lifestyle, he could see Charlotte becoming a convert, at least for the philosophy, if not the cuisine. He thought her recently acquired open-mindedness to the improbable, ensured she would further assess the world of Kali and Fortuna. For him personally, being too far down the conventional fleshpots route to switch to indigestible food, candle light, and incense, walking the road of Grasshopper David Carradine in *Kung Fu*, would be a bridge beyond him.

Roger did however fetch out his copy of the Zombies *Odyssey and Oracle* CD, playing the *Time of the Season* track repeatedly, the goddesses' lasting influence on his playlist.

CHAPTER 19: THE BABE MAGNET

After the PT meeting, Roger examined the A-level business studies curriculum, and prepared some complementary course material, in line with Mister Bryant's requirements, much of it boiler plate and stuff which he quickly worked up into examples of modern business practices. Then he emailed everything to him for print off, so the girls would have the material before the two-hour sessions, scheduled for Tuesday and Thursday evenings over two weeks began, the idea being that the girls would digest the information in advance, and Roger would present some practical case studies regarding the session subject matter, leading into a Q&A session.

* * *

On the first Tuesday evening in October, Roger turned up for the initial session, Wendy having gone on ahead of him with her friends, so not to be seen as teacher's pet. Mister Bryant introduced him to about 15 girls, some of whom were Wendy's friends, including Roxanne Harrison, Abigail Mortimer and Patricia Ellison. Bryant sat at the back of the classroom, also intending to absorb the information, so he could use it for future classes.

At Mister Bryant's insistence, Roger's first session centred on innovative and entrepreneurial skills, but he started with an introduction, a thumbnail sketch designed to answer the question, 'Why should I be listening to you?' It also presented an opportunity to break the ice, with a few funny anecdotes about investment banking, before they got down to the serious stuff. The girls obliged him by laughing at the appropriate points, for each delicately selected tale. Then he began going through some generic examples of innovative and entrepreneurial skills leading to business expansion, with the aid of a whiteboard and an overhead projector, hooked up to his laptop.

They were about 45 minutes into the pitch, when he noticed Roxanne mooning at him, relentlessly. It hadn't struck him before, but like Wendy, she was no longer a girl, her oval-shaped blue eyes huge, her hairstyle quite sophisticated and without doubt, Roxanne had become a shapely young woman. It broke his concentration and he cleared his throat to re-engage the delivery.

"Entrepreneurial skills and innovative thinking are both key to the success of any modern business enterprise," he informed, whilst watching Roxanne out of the corner of his eye. Then he spotted that some of the other girls had the same docile, fixated look, but continued with the pitch. "With the advent of highly geared employee-to-profit ratios, adopted by businesses during the early 1990's, resulting in the replacement of the pyramid organisational structure with a much flatter shape, every employee has become axiomatic to accomplishing company performance." Beginning to feel a little uneasy with the unexpected attention from Roxanne and other feline voyeurs, he had to find something to distract them. Usually, he walked about at the front of a room, when giving a work briefing. He decided to adopt the same technique here to sustain the dynamic, and ensure the girls were concentrating on what he said, rather than on him. "In parallel with this resource-matching to task discipline, there's been a corresponding rise in empowering decision makers with a set of business development, sales and marketing skills, aimed at securing long-term company tenure and growth."

The ploy not working as intended, he grasped that at least half the girls seemed to be connected to his every movement by an invisible wire. If he raised his hand to emphasise a point, he noticed some heads rise and fall, in sync with his movement. It became disconcerting. He felt more like a puppet master than a businessman. Usually, it took all his interpersonal skills to keep groups at work, particularly the traders, focused. In an effort to disengage the slavish connection, he broke off giving further examples of innovative and entrepreneurial techniques, and prematurely opened the session to questions, to make sure the girls had understood the material.

"Right then, let's do a quick review, just to make sure everybody is on the same page. Does anyone have any questions so far?"

To his amazement, at least ten hands shot up, making him retreat slightly. Used to almost dragging questions out of work audiences, the burgeoning eagerness of the business studies class came as a surprise. Worst still, Roxanne, one of the more blatant enthusiasts, added a wink to her waving hand, so he decided to defuse her apparent entrancement by selecting her first.

"Yes, Roxanne?"

"Mister Fraser, will you be doing more of these sessions, next term?"

"Next term," he repeated, staggered by the keenness of the question. "No, erm, as was explained in that flyer Mister Bryant sent out, the idea is to supplement your understanding of the subject matter at the beginning of the course, so to provide a model or a method to interpret the daytime syllabus, in the context of proven business successes."

Roxanne seemed totally unconvinced.

Seeking confirmation, Roger gestured to the business studies master at the back of the room, who dutifully nodded his agreement with the approach, and said, "yes, that is correct."

"But Mister Fraser," opined Patricia Ellison, "don't you think we are going to need refreshers throughout the course....so we don't fall into bad habits, so to speak?"

Clever girl, Roger thought, too damn clever by half. Clearing his throat again, he imagined if this teasing line went any further, Wendy's constricting hands would be around his neck, her reaction in response to the class's outrageous behaviour. Worse still, she might file a report of the occurrence with her mother.

"No," he responded forcefully, "I've constructed the supplementary content to overlay the entire two-year AS and A-level course, so this is a one-shot affair. You shouldn't need any further external material after this." He glanced at Bryant again, half imploringly. "I am right in saying that, aren't I, Mister Bryant?"

"Yes, Mister Fraser, you are….if there are any repeat requirements of the material you are presenting, then I will be taking on that task."

Roger noticed at least half the class had now turned with dagger eyes, to face the business studies master.

Sensing their air of disapproval, Bryant said squeakily, "We had better get on, Mister Fraser."

"Quite," Roger replied, looking more than a little concerned, that indeed he may have misinterpreted Missus Greenwood's requirement.

He continued with more practical and pragmatic examples of innovative and entrepreneurial techniques and skills for a further 15 minutes, before calling a comfort break for the class.

Whilst cleaning off his scrawl from the whiteboard, he suddenly got the distinct feeling of the close proximity of others. Turning about, he found that he had become surrounded by six girls, all looking up at him, wide-eyed and expectant, with Roxanne leading the fox pack.

"Mister Fraser," she began in an uncompromising manner, "we think you should reconsider."

"Reconsider….reconsider what?"

"We think that if we are going to get high grades in business studies," explained Roxanne, "we are going to need your support, at the beginning of each term."

Letting out a half-restrained nervous laugh, he cleared his throat for the umpteenth time, then said, "No, er….by the time we have completed these four, two-hour sessions, I am confident you will have all the information necessary, to avoid falling into textbook answers to examination questions."

Appearing to be disappointed, Roxanne pouted, breathed out nosily and then folded her arms, and began to sway about her hips, his response definitely not to her liking.

Another girl, who he'd not met before, and who he didn't think was a member of Wendy's girl set, then said, "Our parents will be very distraught, if we fail our examinations because you haven't delivered on your promises."

"Promises?"

"Yes," the girl explained, "we understood from Missus Greenwood that you would be doing everything that was necessary, to make sure we are well-prepared for the examinations."

Another nervous laugh leapt from his mouth. It may have been his imagination, but they seemed to be closing in on him. "Yes….well…." he spluttered, with an unconvincing accompanying look, "I think you may be misinterpreting Missus Greenwood's words. I think what she probably said, was that I would help at the beginning of this term….yes, that must have been it."

He'd never considered himself to be a lady killer, in fact the exact opposite applied during his formative years. Roger exuded confidence, able to talk to the opposite sex at will, but he always had to work at it, to get them to swoon over him. He had played the field in the past, but unlike some guys he knew, who were babe magnets, he invariably had to make the first move, the only exception being Charlotte. When they met, it truly had been like the stars had aligned, they kind of instantly fused into a single immutable entity. Having found his soul mate, his wolfing-around days were over. But since they married all those years ago, he seemed to have become more attractive to the opposite sex. Being out of bounds appeared to be an aphrodisiac, even a challenge. Nothing ever happened, he always thought it extremely bad form to cheat on your wife, but it did confirm the illogical behavioural patterns of the female of the species.

Now on the wrong side of 40, he seemed to have become a

DOGHOUSE BLUES

babe magnet himself, but being the source of schoolgirl attraction made him feel extremely uncomfortable, particularly with his eldest daughter in the same room, and she must have noticed the six girls encircling him. Glancing over in Wendy's direction, he saw that sure enough, she had developed that same icy stare of disapproval that Charlotte threw at him, when he incurred his wife's displeasure.

"Excuse me, girls," he requested, removing their tentacles, "I must just have a quick word with Wendy."

Dividing, like Moses parting the Red Sea, they allowed him safe passage, and he briskly moved towards a quiet part of the classroom, with Wendy in tow.

"Oh, Mister Fraser," she expressed in a sarcastic, overly school-girlish voice.

"Not a word to your mother," he said pleadingly.

Wendy tutted, "Huh, they're just like groupies!"

Over the course of the following evening classes, Roger found the schoolgirl crush brigade increased in numbers. After the first session, word went around the school, and for session two, the attendance number swelled to nearly 30, with the final-year business studies students attending, to see what all the fuss was about.

Funny that it had never occurred to him before, he began to appreciate the difference between 18-year-olds compared to 17-year-olds, in terms of their provocative nature. One new entrant in particular, Lolita, nigh on consumed him alive at the break, with her suggestive questions and overt body language.

By the following Tuesday, the ranks had swollen, with 16-year-olds, who were thinking about taking business studies A-level, the following year. Grasping the evening class participants must have arrived well before him, he found them in a huddle outside the designated classroom, talking loudly, which quietened to a series of smirks and girlie laughs, when he came down the corridor with Mister Bryant.

"Good evening, girls," Roger said brightly.

They responded back with a precision, choir-like, "Good

evening, Mister Fraser", the sound booming up and down the corridor, accompanied by more giggles and wicked grins. He could have sworn one of them would eventually turn up, replete with an apple for him, or something even worse.

What he also found amazing was that Mister Bryant seemed even wetter behind the ears, failing, at least on the surface, to notice the scent of a woman-like intoxicating perfume, filling the close physical atmosphere.

* * *

Returning from the office one day, Roger heard Charlotte say, "I understand you've got quite a fan club at the school."

His immediate and uncharitable thought was that Wendy had dropped him in it. But Charlotte went on to say she bumped into Abigail Mortimer's mother in Waitrose, who had practically frothed with fervour and thanks, for helping her daughter get to grips with the business studies A-level. Roger breathed a sigh of relief, going on to assure his wife that though the sessions afforded him some personal satisfaction, nonetheless, he would be glad when his commitment became fulfilled.

* * *

As the final evening class approached, he became very thankful that the finishing post beckoned, and even gladder he had not signed up for more sessions, later in the school year, as he had momentarily thought he had done at the first session, as had most of the girls.

For the second hour of the last evening, the axiomatic role of branding in revenue generation became his theme. He had already provided some examples in the material emailed to Bryant, which he printed and distributed before the event.

They were having the usual interactive session. The girls all fired up and prepared to ask exacting questions, with Fraser controlling their exuberance as best he could. Going through some successful classic branding examples, like Coca-Cola and Microsoft, for once he managed to retain the girls' focus, without the lecture descending into lewd and suggestive territories. For a change, Fraser began to enjoy himself, whilst Mister Bryant smiled away, conjuring up visions of him teaching the same material, and winning everlasting approval from Missus Greenwood, leading to a promotion. To balance the topic, Fraser then turned to some howlers, his intention to get the girls to see the fine distinctions, often determining the difference between branding success and failure.

"One of the worst examples of re-branding which went dreadfully wrong, was the instance of the Marconi company name being replaced, by that of its corporate owners, GEC," Roger began earnestly. "Marconi were synonymous with high-tech telecommunications and computer systems, whereas the parent GEC's pedigree came from heavy electrical engineering."

"Mister Fraser."

It was Lolita.

"Yes."

"Would you say that school uniforms fell into the category of bad branding?"

"What....what do you mean?"

"Well, most girls would prefer to dress, as we are this evening. Does that mean the requirements to wear school uniform have been, to use your business term, positioned badly?"

Scratching his head, trying to make the connection, he replied, "we are talking about industrial-scale business branding....not whether the success of getting girls to wear school uniform, is an exercise in classic branding."

"But Mister Fraser."

It was Roxanne Harrison.

"Earlier, you were saying that product modification in response to market demand has often improved brand integrity, and therefore market awareness."

They might have looked like life-wrecking sirens, but they were very switched on, very bright, and most certainly intelligent enough to absorb his material, able to ask testing questions, and make correct observations.

"Yes...." he protested, "but I don't see what this has to do with school uniforms."

Coming back in, Lolita advised, "Girls modify their school uniforms to make them more attractive, more fashionable. Doesn't that improve the brand image?"

"Well, yes," he conceded, "but I can't quite see where this is going."

What the hell has this got to do with GEC anyway, he thought?

"Isn't branding all about creating demand?" suggested Lolita.

"Yes but...."

"Well," she pressed interrupting, and standing up to reveal a skirt so short, it would embarrass even the Guatemalan husband-hunters, "the girls modify school uniforms to create market demand."

"Yes, well....you've proved your point," he flustered, "now, can we please get back to GEC?"

Directing a glance in Bryant's direction hoping for support, Fraser noticed the business studies master appeared to be still recovering from Lolita's leg display. Bryant's mouth had opened and his glasses were steamed up. Roger coughed to catch his attention, but like Elvis, he had left the building, at least in the metaphorical sense. It appeared that Bryant's balls had finally dropped, and he had suddenly become aware there are certain key differences, between the male and female form.

As the girls began to get geared up for their next onslaught on his sensitivities, Fraser said, "Now, where were we?" giving up on Bryant, and trying to re-engage his concentration.

"GEC," confirmed Wendy, with a reprimanding expression.

"Thank you, Wendy," he replied graciously, flashing an endearing smile at his daughter, which she didn't return.

Recognising the warning signs from previous sessions that preceded the approach of bedlam, and beginning to lose class control, yet again, he thought it would be a good time to neutralise the salacious banter with a quick recess. "Before we go on, girls," he extolled, "let's have a two-minute comfort break."

Before the most determined girls could surround him, as they usually did at breaks, he used his rugby skills to body-swerve around the oncoming man-eaters, and head for Wendy.

"They are only doing it," she informed him, "because toying with you represents a challenge to them."

"And I suppose if I were taking them for French, they would all be posing as Irma la Douce?"

"Probably."

"Thank God this is the last session. If I'd had any notion it was going to be like this, I would never have signed up for it."

Laughing with abandon, Roger's daughter basked in her father's acute discomfort.

"Don't worry, Dad." She reverted to schoolgirl temptress tone. "Er, I mean, Mister Fraser."

Looking over at Bryant again, Roger observed that he seemed to be coming out of his trance. Cleaning his glasses and mopping his forehead, it appeared that Elvis had returned for an encore, but Roger could see the young teacher would be no bloody use to him whatsoever, in keeping the foxes focused on the subject matter.

Time for the final round. Fraser called for quiet, and the girls resumed their seats. Feeling more like a ringmaster than a businessman, he thought that somehow he must regain complete control over the girls' fondness, to stop the subject content moving down scandalous blind alleys of their choosing.

Raising himself to full height, he tried the authoritative approach, hitting the class with his most stern face. "Okay girls, to continue….GEC also owned white-goods manufacturers like Hotpoint. After being re-badged and thereby re-branded under the GEC moniker, with the Marconi name dropped in its entirety overnight, established Marconi customers thought they would be approached, to buy Hotpoint washing machines and spin dryers." Pausing, he quickly scanned round the class. The girls seemed to be absorbed in the self-imposed afflictions of GEC. His uncompromising approach appeared to be working. "On the face of it," he continued with growing confidence, "quite a macabre, even hilarious outcome. But in terms of market perception, it damaged the Marconi kudos, leading to a downturn in company revenues. GEC soon restored the status quo, and with the Marconi name reinvested, the Marconi divisions of the GEC empire flourished again….This is an archetypal example of how brand is so important to customer perception, and thereby revenues and profit."

Satisfied that he had accomplished his aim, he spied out over the class again to see reasonably attendant faces, all tuned in to his theme, then a hand shot up from the middle of the classroom, Roxanne Harrison again, looking all innocent, and butter wouldn't melt.

"Yes, Roxanne," he said somewhat tersely.

"Mister Fraser," she opened in an evocative manner, "would you say that branding is key to the successful business of say….women's lingerie?"

Oh Christ, he thought, what potentially controversial waters is this going to lead into? First, provocative man catching school uniforms, now lingerie.

"How do you mean, Roxanne?" he asked, sensing a loaded and redolent flavour to the question.

"Well," she began, as her huge eyes rolled in a continuing attempt to feign innocence, "to sell lingerie products in volume, shouldn't the brand be associated with women who can use their natural assets, to show off the products?"

"That's an excellent question. Yes, I think in terms of promotion, a lingerie supplier would use attractive models, to best display the attributes of their products."

Whoops, in his enthusiasm to applaud Roxanne's suggestion, he had fallen right into the trap.

She stood up at an oblique angle, hands on hips, and said, "Do you think I would make a good lingerie model, Mister Fraser?"

Before he could answer, Patricia Ellison also stood and wiggled. "What about me, Mister Fraser?"

Then Lolita and two other girls posed the same question, each squirming around on the spot, making suggestive movements. He began to understand why male teachers got snared by jailbait.

Just when he thought the business studies master had fallen asleep, Roger suddenly heard Mister Bryant say, "Okay, settle down, girls. I think you are beginning to overload Mister Fraser."

Overload me, Roger thought, how about stomped all over my nervous system, and trampled me half to death. I signed up for skills and knowledge transfer, not man baiting.

Knowing they had just about tested his upper limits, the girls became passive. With normal service resumed, he went on to cover more examples of the power of branding.

With just five minutes to go before the final session concluded, and when he could see the finishing flag, waving to him in the near distance, Missus Greenwood suddenly made an unexpected appearance. All the girls stood up as she entered the classroom, as did Mister Bryant, and for some irrational reason, Roger stopped speaking, and virtually stood to attention, like he was back in the sixth form.

"Good evening Mister Fraser, Mister Bryant, girls," she said, the hallmark of approval, glistening all over her face.

"Good evening, Missus Greenwood," everyone replied in unison, Roger included.

She came to the front of the class, and stood next to him.

"Well, girls, I hope you all appreciate Mister Fraser's efforts, in polishing your capabilities to accomplish the top A-level grades in business studies." She smiled at Fraser, as if about to award him house points for gold star performance. "I've been hearing some excellent reports from many sources, and I am pleased to announce that Missus Fraser has agreed, that Mister Fraser will be taking similar sessions in the future."

Roger thought that he must be dreaming. He could have sworn she just said, 'Missus Fraser has agreed, that Mister Fraser will be taking similar sessions, in the future'. He let it sink in. No, he wasn't dreaming, his ears were not deceiving him.

He could almost feel the groundswell of approval wash over him from the class, as the girls' faces apart from Wendy's, now turned from dutiful respect for Missus Greenwood, to those of jubilant, smiling St.Trinian's look-alikes, granted another fun-filled bonanza by a great deity.

"What?" Roger exclaimed, the blood draining from his face.

"Yes, I knew you would be pleased, Mister Fraser," Missus Greenwood began to explain. "I telephoned Missus Fraser this evening, offering my thanks for your services, and said how much you were enjoying the experience. She said if you were that happy, she didn't have any issues with you helping the business studies class out again."

Troubleshoot your way out of this one, he thought to himself. Then looking to his front, he saw row after row of little vixens, licking their lips and rubbing their hands, apart from Wendy, who had that satisfied look of *touché*, something she inherited from her mother.

CHAPTER 20: GREENWICH PARK

After the rigours of the Big Lebowski visit, and the pain of his A-level business studies evening classes, Roger needed some recuperation. He suggested to Charlotte that they take a family trip to Greenwich Park, at the weekend. Sounded good to her, and the more junior members of the family, so it got the thumbs up, and preparations were made for a start on Saturday morning, straight after breakfast.

Before they could set off, a knock at the front door drew Roger's attention. Answering it, he became confronted by a Phil Daniels lookalike, from his role as Jimmy in *Quadrophenia*, wearing a Lenin revolutionary style hat, and what looked like a bus conductor's bag, slung diagonally across his body, from his left shoulder. Leaning at an acute angle, against an imaginary post, his mouth half-open, and his eyes glassy, presumably through over-indulgent ecstasy tablet consumption, Roger thought Jimmy seemed to be extremely short in the brain cell domain.

"Yes, can I help you?" asked Roger.

"Errr….Avon," Jimmy said from the side of his mouth, in a low-register South London accent.

"Yes?" Roger asked again.

"Errr….Avon."

"Yes, what about Avon?" he replied irritably. "Do you mean the River Avon, Avon Tyres?"

"Err….Avon."

"Yes, we've established it's Avon, Avon what?"

"Errr….Avon Cosmetics, innit?"

"Avon Cosmetics innit….what does that mean?"

Jimmy peered at him, as if he'd been asked to explain the intricacies of Einstein's Theory of Relativity.

"Huh," he uttered, screwing up his gaunt face.

"I'm asking," Roger pressed, beginning to lose his cool, "what do you want?"

"Oh....cosmetics....wanna buy some cosmetics, mush?"

"Cosmetics," repeated Roger, stepping forward in a threatening manner. "Are you trying to imply I need cosmetics?"

"What....huh?"

"Never mind....what precisely is it you want?"

"Er....er....Avon."

Resisting the temptation to throttle him, Roger went for plan B.

"Charlotte," he shouted, whilst looking at the Phil Daniels impersonator disparagingly. "It's someone for you."

* * *

The journey to Greenwich became quite an unexpected pleasant and enjoyable affair. For once, the Minister for Transport had decided not to torture weekend motorists, with mile upon mile of cones on the A2. No one cut up the MPV, and they zinged along at a steady 70. The kids weren't asking awkward questions, and Charlotte didn't lambast Roger, although she had not been exactly chuffed, with having to deal with Jimmy.

Surprised to also find there were no disconcerting, wandering lane-to-lane, half-asleep juggernaut drivers, and annoying, pot-smoking, 'Chelski'-supporting boy racers in his path, Roger launched into several verses of *I got the Chicken Shack, Fleetwood Mac, John Mayall can't fail blues*, without interruption.

So used to playing motorway dodgems, and hurling abuse at those who incurred his displeasure, remarkably, he found the lack of pesky road users bewildering. Often he would be bombing along the motorway in the M3, doing a steady 110, when in his rear view mirror, he'd see some wide boy West London oik, in a 1.3 Escort or Astra van, flashing him to move over, and mouthing to 'Get out of the fackin' way, you cant'.

DOGHOUSE BLUES

God knows how the engines in those things never exploded, he often thought, since the rev counters must have kissed goodbye to the red danger zone, way back when the vans were doing 80.

They parked up, and Roger fed the meter enough pound coins to sponsor the entire London Marathon, before they walked off in the direction of the Royal Observatory.

From the Greenwich Park balcony, at the top of Blackheath Avenue, looking north across the Thames, he could see the firm's offices at Canary Wharf.

"If it wasn't for that hideous financial centre," observed Charlotte, "we would be able to see the Olympic stadium at Stratford."

"Hhmmm," he responded meekly, not rising to the bait.

"Aren't they using Greenwich Park for some horse event?" James asked.

"Yes," confirmed Charlotte, "equestrian events."

"Didn't that cause a furore with local residents?" questioned Wendy.

"Yes, that's right, Wendy," Roger replied. "Some trees, which were over 100 years old, were cut down to stumps to make way for the dressage, or Paralympics equestrian, or something like that."

"Oh, yes," James confirmed, "look over there."

They all turned in the given direction, and sure enough, where once there used to be mature oaks and sycamores, now only grotesque stumps filled the landscape.

"Small price to pay for the Olympics," stated Charlotte.

"I thought you were a New Age tree hugger," exclaimed Roger.

"I am," she confirmed, nearly biting her bottom lip at the apparent dichotomy, "but sacrifices have to be made for progress."

Coming up from the National Maritime Museum, they saw a band of locals with placards, heading towards the Greenwich Theatre area, through the park. Shouting slogans in unison, about carting Sebastian Coe off to the Tower of London, and impaling his head on Traitor's Gate, it became clear no love was lost between them and the Olympic Games delivery committee.

"I think these people would disagree with you, Mum," contested Wendy.

"The Olympic Games will be good for England," insisted Charlotte, resolutely.

"Oh, on what basis do you say that?" Roger enquired.

"It will bring in lots of overseas revenue into the economy, and leave legacy buildings, which can be used by the general public."

Economic business justification was something Roger Fraser dealt with on a daily basis, and his wife's assertion had no foundation in fact.

"So let me understand this correctly," he clarified. "The justification for funding the 2012 Olympic Games development from the taxpayer kitty, and supplements on London Council Tax, was on the basis that the investment would be recovered, and even a profit made, through foreigners flocking to the games. Is that correct?"

"Yes."

"But Charlotte," Roger began to argue, "according to the holier-than-thou BBC, all the tickets have been sold to British residents, so where is the return going to come from?"

"Yes, but, but....oh, Roger, not everything can be measured, in terms of profit and loss. Some things have to be bank-rolled, out of the public purse."

"They said that about the Millennium Dome," chipped in Wendy. "But it never paid for itself, and was sold for virtually nothing to the private sector."

"That's right, clever daughter of mine," her father supported with pride. "Come on, Charlotte, all these high profile-public ventures are there, so that civil servant fat cats, and selected friends and advocates of the government of the day, can get very rich. That's the key reason, why Blair sanctioned the Olympic Games bid."

"You're just anti-New Labour," Charlotte accused, "like my

mother."

"Not true," Roger protested, "long ago, in my early-twenties, I gave up on all three main parties, because they have agendas, designed to benefit themselves." He opened his eyes wide at Charlotte inviting a reply and expecting a virulent retort, but she stayed silent. "Oh, they may fly the synthetic flag of social justice, and all that fashionable, politically correct rubbish, or staunchly play the patriotic card, but that's just fluff, surface gloss by which politicians get elected, and terminally stupid and gullible voters get caught up in. As Davina says, after that it's just one long gravy train, for the main protagonists and their hangers-on."

"That's a very anti-Keynesian view, Roger," jabbed Charlotte.

"That's a rational and realistic view," he countered. "Besides, Keynesian philosophy is just nonsense, yet another chic theory, designed to justify an even bigger public sector, funded by more and more national debt, to support the privileged bureaucrat stratum. Why should the taxpayer fund the political classes' ego trips, and feather their nests?" Again, Charlotte didn't answer. Inwardly, she knew Roger's assessment to be true, but would not be forthcoming with an admission. Recognising he still had the chair, unopposed, he sallied forth again. "I belong to the realist party. We don't have any candidates or a manifesto, but you will see us, every day of your life. We are the people in the private sector, who actually provide the economic foundation for all these grasping, mendacious, artificial do-gooders to fund their hypocritical agendas, many of which have fuelled the national debt crisis."

Feeling the need to defend her recently-adopted Keynesian stance, Charlotte pushed, "Oh, Roger, that's a very callous way, to look at things. Sometimes, you can be very intolerant of progressive politics. We have to be very careful, not to go too fast, relieving the national debt. That's why public works are still on the statute."

Shaking his head dismissively, Roger became tempted to let

fly with a reality check, but instead chose to sustain the measured approach.

"That sounds like a Vince Cable statement, more driven on by populist vote catching, than realism," he insisted. "The only way to relieve the national debt is to earn foreign currency. That means instigating a strategy, to prioritise winning overseas trade. Export manufacturing, professional services and tourism. They are the three saviours, which will bring new wealth into the country, and drive down the structural debt." Glancing at Charlotte, thinking she would reply, once again his wife remained tight lipped. "Public works only draw on existing Treasury funds," he stipulated, "or worse still, they are financed by even more national loans, exacerbating the pain. It may make David Cameron popular, but a huge public building programme will just add to the spiralling debt crisis, unless we earn foreign currency." He stopped, looking around, to also include the children in his final comment. "As I've said before, any fool can spend money. It's money creation the country needs, and I'm not talking about quantitative easing. That's just a plaster, over an already gaping wound, the politicians' way to suspend disbelief."

"Dad's actually right, Mum," opined Wendy. "I talked to Michelle about the debt crisis, and she said the same thing."

Appearing near to exasperation, Charlotte said, "I can't win with you, or it seems Wendy on this one, can I?"

"Daddy's used that word hippo-crit-t-cal again," reprised Heather, as if reproaching one of her errant Weakest Link contestants.

"Yes, sweetheart," confirmed Charlotte, with an intimidating look, aimed in her husband's direction.

"Why are grownups hippo-crit-t-cal, Mummy?"

"Oh, Heather, we've only recently been through this one, the night of Wendy's birthday."

"Yes, but I didn't understand it then. And I don't, now."

"Heather," assured James, "Wait until you are my age, then you will understand why grownups are hypocritical."

Scowling at him, his mother retorted with, "Yes, thank you, James. We can do without the teenage satire take on adult behaviour."

"Oh, look," announced Wendy, "those placard-waving protestors are coming this way."

Sure enough, the local branch of the preserve Greenwich Park society made its way towards Greenwich Observatory, less than 100 yards from where the Fraser family stood. Appearing to be in high spirits, the protestors forged forward with vigour, their faces reddened by a combination of chanting, and the effort needed to climb the hill to the observatory.

"I'm going to have a word with these people," stated Charlotte, with a look of determination, last worn by Joan of Arc.

Immediately, Roger became alarmed. He generally went out of his way to avoid controversy or at least thought he did, according to some of his more empathetic friends. In Charlotte's apparent state of agitation, that of favouring the levelling of Greenwich Park in its entirety, to make way for the Olympics, he could only see potential conflict, fast looming into view.

"Now Charlotte," he pleaded, "we are here for a pleasant day out, not to fly the flag for Sebastian Coe's Olympics delivery team."

She gave him one of her grievous Medusa looks, guaranteed to turn mere mortals like Roger to stone, if he persisted with his remonstration. "There are some things I feel very strongly about," she told him, "and the Olympic Games is one of them."

"Is Mummy going to fight with the protestors?" enquired Heather.

"Not while I still have breath left in my body," Roger replied. "Now Charlotte, come on, let's go inside the observatory....that's the main reason we came to Greenwich."

"That can wait," she determined.

He'd seen his wife like this on other occasions. Once she had her mind set, on a course of what she considered to be morally justified action, not even a brigade of the Queen's Lancers could stop her. He watched in horror, as the Greenwich Park-loving contingent reached the balcony area, shouting their slogans, and punching the air with their placards, Charlotte looking purposeful, hands on hips, legs slightly apart, observing the oncoming entourage.

"Now, darling," he urged, "let's be sensible, let's….oohff." His sentence became curtailed by a back-elbow move to his ribs from Charlotte, which would have made Mick McManus proud.

There must have been at least 30 protestors, but any bookie knowing Charlotte's fighting form would have been giving odds on a Fraser victory. Once convinced of the rightness of the cause, not even Vlad the Impaler could deflect her. She stood in front of their intended path, holding her hand up, like a septic traffic cop marshalling a four-way interchange in Los Angeles, whilst the other Fraser family members, plus several other curious bystanders, watched proceedings.

The lead protestor, a medium-sized homo-sapien with a large moustache, Roger reasonably thought maybe Guatemalan, dressed in a paisley Rupert Bear coat and moving with a determined stride, sensed an objection coming his way. He came face-to-face with Roger's wife, a few other protestors coming to a standstill behind him, whilst the rest filtered forward around them, war cries beginning to falter, up and down placard motion slackening to a halt, realising someone wanted to question their motives.

Fixing her icy gaze on the lead protestor, Charlotte probed in a waspish voice, "Are you against the Olympic Games?"

"No, madam," came the reply, "but we are against the wanton destruction of our environment."

Persisting, she demanded, "don't you understand that some sacrifices are necessary, for the games to take place?"

"Yes, but why destroy Greenwich Park, when there are plenty of ex-industrial brown-field sites around Stratford, which could be converted for the equestrian events, and then reused, after the games are over."

Mmmm, a very sound answer, Roger thought to himself,

difficult to argue with that one.

"The Olympic Games budget is only so big," countered Charlotte, "and some existing locations have to be used, to keep costs down."

That also was good, thought Roger. His wife had obviously taken his view of economic realities onboard.

"Madam, do you actually reside in Greenwich?" the lead protestor asked.

Oooohh, Roger thought, the archetypal show-stopper card.

She glanced away from her adversary for a moment, clearly searching for tangible straws, Roger knowing the question had troubled her sensibilities.

"No, I don't, but that's irrelevant," she maintained.

"No, it's not," said a rather large woman protestor with a flushed complexion, who pushed the Rupert Bear attired man aside to confront Roger's wife.

Fixing Charlotte with a stare of complete disdain, her eyes traversed up and down, taking her in, weighing her up, making a judgement as to whether she would prevail, if it came to violence. She squared up in front of Charlotte, hands on hips, almost beckoning her to make the first move. Charlotte stood her ground, unflinching.

"If your local park was being destroyed," challenged the large woman, "to make way for a bunch of toffee-nosed horse riders, you too would be up in arms."

Taking one step forward, Charlotte replied, "No, I wouldn't. I can see the bigger picture, and thereby the national benefits."

"Oh, it's so easy to say that," forwarded the large woman. "It's so easy to take a laissez-faire view, when it's not you, who is affected. Haven't you noticed….the trees have been cut down? That is nothing short of government-authorised vandalism. Is that what you support, you stupid woman?"

Oh dear, thought Roger, if there was anything guaranteed to ignite Charlotte's volcano, it was to paint her as a stupid woman. He gathered the kids around him, not to protect himself, but to protect them.

"What did you say?" demanded Charlotte, clenching her fists.

Her opposite number took a step forward. "I said, is that what you support, you stupid woman?"

Growling, Charlotte launched into her adversary with a flurry of flailing fists, but her opponent seemed up for a fight, and responded back in kind, equalling 'Sugar Ray' Charlotte's wind-milling tactic.

So gutsy with self-belief, fear was something that did not come into Charlotte's reckoning, and never diluted her resolve. She retained Roger's everlasting admiration and love, even when he didn't agree with her. However, despite his perceived bookies' faith in her, to prevail against overwhelming numbers, it was definitely time for him to intervene.

"Wendy," he instructed, "hold Heather's hand. James, stand in front of your sisters. Your father has to reveal his red and blue under-suit."

Armed with his peacemaker expression, 'Superman' Roger strode forward into the melee. "Excuse me, excuse me," he entreated, as he diplomatically pushed people aside.

"What do you want?" he heard to his left, from another irate protestor.

"Just coming to extricate my wife from hostiles," he replied, smiling at the questioner, who did not appear too empathetic to his cause.

By now, Charlotte had her foe in a headlock and was trying to force her to the ground, presumably, to use a rugby changing-room fighting term, 'ease her' into submission. Then he noticed more scuffles had broken out, between the protestor group members and other bystanders. Clearly, Charlotte had some support.

As he reached his wife and her fellow gladiator, the large woman protestor was about to deliver a punch. Charlotte saw it coming, ducked, and the uppercut caught Roger perfectly. A good solid punch with plenty of weight behind it, he kind of walked into, multiplying its effect, it sent him recoiling back.

Wincing in pain, he then felt a shove in the back sending him to the ground. As he fell his head bounced against a park bench. Oblivious to her husband's fate, Charlotte continued exchanging blows with her opponent.

He heard Heather scream, "They've killed my daddy, they've killed my daddy," but he knew Wendy would be holding her back. Then everything went very black.

Starting to come around, Roger's bleary sight revealed various people, being questioned by the police. It looked like plod wanted to talk to his wife, as well, but she appeared to be keeping them at bay, with her pointed toe boots and trusty umbrella.

While Wendy mopped his brow to aid recovery, he heard Heather shout, "They're trying to take my Mummy away."

For a split second, he became convinced that he lay in a tremulous dream, and would awake at any moment, without his head feeling like a moose in rutting season, had used it for butting practice.

Then he heard James say, "Should I call Uncle Steve, Dad, to get Mum bailed out, if she's arrested?"

That's all he needed, Steve Hunt coming to the rescue in the guise of latter day crusading civil rights solicitor, with a social conscience he knew he didn't have, and in the process, having enormous fun at the Frasers' expense, then recounting the embarrassing details to all and sundry at Kappa Corinthians.

Swimming in the delicate throes of recovery, and trying to rationalise what had occurred, Roger had just about regained full recollection of events, when a policeman came over and said, "Are you alright, sir?"

Still struggling to achieve full compos mentis capacity, but feeling the primordial need to be manly, Roger decided to be at least halfway macho, and bullshit him. "Yes, I'm fine officer, nothing I haven't experienced on a rugby field."

Screwing his eyes up, the policeman stared at him with an apparent look of sympathy, Roger assuming because of his prone state, but then he said, "I understand you are the husband of that lady, who is trying to kick my colleagues, sir."

Focusing on the hullabaloo, Roger saw three burly policemen, doing their best to restrain Charlotte, whilst at the same time avoiding her lethal pointed boots and rapier-like umbrella.

"Yes, that is my wife," he confirmed, in a half-melancholy resigned voice.

He was pretty sure that he heard the policeman respond in a whisper, with, 'You have my sympathies, sir,' but he could have been wrong.

Stooping down, the officer of the law said in what Roger considered to be an extremely considerate tone under the circumstances, "Well, sir, we will have to caution her, along with a further 12 people for disturbing the peace, if she doesn't stop beating up my colleagues. She seems very agitated….could you come over, and help calm her down?"

"Certainly."

With the law's help, Roger got to his feet, and made his way over to Charlotte, still doing her martial arts act.

"Charlotte," Roger barked in his most serious tone. He raised his right hand, in a gesture for her to stop.

She caught sight of her husband, but carried on her one-woman policeman demolition.

"I think you've made your point," he told her. "Now if you don't stop kicking out at the police, they will arrest you for disturbing the peace."

His words struck home. Her swishing umbrella action slowed, and she relented. "Alright," she told the policemen. "You can let me go."

Looking thankful, three heavy-set law enforcers released her, muttering that they would rather deal with a bunch of football hooligans or drunken Scotsmen, than sustain the encounter with Roger's wife.

After dispersing all combatants and spectators, the police climbed back inside their Black Maria, and headed for their next crowd control assignment. Apparently, a temperance society protest had got out of hand in the quaint and leafy South London suburb of Bexleyheath, and the tea-supping, church-going devotees of societal virtue, who would normally shun violent acts, had become involved in a gruesome riot with local real ale supporters.

Roger and his family made their way back to the MPV. Greenwich Observatory would have to wait, for another day.

Back in the vehicle, appearing shame faced and repentant, Charlotte said, "I'm very sorry, everybody, I just got carried away."

"That's all right, darling," Roger said, whilst feeling the bumps swelling, on his chin and forehead. "These things happen."

"I don't know what came over me," she confessed. "I suppose I just saw red, when that woman implied I was stupid."

"Forget it, Mum," implored Wendy.

"I thought you were very brave and daring, Mummy," added Heather.

Turning to face their youngest, with a tear in her eye, Charlotte replied in a soft voice, "Oh, thank you, darling."

"By the way," began to inform James, with a slight air of menace building in his tone.

"What?" his father enquired.

"I got the whole thing recorded with my iPhone video app."

"You haven't posted it on YouTube, have you?" asked the retired combat-sports mistress.

"No, Mum….not yet."

Charlotte and Roger glanced at each other, thinking the same thing.

Looking sternly at their son, Roger asked, "What do you mean, not yet?"

"Well….I was thinking we could do a trade."

"What kind of trade?" asked Charlotte, beginning to smell a

tricky situation.

"The kind of trade that grants Wendy, Heather and me what we want, in return for not posting it on YouTube."

Well, well, well, Roger thought, his son had started to develop negotiation skills. That would be useful to his future career, whatever it may be.

"Why, you little…." Charlotte snapped at James, her anger beginning to swell again. She made a grab for his phone, demanding, "James, give me that iPhone."

"Ah, I thought you may say that," James retorted, his air of menace building into assured confidence. "I've already wrapped the video in a secure file, and sent it to my mate Neville Matthews, with instructions to keep it on hold. He can't open the file, so your secret is currently safe."

"Clever little sod, aren't you?" remarked Charlotte, ruefully, wanting to reach for the iPhone again, or it could be their son's neck, but persuaded herself it would be a futile act.

She stared ahead momentarily, as if weighing up her options, but swiftly concluded there were none. Turning to peer at James, with the look of defeat emblazoned on her face, she said, "Okay, what's the price of your discretion?"

"Well," James replied, "the list is extensive and very deep."

She glanced at Roger, mouth open, disbelief now written all over her face. "I'm beginning to appreciate how you must feel, when you get into trouble inadvertently."

"Yes, darling," he said tenderly, "it looks like we are both in the nasty stuff this time, jammed up a creek without a paddle between us, and the wolves are circling."

For once, both Roger and Charlotte had the Doghouse Blues.

THE END

BLACK ROSE
writing™